EDWARD STEVENSON

# 0 Days Off

The information given in this book should not be treated as a substitute for professional medical advice; always consult a medical practitioner. Any use of information in this book is at the reader's discretion and risk. Neither the author nor the publisher can be held responsible for any loss, claim or damage arising out of the use, or misuse, or the suggestions made, or the failure to take medical advice or for any material on third-party websites.

Edward Stevenson

info@zerodaysoff.co.uk

www.zerodaysoff.co.uk

First edition

ISBN: 9781726789479

This book was professionally typeset on Reedsy.
Find out more at reedsy.com

*Dedicated to the two women who gave me the strength to write this book –*
*your pain means others will live with less.*

# Contents

IV   Nutrition

V   The Physical Body

VI   The Authentic Entrepreneur

VII   Conclusion

# Acknowledgement

Due to the isolated journey that this book has taken me on, there are fewer people to acknowledge than might be expected in a different kind of book. The people who have remained closest to me on this journey are also acknowledged throughout without being named.

I would like to thank my editor, Sandy Draper, for taking what was a passionately written story and turning it into a real book. This book took me more than 10 years to write and, upon completing the first full draft, I was hesitant to get it professionally edited. I wondered whether someone who hadn't accompanied me on any part of my journey could add value without disrupting the authenticity of what I'd written. However, deciding to work with Sandy turned out to be the best decision I could have made and transformed what I'd created myself into something that I could deliver to others. I'd also like to thank Christina Roth for giving it the final touches.

There is also one more person that I'd like to thank, someone who won't read this book until many years after it's published. To you, my son, I want to express my deepest gratitude for always understanding why I couldn't be with you as much as I desperately wanted to. Repeatedly leaving you was the hardest thing I ever had to do, and only when reunited does my heart become whole again.

At only six years old, you always accepted that I had to write this book because, as we talked about many times together, 'Daddy is trying to help other people with a sore tummy.' But regardless of how much this book has consumed my time since the day you were born, nothing will ever be more important to me than you. I love you more than any written word can express.

# Introduction

## No Way Out

6,307,200.

This is my number. It is an approximate number, but its exactness has little relevance because it represents the number of consecutive minutes I've endured chronic pain. Without a break, without respite and, for a long time, without knowledge. The number also represents how long it has taken me to write this book: 4,380 days, or 12 years.

As you'll discover, these thousands of days also equate to an extensive education in nutrition, exercise, the inner workings of the mind, and how to achieve fulfilment in life.

I have a digestive illness, which causes pain on the left-hand side of my abdomen in the upper region of my stomach. The pain is physical, but the sheer magnitude and relentlessness of it have come with a high mental and emotional cost. Pain has altered my personality and took away much of my joy in life.

I once described the feeling as being tortured by two people simultaneously: one burning the inside of my stomach with a lit match and the other ferociously scratching at the same place. Undesirable at best and unbearable at worst. What triggered the pain is a mystery; it has confused a host of medical doctors and holistic practitioners. Why did it happen? How did it happen? What is it? No answers have ever been forthcoming, despite my relentless search. Day after day, month after month, year after year. I desperately wanted to find a cure. I desperately wanted the pain to stop. I desperately wanted to live again.

My search for a cure lasted more than a decade, and despite everything, there seemed no way out. It didn't matter what medicine I took, which therapies I tried, or how much I adjusted my diet, I couldn't figure out how to reduce the pain. I often felt like I was grasping on to a thin branch of hope, with the limb ever weakening through the passing of more time.

I tried to stay optimistic and looked toward a possible light at the end of a very long tunnel. But that light just seemed to fade a little more each day. I lived in a state of denial, as I kept telling myself that one day, I would reach that light. One day, I would live without chronic pain.

Then year seven went by. And year eight. And year nine . . . each year taking another part of my inner strength and motivation.

Battling illness for such a long time could only ever lead to one eventuality – exhaustion. Eventually, I became tired of fighting and persevering every day. What was the point of being alive, if every day was a day of pain?

Suicide is a dark subject, often taboo, but I hope to offer a different perspective in this book because reaching this extreme point – where life seems futile and hopeless – can also represent the point at which a particular type of change occurs – authentic change. I believe we all seek authentic change because it's lasting and cannot be easily undone, but often we achieve it only when we reach a precipice in life, and we feel like we're out of options.

## Seeking Lasting Change

My own journey of self-discovery is one of many relationship changes. Not with people, although the effect of pain on relationships is considered in detail, but rather with the non-tangible.

The most profound difference – and the one that was the catalyst for other changes – was with the pain itself. This is what took me back from the precipice. When standing at the edge, I felt a seismic shift inside of me and realized that if pain could be a teacher in my life, then

I was learning every single day. What an extraordinary waste it would be if I didn't share everything I was learning.

I can say with total honesty there is no bias in this book. There is no agenda or motivation to prove a point. It's just a true story about living with chronic pain and the lessons learned along the way. However, this knowledge may not only be useful for chronic pain sufferers alone as the subjects of the mind, nutrition, exercise, and personal growth are all of universal interest.

The information relating to the mind is reflective of the teachings provided to me by my mentor: an extraordinary person who has asked to remain anonymous. He's been my teacher, guide, friend, father figure, inspiration and someone who has walked side by side with me on the long and painful journey writing this book. No word can singularly describe him, so I simply refer to him as my mentor throughout.

I believe you'll find the information relating to nutrition both intriguing and controversial. It highlights that what we are taught about nutrition is often outdated, flawed and influenced by industry. You may find what is disclosed surprising, shocking and yet extraordinarily simple.

The information relating to physical training reflects my own knowledge and is based on a lifetime of enjoying sports, as well as some valuable principles which living with chronic pain has taught me. Exercise is a natural painkiller and one that I've relied upon for years. Without it, I never would have made it this far.

Beyond the core subjects of the mind, nutrition and exercise, I've also included my own journey towards becoming an entrepreneur. I felt this important because it highlights an incredible irony in my life:

*My lifelong dream to become an entrepreneur and create something of value in the world wouldn't have come true without experiencing so much pain.*

## Why I Wrote This Book

No one wants to experience pain, but it can be the very thing that pushes us to reach our potential. I certainly never wanted to live with so much pain in such continuity, but I can't deny how much that it has taught me – anybody who stayed in class for more than 4,000 days in a row would get an incredible education.

My wish for this book is that it helps you improve the shape of your life as a whole. Not just your body and not only your mind. Even though I can't claim to have found a cure for my own health condition, I can say that the progress I've been able to make entirely on my own without painkillers or medicines is astounding.

*0 Days Off* is a story about life, love, loss, death, health, spirituality, personal development, finding purpose, relationships, risk, and so much more. What's important to remember, as you read this story, is the evolving nature of it. I am not the person I was when I started writing this book nor am I even the person I was yesterday.

I am simply someone who keeps learning – a student of life and a student of pain, which are perhaps the same thing. As Socrates once wrote, 'The only true wisdom is knowing you know nothing'.

What I wanted to retain throughout the book was a real-time tone of writing. One which emphasizes how I was feeling as I was going through this journey with pain. I express both positive and negative emotions, even though I've now been able to let go of the past, accept all that has happened and live more presently. In that time, I've endured more physical pain than I'd ever wish on anyone, but it's a pain that has become my ultimate teacher in life. As Eckhart Tolle wrote:

> *'Even within the seemingly most unacceptable and painful situation is concealed a deeper good, and within every disaster is contained the seed of grace. Acceptance of the unacceptable is the greatest source of grace in this world.'*

By learning from pain, I have learned to live with less pain. The story of which I'd now like to share with you.

# I

# Life Before Pain

*When life becomes too serious, the quality of life diminishes.*

# 1

# A Life of Fun

When I started writing this section, I had to think long and hard about what to include. I aim to reach as broad an audience as possible and help them in some way, but I wondered whether we might get off on the wrong foot if I was too open about my past. Then I realized that this book is not about living a flawless life. It's about creating authentic change.

*Change can only be real if the future is different from the past.*

I've made many mistakes along the way, but I believe there is so much learning to be found in them. What matters is whether we can suspend self-judgement and accept that human beings are flawed by nature, so errors are unavoidable.

My life has changed enormously. When hammering back another vodka during one of my many late-night benders in my 20s, I would never have imagined that I would end up meditating and restricting myself to room temperature still water. But that exemplifies just one such change – the truth is that my whole world has changed.

But it wasn't all bad. It wasn't all naughty. The single life of a young man travelling the world is one of total freedom. And my misgivings were mostly associated with that of a typically selfish male whose priorities were drinking beer and chasing women. As well as the occasional dip into recreational drugs. I remember sending a message to a friend as the sun came up after another alcohol-fuelled and drug-fuelled night out, saying:

*We don't create memories . . . they create us!*

Granted, I was heavily intoxicated, but I still retain a fondness for these words. Although they aren't ones I live by today, because I live much more presently, they do reflect how much fun I was having. So much fun, in fact, that I'd find letting go of this lifestyle incredibly tricky later on.

When I was sitting by my mum's bedside, during one of what were to become frequent hospital visits, she told me that the longer I lived this philandering life, the more difficult I would find it to leave behind. They were wise words, she was right.

Did I listen? No. I was having too much fun.

My mum was incredibly special to me – that will become abundantly clear through this book. She was my hero in my life, and I can't put into words just how strong a bond we had – one that began 40 years ago, in a small Scottish town called Annan.

## A Small Town in the Centre of the World

Annan sits directly on the border between Scotland and England, with a population of 15,000 to 20,000. It really was a case of knowing practically everybody when I was growing up. Doors were left unlocked, and there was a real sense of community.

My primary school was only a five-minute walk from home. It was a Catholic school, and although we weren't an overly religious family, we did go to church almost every Sunday. I had a great group of friends and

4

was an early starter when it came to girlfriends. I was more committed and loyal back then than I ever was as an adult. Perhaps like many people, I lost my childhood honesty and innocence somewhere in the transition to adulthood.

Growing up through primary school, I recall life being good despite a distinct lack of tranquillity at home. My parents had a difficult marriage, and my mum ended up hating my dad with a fierce passion.

Although this was a reality, the fighting just became something of a norm. So, for my brother and me, it was nothing new to hear them screaming at each other or see my mum looking miserable. I never thought that this in any way corrupted me, and I don't use it as an excuse for never getting married, but I did later learn how influential our environment can be when we are young.

Despite the conflict at home, I didn't think I had any reason or justification for complaining. I was one of the more popular kids at school, which continued when I moved onto secondary school, and I always had lots of friends along with usually having a girlfriend. I remember one friend asking me, 'Who's your girlfriend this week?' A humorous question about the frequency to with which I chopped and changed.

This promiscuous lifestyle would later become damaging, but at this time, I lived with youthful freedom and didn't take life too seriously. I think many of us lose this sense of ease and liberty as adults.

Overall, life was good in Annan, although there was a drawback in living in such a small town. Bullies! No matter how many times a member of a known family of bullies would grow up and move on, there always seemed to be another one ready to take his or her place. The same families ruled the streets for generations.

Gaining status on the streets of Annan was based on three things: how tough you were in a fight, your popularity with the opposite sex and your sporting ability. This generally being the order of priority. I was below average, outstanding and good. I was never the best in a fight (although toughened up), I always had a girlfriend, and I loved sport.

## Early Passions

As my teens progressed, football became my game and helped shape my character. Discipline, leadership, working as part of a team and learning how to deal with losing were all valuable lessons that I learned through football. Although my friends will vouch for the fact that I never got much of a grasp on the dealing with losing part. I was a very sore loser.

Annan's local football team was called Annan Athletic. It was a fantastic club and having joined at the under-12 age group, I stayed with it all the way through to playing for the senior teams before I left to go travelling at 22 years old. I will never forget being 17 and playing my first game for the senior team. I got paid £20 and felt like Ronaldo!

Along with my interest in sport and fitness, however, was my keen interest in chasing girls. Once I moved past the age of 16, I also discovered drinking alcohol (or a bit before that age if I'm honest). Perhaps not surprising that I managed to earn the nickname 'Georgie', after the late, great footballing legend George Best, when I was playing with Annan Athletic.

Unfortunately, I knew the name was more associated with my ability to play a football match with a hangover and chase girls than about my talent as a footballer. I was a good footballer, and perhaps with more discipline I may have carved out some kind of career, but like many teenage boys, I was easily distracted. I remember one of my coaches saying to me, 'If you can play like this with a hangover, imagine what you can play like sober.'

It was said with a friendly jest, but these two very distinct and opposing parts of my life – sport and fitness versus partying and womanizing – would end up being hugely influential in my later life.

As much fun as I was having, I was never going to reach my potential playing around. Something would have to change in my life. Whether by my own hand or something else.

## The Follower Turned Leader

Although football and an active social life helped to develop my personality, I still look back at myself as someone who lacked self-confidence when I left home at 18 and went to Stirling University. I showed a willingness to get out there on my own but inside had a lot of fear and self-doubt.

There was a strange confidence-no-confidence thing going on. I had an urge to do more with my life and was willing to get out into the world but felt myself shrinking when criticized or put under pressure. The shrinking never quashed the urge, though, and I retained an empty feeling.

> *What I didn't know then is that it would be pain which filled this emptiness.*

Where I did find some fulfilment during those four years at university was in two profound experiences. One was an exchange semester in the South of France, which satisfied my adventurous side, and the other was being appointed captain of Stirling University football first team. This satisfied my growing desire to do more and be a leader.

My exchange trip landed me in a stunning location called Juan-les-Pins. I ended up living in a tiny studio apartment with two other students from Stirling – it was cramped but fun. Because we were exchange students, we didn't need to study too hard, and my time was spent more on socializing, travel and playing football for the university I attended. That and embarking on a globetrotting tour of promiscuity with girls from all over the world.

I just figured if not now, when? Which is what I said to myself for the next 10 years.

When I got back to Stirling for my fourth and final year, I switched to a very different mindset. Again, this highlights the two very distinct parts of my character. One side living the party life and the other getting down to serious business. Stirling University hadn't won the football national championship in more than 20 years. I wanted to change that as captain.

I introduced and stuck with specific policies based on the best players playing along with those who trained the hardest. No more picking friends or trying to win a popularity contest, which I believed was the downfall of previous team captains. I learned a great lesson about leadership through this, which is that distance is sometimes needed between a leader and the team. I was willing to make that sacrifice.

By the end of the season, I was holding the trophy for the Scottish National Championship aloft. We could even have won the British Championship too but for some unfortunate luck in the quarterfinals. Despite some mixed emotions at the end, due to the loneliness of leadership, it was a beautiful moment and one I'll never forget.

*Sacrifice leads to reward.*

I'd done what needed to be done as a leader, and we had won. Perhaps if my wilder side hadn't been as strong as my disciplined side, then I would have gone on to pursue some kind of coaching path. But that isn't how my life panned out. As much as I had an urge to do more, I also had an urge to pursue adventure.

# 2

# The World Is My Oyster (An Aphrodisiac)

After university, I worked day and night to save up and go travelling. My first stop was Sydney in 2003 and, although the next 15 months wouldn't be kind to my liver, they were to be some of the most fun I've ever had.

The peak of fun in Australia was spent travelling the east coast. We started in Sydney, went all the way up to Cairns, and settled back down in Brisbane. By the time we got to Brisbane, there were 15 of us travelling together, and we somehow managed to persuade an estate agent to rent us a house. We conveniently forgot to say how many would be living there and I think we defined it as three people with the occasional person (or 12) staying over.

We lived to party and we spent every penny we earned on drinking alcohol, eating or paying rent. The theme of trying to get laid as often as possible continued, but as there were girls in the group too it certainly wasn't a male pastime only. It was basically just a free time in our lives when we couldn't care less about the future.

To maintain this lifestyle, though, we did have to work, and some of the ways we earned money were borderline ridiculous. In Cairns we decided against getting jobs and just focused on winning sporting events to sell the prizes. We surprisingly did it consistently enough to give us our $20 daily budget: $10 on accommodation, $6 on alcohol and $4 on food. Eating was always the least important.

In Sydney I talked my way into getting a job as a cocktail barman, even though I'd never poured a pint, and somehow stuck around long enough that I ended up running the bar. It wasn't exactly glamorous though, as the bar was in a rough area, and dayshift every morning included serving the alcoholics who tended to wet themselves on the seats and put their mouths under the beer taps when I wasn't looking. So not quite Tom Cruise then.

We had some great times but perhaps the memory that sticks out most, or sticks on most as the story will unveil, is when a few of us went to Fraser Island and decided to make a friendship pact. In short, we got drunk, started a fire, heated some toy crocodiles to no avail (seemingly plastic melts in fire), then settled on using a fork to brand ourselves.

The next morning, three of us woke up with substantial skin burns on our arms. There were four of us in the group, but one had somehow managed to escape his turn. Bizarrely enough, the idea of four friends and the four prongs of a fork made some kind of sense. Had the fork just touched the arm momentarily, then four thin lines would have appeared. However, the execution varied considerably from the 'amazing idea', though, as we held the fork on for about 30 seconds to the smell of burning skin and the sound of agonizing screams.

We did gain some notoriety, though, and even ended up on national television in Australia. Somewhere in the TV archives the 'fork boys' live on.

My 15 months in Australia were wild and free, but by the end of it, I was partied out. I didn't feel ready to go home, though, so I decided to get off the beaten track and ended up in South Korea.

## A Change of Scene – But Not Pace

Arriving in a small city called Gumi, I honestly wondered what I'd got myself in for. When a young Korean boy started crying as I looked alien to him, I knew I wasn't in Kansas anymore.

My job was teaching English to Korean students and, despite my best intentions for going there, I got off to a familiar start. I arrived on a Thursday, was taken out by the other teachers to a local bar on Friday, slept with a Korean teacher that night and by Monday she was fired. I only got a slap on the wrist and, although I was embarrassed by the inequality, I was just relieved to still have a job as I was broke.

Traditional barbecues, karaoke, lots of travel, teaching and sport made up my time in South Korea. These two worlds once again dominated my life, as I worked hard and trained hard during the week and partied even harder on the weekend. I took a different direction with exercise, though, due to the limited opportunities to play football. I joined a local boxing club.

The training was extreme, but I loved it. I trained six days a week and usually for three to four hours per day. My coach wasn't keen on body fat, so he literally used to punch it out of me. Fat bruises easily so he would put me in the corner of the ring, ask me to hold the ropes, and then proceed to punch my abdomen continually. The more bruising there was, the more body fat I had to lose - an effective form of motivation!

When he wasn't punching me, he was running on my stomach. Literally. I would lie down in the ring near the ropes so that he could hold on, then he'd run on me to strengthen my abs.

It was nuts, but I really did love it. The more extreme the training, the more it fascinated me. And as a result, my physical conditioning was excellent. My body fat was at an all-time low, and I really got engaged in the sparring sessions. The only drawback was that my boss at the school wasn't keen on my consistent black eyes.

I kept telling my coach to stop giving me black eyes because I was getting into trouble at school. He told me I wouldn't get black eyes if I kept my guard up – fair enough.

## More Adventures

My year in South Korea ended in autumn 2004, and I wanted to embark on one more adventure before timing my arrival back home for Christmas to see my mum. So, I applied for a position in Japan and landed a job teaching at a University in Yokohama to end almost three years of travelling. A period in which I had also squeezed in some other wild adventures to countries like Thailand and Malaysia.

Before arriving in Japan, I had a three-week gap to fill, so I went to Bali. When I got there, I found it to be a bit too much like the Australian version of Ibiza and moved on quickly to the Gili Islands. There were more stories of promiscuity, but to avoid the risk of becoming repetitive, I'll focus on one memory that carries a lot more depth.

While sitting by my beach hut on the main Gili Island, I one day noticed smoke billowing out from behind me. A fire had broken out a few huts back, and it was beginning to get dangerously out of control. In response to this, a human chain had started to form between the sea at the edge of the island and leading up to the fire – it was a wonderful coming together of people from all over the world.

I jumped in and did my part, but I wanted to get closer and really help put out the fire before it destroyed everything. As I clambered into one of the huts, two gas canisters were sitting there. It was one of those 'deer in the headlights' moments and I just froze, waiting for the inevitable explosion. Thankfully they turned out to be empty.

Eventually, we got the best of the fire and finally put it out. It was then I saw one of the most profound contrasts in human behaviour. Once the blaze was out, the locals just got about rebuilding. Some of them had literally lost everything – all of their belongings along with their homes. But I never saw one of them complain, cry or seek pity. They just accepted what had happened and immediately got on with it. Nobody had been hurt, and they seemed to find no value in dwelling on the past or what material possessions they'd lost.

In total contrast, an American tourist had lost her passport in the fire. She was in floods of tears and inconsolable. Literally on her knees crying. The locals had lost their livelihood, and this tourist had lost a travel document.

It was an extraordinary education in life. One that I would lose sight of but eventually return to.

When I finally made it to Japan, I retained the same lifestyle by partying at the weekends and boxing throughout the week. After about a month at the university boxing club, though, something strange happened – the coach asked all the other boxers to line up and apologize to me. He hadn't realized that I was a teacher, and he wasn't happy that I'd been cleaning up the gym at the end of each evening with the other boxers. It was an unforgettable show of respect and one which we could do well to learn from in the West.

**'Teacher' in Japanese means 'sensei' and 'all' teachers are given great respect.**

When it came time for me to leave, which also marked the end of my world adventure, all my students organised a night out and party for me in Tokyo. It started with dinner and ended with the usual karaoke. What blew me away was the outflowing of emotion – many tears flowed, and thanks were given for my passion shown as a teacher.

Teaching. Coaching. Adding value to the lives of others. It seemed as if this would be my destiny. Perhaps it would eventually be. But I would become very lost along the way.

## Back Home Again

I landed back in Scotland in December 2004 and embraced my mum. It was a beautiful moment. I was so pleased to see her. I couldn't, however, notice just how much older she looked than when I'd left. Time had passed, but there was more than that. Her health had visibly deteriorated.

Before I'd left to go travelling, my brother and I had helped Mum move back to Clydebank – a city near Glasgow where she grew up. Annan and the house we lived in with Dad before he left were filled with painful memories, and Mum wanted to go back to her home. There wasn't much money, so she took a council flat in a high-rise building. It was far from luxurious, but my brother told me she seemed happier and more at peace being away from Annan.

I couldn't stay with Mum for too long because I needed to get some sort of career started. My passion for coaching and teaching was accompanied by a dream of becoming an entrepreneur. Although different, the characteristic trait I found was that of trying to add value to the lives of others.

I moved to London in January 2005, and that is where my path to entrepreneurialism began. It was one which would lead me through a lot of struggle and pain, before I finally became an entrepreneur in 2017.

The period between those years is very different from those which preceded them. My battle with chronic pain started in the summer of 2007 and, to this day, has never stopped. But despite the hardship, I now admit the value it has brought to my life.

Clearly, as this summary of my youth shows, I lived a more selfish life. I don't say this with self-judgement but rather with the acceptance that it was all about me and my fun. The pain took away this fun but also brought about an incredible amount of learning. How I life my live today is unrecognizable compared to how I did in the past, which shows that change is achievable for any of us.

It's not all about me anymore and it never was – I just acted as if it was. I've given everything to *0 Days Off*, and my wish is that what is written in the following chapters is meaningful to you in some way.

**To save one person is to save the whole world.**

14

# II

# Pain and Purpose

*Pain is not just a teacher. Pain is the ultimate teacher.*

# 3

# My Pain – I Am Different

The nagging urge to do more with my life made me feel like I was different. Not special, just different. There is no doubt this was illustrated by lust for adventure and a shallower desire to be the centre of attention. No matter where I went or what I did, though, I couldn't fill this sense of emptiness. There just seemed to be a never-ending need for more.

Although my understanding around how to authentically fill this emptiness has improved, my path to doing so isn't one I would have chosen. For it is one marked with struggle related to an extreme digestive illness so sensitive that even a glass of still water can trigger it. It is an illness that I simply refer to as 'my pain'.

I've learned a lot about what increases my pain, such as food and stress, but my condition has never been diagnosed. No practitioner has ever been able to explain its cause or why I don't respond to any medical treatment.

The fact that food and drink worsened my pain was also a curse. How could I not eat or drink? Then there was the paradox related to stress because the more pain I experienced, the more stress I endured. All of this left me feeling confused, and the only thing that seemed clear was that the pain never stopped.

I woke up in pain, I went through every moment of every day in pain, and I went to bed in pain.

Like so many other people who suffer from a pain-related illness, sleep was always a welcome respite. But as many chronic pain sufferers will testify, real rest can often be hard to come by.

## The Only Option

Despite facing what seemed like an unwinnable battle, the only option was to fight. What choice do any of us have when we fall ill? This fight manifested in a search for a cure or at least finding some way of reducing the pain.

Doctors, therapists, medicines, supplements, alternative remedies, diets – I exhausted every avenue of exploration. 'Exhaustion' being the prominent word in what I call my '10-year search' between 2007 and 2016.

A decade is a long time. But when put into days it seems even longer; 3,650 is a frightening number when it doesn't result in a cure.

Each time I visited a new practitioner, I was reminded of how different I was and how, ironically, I no longer wanted to be the centre of attention. I'd spent most of my life trying to be different but would have given anything to be just another face in the crowd.

Every time I asked a practitioner if they'd ever seen anything like my condition before, they answered, 'No.'

It was disheartening, to say the least.

At the end of my 10-year search, I decided to stop searching for a cure. It was clear that nothing was working, and nobody could help. The responsibility lay with me, and I was on my own. A horrifyingly daunting prospect, but one I had to accept.

***Acceptance represents the first step to progress.***

## A New Definition of Success

When I reached this point, I looked back at the time I'd spent. All those failures. All that effort. I realized that even if I only documented the things that didn't work, I would still have more than enough content to write a book. Perhaps this could at least help other people save some time by avoiding my mistakes.

Even though I couldn't find a cure, I later realized that this decade of failures hadn't been wasted. Edison failed 1,000 times before he discovered the lightbulb, and each of those failures taught him something. I'd failed 3,650 times (10 years in days), but I'd learned something every single day. At least I was in good company.

After my 10-year search, I had my own lightbulb moment as I realized that my definition of success in overcoming my condition was flawed because defining success as finding a cure would most likely lead to eternal failure. Redefining success as achieving progress, however, could lead to a better quality of life.

What did progress need to mean? It was essential to understand this and realize it didn't mean having a setback or improving every day. What it meant was achieving progress in life as a whole. Growing as a person and using what I was learning from my pain for a higher purpose.

How I've been able to achieve this progress is the central story in this book – a story which started in another foreign land – Bratislava, Slovakia. But this time, the fun was coming to an end.


## A Different Sort of Tour

Lying on an operating table in a hospital in Bratislava, with the doctors and nurses speaking broken English at best, a thought crossed my mind: 'What on earth am I doing here?!'

This thought turned to white-faced fear as the lead doctor informed me, in the best English he could muster, that following an endoscopy he'd found a problem – quite a grim one by the look on his face. One which gave me a 50 per cent chance of getting oesophageal cancer.

When I got home to my flat that day, I did what most people in modern society do when panicking about a health issue and searched through Google to find information. And the more I read, the whiter I became. The mortality rate of oesophageal cancer was scarily high, and the overall outlook was dire.

A 50 per cent chance?

The flip of a coin?

It all began with a simple sore throat, which was so persistent that I decided to go see a doctor. She believed the issue was due to acid rising up through my oesophagus to my throat and causing inflammation, which was confirmed by an endoscopy. The rising acid – although not usually life-threatening – is known as acid reflux.

So, what is the link between acid reflux and cancer?

The specific problem the doctor identified was that the mechanism at the top of my stomach/bottom of my oesophagus wasn't closing correctly. The core function of this mechanism is to allow food to pass into the stomach, as well as prevent corrosive stomach acid leaving. If this corrosiveness comes in to contact with cells in the body it isn't supposed to, such as the oesophageal area, then it can become damaging and lead to a precancerous condition called Barrett's esophagus.

Engrossed in fear, I took a medicine known as proton-pump inhibitors without question. However, it didn't stop with just the prescription as I then embarked on a whirlwind tour through the Slovak health system, which resulted in many madcap situations. It's not a tour I'd like to do again, nor even one that I willingly signed up for in the first place.

I went on this tour because the medicine didn't reduce my pain. More visits to doctors and tests ensued. During one procedure, a polyp was found, which wasn't good news for my toss-of-the-coin cancer odds. The doctor suspected it could be cancerous so sent me to the hospital to have it removed and analysed.

As I had limited Slovak language skills, I wanted to get to the hospital early, so I arrived at 5 a.m. for my appointment. There was, however, absolutely nobody around. It was like a post-apocalyptic scene from a horror movie.

When I finally bumped into a nurse, she didn't speak English but ushered me into a changing area behind a curtain and handed me a gown. There was no attempt to understand why I was there or who I was meant to be seeing – just a few finger points to indicate I needed to change.

So, I did. I took off my clothes.

She then picked up my clothes and walked off.

'Hold on a minute', I thought, 'was that even a nurse?'

Standing there with only a thin robe to cover me, I had little choice but to set off through the hospital to try and find some sign of life. What a bizarre sight I must have been – a Scotsman strolling through a Slovak hospital with his ass showing and repeatedly saying one word, 'polyp'.

I'm surprised they didn't direct me to the psychiatric ward!

Eventually, I did end up in a hospital bed. I had no idea whether I was in the correct ward or not, but I figured at least they knew I was there. So, I waited. And waited. And waited. One day passed. Then another. The only contact was when my meals were brought to me. It was truly bizarre.

Finally, on the third day, an English-speaking doctor came to my bedside and asked, 'Why are you here?' I didn't know whether to laugh or cry. I explained the situation, and he was then able to confirm that I would have the operation later that day.

When the moment came, I was taken into a room to see the surgeon, who thankfully spoke good English. He then proceeded to politely tell me that they had decided not to remove the polyp because the hospital didn't have the budget.

In shock and a state of desperation, I did the only thing I could think of and offered to pay cash! I sat there wondering how much money I could withdraw from the nearest cash machine.

My offer was rejected and my 'short-break' in a Bratislava hospital came to an end, but not before being forced to stay one more night. Why? No idea. Perhaps I should have read the brochure.

When I went back to see my regular GP the following week, he was mortified due to the cancer risk. He called in a favour and booked me into a different hospital, where he knew the surgeon personally. He told me, 'Don't worry, it's not yet midnight . . . it's only five to [midnight].'

Not quite sure how I was supposed to take that.

I arrived at the other hospital and was taken in straight away. Before I knew it, I was lying on my side on an operating table. I was quickly sedated – or rather semi-sedated – and then had the pleasure of watching the blood pour out of my mouth. It wasn't painful. It was just crazy. Most importantly, however, the polyp was out and could now be analysed for cancer.

Needless to say, after everything that had transpired, I didn't fancy hanging around. So, I persuaded the nurses – mostly through sign language – to let me go home early. I got out of bed, packed up my things, made my way to the exit, then collapsed at the door. My eagerness to leave was, in fact, too eager. I was severely dehydrated and still partially sedated.

My bed in the ward had been quickly reallocated, so there was no other option but to crawl onto a random free bed in the hallway. I just lay there drinking sporadic cups of water that were brought to me by the nurses, who didn't really seem that surprised that I was lying on a bed fully dressed in the hall near the exit.

Perhaps they were used to seeing escapees!

As soon as my legs could carry me, I was in a taxi and heading back to my flat. I'd gone two rounds with the Slovak health system but was still on my feet.

Or just about.

## No Cancer, But No Change

Despite the craziness of all of this, I shortly afterwards received confirmation that the polyp wasn't cancerous. I was no further forward with my pain, but I was relieved all the same.

What was shocking was that despite my bizarre and frightening journey through the Slovak health system, I continued to work hard and play hard. Regardless of the cancer odds and everything I'd been through, I didn't change my lifestyle. I still took no responsibility for my own health and left it in the hands of doctors and pharmaceutical drugs.

I made continual excuses for myself about how hard I'd worked to get to where I was, and I kept telling myself that if I could make enough money, then I'd be able to buy back my health through the best healthcare.

Every time I had a night out, I thought, 'What's one more beer . . . What's one more shot?'

But it never was one more. There was never any sense. Any control. One drink became two drinks, and this always led to getting drunk. Even the healthier side of me – my physical fitness and work ethic side – wasn't in synergy with taking care of my health. On the work side, I was at the point in my life where I wanted to 'make it', so I knew I had to put in mega-hours. Mega-hours which resulted in mega-stress.

On the fitness side, I'd joined a football team with a fantastic bunch of lads. As my Slovak language skills were limited, I found it far easier to join in socially when alcohol was flowing after the game. So, although the football was much better aligned with taking care of my health, the aftermath wasn't.

Still, I treasured the one season I played with BCT Bratislava. I gained the nickname of 'Running Man' due to my insatiable energy in midfield. It always made me smile when the coach would give a long speech in Slovak with my name cropping up regularly, only for this to be translated by a teammate to, 'Just run'.

## A Different Sort of Pain

I played only one season for BCT because my time in Slovakia came to an abrupt end in the summer of 2009. Mum had fallen very sick and my brother called to tell me that she had only 24 hours to live. I broke down in tears and begged him to tell me that there was still hope, but the tone of his voice was too honest. Therefore, I pulled myself together and rushed back to Scotland to say goodbye.

When I got there, I apprehensively walked into the intensive care unit to see my mum lying there. Her reaction upon seeing me was so typical of Mum when she said, 'You silly billy, you came all the way back from Slovakia for me.'

Mums will be mums.

Even though she was conscious, she wasn't through the worst of it. We were on tenterhooks for days, while the doctors pumped what I can only describe as 'black tar' out of her system. She'd been a heavy smoker for the best part of 40 years, and it had taken its toll.

Mum's condition eventually improved, and we all agreed she would need someone to stay at home with her. My brother had already been through a lot, so we decided I would do it. I went back to Bratislava, said my goodbyes and moved back in with my mum in Annan.

I stayed for three months before returning to London, but this was nowhere near enough. The truth was that I prioritized my career over caring for Mum. Considering how close we were it was strange that I didn't just stay in Annan and get a job. The only explanation I can give is that I hadn't changed my life, despite my own battle with illness, and therefore hadn't changed my mind. I was chasing material gain and living more selfishly.

No matter how much money I earned, all Mum really wanted was time with my brother and me. Although this is a profound lesson that I can't reconcile with my mum in person, I've learned to apply this to my life today.

## Needle in a Haystack

After three months with Mum, I headed back to London in October 2009. Along with searching for a new job, I had to re-engage with my own health issues. My pain had worsened with the recent emotional stress, so needed immediate attention. Whereas before, the pain was aggravated mostly by heavy drinking and eating junk food with a hangover, it had now progressed to becoming a problem whenever I ate or drank anything.

But still, I didn't take responsibility for my own health. I jumped into the UK health system and pursued the same avenue of doctors and medicines. I still wanted them to change the magnitude of my pain, so that I didn't need to change my life.

For the remainder of 2009 and throughout 2010, I endlessly trawled through diets, nutritionists, alternative therapies, books, pamphlets, tests and just about anything that I could get my hands on. None of it worked, and a lot of it was nonsense.

But, with no other choice, I had to choose whether to keep going or give in.

On top of this dedication to food research, I was also doing all sorts of other things: pH tests, alternative remedies, intolerance tests – anything and everything. I was spending money left, right and centre, but nothing was working. The, 'it's only £10' rip-off options on the Internet were quickly adding up. As was the amount I was spending on seeing therapists.

When I went to see one nutritionist, she gave an honest unveiling about the size of the task I was facing:

> *'We are probably 100 years away from understanding how the human digestive system truly works. We are still only at the tip of the iceberg.'*

I thought I was looking for a needle in a single haystack, but it turned out that there were loads of haystacks. In fact, it seemed like there were fields of haystacks over acres of farmland. My chances of finding the needle were minuscule to say the least.

At the beginning of 2011, I started to at least begin to accept that I had a serious illness. I'd never been brave enough to describe it as serious, nor even as an illness, because nobody around me treated me as if it was. Part of this was my own doing as I persisted with the same damaging lifestyle, and part of this was reflective of my social circle.

As 2011 wore on, I can remember the exact moment when I thought, 'Am I really going to be in pain like this for the rest of my life? Wake up in pain, go through every minute of every day in pain, and go to bed in pain?'

My resistance to change reflected my unwillingness to let go of my lifestyle. But it also reflected fear. I was afraid to change. I was afraid of change.

By the end of 2011, I had ticked a whole host of other boxes in my search for a cure. I was following a 'free-from' diet and avoiding gluten, dairy and wheat. I was even drinking gluten-free beer and bringing my own to the pub. Although, all that did was highlight my continued persistence to resist change.

I also registered with the University College Hospital in London, which specializes in gastrointestinal diseases, in the desperate hope that a doctor would give me a 'magic pill' to take away my pain. I tried supplements by the bucket load and signed up for various alternative tests, including a 'microbiology profile' and a 'gastrointestinal profile'.

I didn't understand what they meant then. I still don't know. I do know they were expensive and didn't highlight anything useful.

## More Pain and Grief

The following year, 2012, got off to the worst possible start. Despite Mum miraculously pulling through the scare in 2009, she finally lost her battle with emphysema in January 2012. The truth was, she'd had enough. It was only much later when I got close to my own breaking point that I realized just how far she'd been pushed. She too was living in chronic pain every day, and on top of this, was housebound and stuck on oxygen.

When I arrived back in London in 2009, my focus was so fixated on my own pain, that I didn't take enough notice of hers. I didn't spend enough time with her or sit and listen to her. But although this is a selfish admission, the reality is that this is what pain can represent – loss, destruction and sadness.

As the most important person in my life slipped out of this world, the person who would become the most important in my life was brought into this world. In April 2013 my son was born, and his mum was one of the real gifts of my time in Slovakia.

I met D on another drunken night out, although she was anything but another notch on the bedpost. I found myself caught between two worlds with my old life dragging me back and this new sensation of love. I was just never courageous enough to embrace it and let go of my past. Unfortunately, I never appreciated what I'd found and eventually lost it.

Considering my mum's earlier words of warning, I guess there was an inevitability to this.

Despite one event of tragedy and the other of joy, neither changed the situation with my pain. It was there each and every day without a break. And even though the birth of my son was a moment of great happiness, I was in so much pain through the stress of the birth that I couldn't even stay in the hospital that night. Instead I went back to our flat as a newly crowned father and collapsed into bed with tears streaming down my face.

The tears should have been those of joy, but they were instead those of anguish as the physical pain was so bad.

This magnitude of my pain during my son's birth was also accompanied by a dire financial position. My job had ended very badly in Bratislava, with what I thought at the time was an entrepreneurial business, and I had retaken the plunge with another small business. I followed a non-linear path to becoming an entrepreneur and looking back, I now realize just how much fear I had about setting out on my own.

The pain would change that.

## Uncertain Times

When my son was born, the business wasn't thriving. As a show of my commitment to try and help it survive, I took a significant pay cut. This was an example of how, even though my pain had caused a cataclysmic effect on my life, I continued to dedicate myself to work. Strangely, my pain and work held some synergy of seriousness, and suffering never stopped me working hard.

My dire financial situation meant that we didn't have our own flat when our son was born. We were renting a room with flatmates and it was far from an ideal way to be welcoming our first child into the world. But D never complained and, if anything, she continued to show compassion towards me as I juggled illness, fatherhood and work. Eventually we scraped together enough money, and by the time our son was six months old we had our own place.

One memory that sits well with me during that period is how I refused to use the inheritance money from Mum's estate to pay for rent. It was a modest sum but would have been enough for a deposit and a couple of months' rent. Instead I donated the money to the International Childcare Trust, which is a charity that I'd completed cycle rides for across Cambodia, Kenya and Nepal.

That is where Mum's legacy now lies – helping underprivileged children.

Again, D never complained, despite our living situation, and completely supported my decision. What is strange when I look back is that D had so many of my mum's best qualities, yet I couldn't seem to see it. Or rather I could see it but was too ignorant to appreciate it.

## No Day Off

Despite getting our own flat, there was an unavoidable reality that we all face with pain – a change of location doesn't mean a change of pain. The two years of 2013 and 2014 included more desperate attempts to improve my health but, as always, the pain would not relent. There was no day off.

I really was willing to try anything, and when I reached the point of lying on our bathroom floor doing dodgy homemade liver flushes and enemas, an old familiar thought came to mind, 'What am I doing here?'

My level of desperation that I'd reached is perfectly excmplified by a therapy that I signed up for in late 2014. It was called a faecal transplant and was promoted as a revolutionary way to solve many gut issues. The official description is transplanting the biology of a healthy person into a patient to reset their internal workings.

The crude description is having someone else's shit stuck up your backside!

Once again, the result was the same. No improvement in my health but a much lighter wallet. This time to the tune of £4,000. It turned out to be some expensive shit!

As much as all of this sounds like a combination of naivety, stupidity and utter madness, it was none of these. It was desperation. And this is what pain can do: drive you to extreme lengths even when the chances of success are so slim.

I will always remember my brief conversation with a woman who was going in before me for her faecal transplant appointment. I had to catch two trains to the clinic, which was just outside of London. She'd flown over from Chicago.

With another failure under my belt, I reverted back to the medicinal world in 2015. I went back to University College Hospital in London and underwent more endoscopies. Surprisingly, the results were very different from what I'd been told in Slovakia. My risk of oesophageal cancer was much less than expected, and there was no point in taking more acid-suppressing medicine. However, as much as this was good news, the doctors still couldn't shed any light on what was triggering my chronic pain.

Being fair, they tried their best. I truly believe that. The doctors tried all kinds of medicines and I simply didn't respond to them. I was once again left with fear and frustration, but during what was to be my last medical visit, I did appreciate the feedback from one doctor when he said:

> *'Doctors will try to solve your problem through medicine. Nutritionists will try to solve your problem through food. Therapists will try alternative methods. And unfortunately, you are in the middle of this, trying to make the best decisions you can.'*

He admitted that there was nothing more he could do, so we shook hands and parted ways. The needle in the farmland of haystacks had just become a needle in the Sahara Desert.

## Harsh Realities

The year of 2015 came and went. Simply put, it was just another year in pain but ended with one of the harshest realities of the struggle that I'd endured, and the effort that I'd put in. As our son was almost three years old, he was at a lovely age for Christmas, so I was desperate to try and enjoy the day. At the beginning of December, I therefore set out my master plan to be in better condition for Christmas day:

Over the next 24 days, up until Christmas Eve, I completed 12 yoga classes, six treatments of acupuncture, two psychological sessions and one appointment with a nutritionist. I also underwent one colon cleanse. On top of this I monitored my diet meticulously and didn't drink alcohol (I had quit drinking by this stage).

At a total cost of about £1,500, as well as the time it took on top of my work, I literally couldn't do anymore.

Then Christmas day finally arrived. I awoke with what optimism I could muster and tried with everything that I could to enjoy the day. I allowed myself to modestly indulge in food and give myself a day off.

But taking a day off wasn't on the menu. It wasn't allowed. It was never allowed. It was a real disaster and the preparation ended up being for nothing.

What I didn't fully appreciate then, which I do now, is that my pain doesn't care about preparation.

If I take a day off, I suffer.

That message was delivered loud and clear on Christmas day of 2015.

When I made it through to 2016, I decided that enough really was enough. Not only had the 10 years between 2007 and 2016 been physically, emotionally and mentally exhausting, they had exhausted me financially. I calculated that I had spent around £10,000 per year over that period. Put differently - £100,000. And for what? To wake up with the same searing pain every day. If not worse.

And so, there it is. 10 years gone in a heartbeat from one perspective, and a soul-destroying eternity from another. Would I ever find a needle in the haystack, which became a 100-acre farm then a needle in the Sahara Desert?

Or was I looking for the wrong needle?

# 4

# Pain – One Name but Many Types

Having laid out my own individual journey with pain, let's explore what pain is before exploring the three core foundations of health:

- Mind
- Nutrition
- Body

I now know pain very well, but despite the unique characteristics of my own condition, it isn't unique to me. It's something that we all experience at some point in our lives – from the youngest to the oldest, pain is a part of life.

There are varying types of pain, but all are made more complicated if they cannot be seen. Whether the pain is emotional, physical, mental or even spiritual, if it occurs on the inside, further challenges arise. Consider the reaction of passers-by if they saw someone lying in the street with a broken leg compared to how they would react if they saw someone looking sad. People would feel far less urge to stop and help the person who looked sad because they wouldn't be able to see the depth of pain being experienced.

Different types of pain can also be interlaced, with one influencing another. Physical pain is one pain I know best, but after thousands of days of experiencing physical pain, emotional and mental pain have become added burdens.

When we think about pain, we think of it as something we want to get rid of as quickly as possible. We are naturally conditioned in this respect. It's almost like pain is a disease that we 'have'. But when I describe my own condition, I don't say that I 'have' pain. I say that I am 'in' pain. This is because pain is an experience rather than a disease.

During my research, my mentor gave me a book titled *Understanding and Healing Emotional Trauma*, by Daniela Sieff, which includes a valuable description of what pain is. It isn't a description in the absolute sense, but it provides a useful base for me to broaden out the subject of pain:

> *'Pain evolved to tell us that damage is occurring; it also evolved to be all-encompassing so as to motivate us to do everything in our power to get away from the source of that damage.'*

My own long-term journey with pain has brought me to conclude that the above can be broken down into two key areas. The first one I agree with, and the second one I question. Let me elaborate.

Throughout my 10-year search, I simply saw pain as a problem. It was the enemy I needed to defeat. I was persuaded my only chance for happiness was to extinguish this pain. What I didn't consider was that my pain represented a form of warning. A warning that there was much deeper damage occurring in my life. Damage that included, but also went beyond, the physical. Damage to the mind as well as the body.

### Pain is a type of alarm.

Imagine a family fast asleep upstairs in their house, when a fire breaks out downstairs in the kitchen. The fire alarm goes off, which wakes everyone and alerts them to the danger. The warning tells the family that there is something wrong. There is a threat to their health – one that may even cause death.

Now imagine the same situation without the alarm. The fire breaks out in the kitchen, the family remain asleep and oblivious to the danger. Initially, it doesn't cause too much damage, but as it starts to smoke and spread, the blaze creates more destruction.

By the time the family realize what's going on, it's too late. There's no escape, and there's no way out. At best, they may experience horrific injuries until rescued, and at worst, they may lose their lives. The point is that the alarm isn't there to endanger them but to alert them of potential danger.

This is what I finally realized with my pain. By spending 10 years trying to find a cure for my pain, I was trying to turn off an alarm in my body. I was ignorantly trying to silence the very thing that was alerting me of danger and telling me that damage was occurring.

## The Value of Pain

It's essential to be very clear – this shift in thinking about pain is far from easy. Especially if the pain is severe and persistent. I would never have believed in my darkest hours that I would learn to consider pain as something of value. In fact, it was the continuity of my pain over such an extended period that pushed me to explore the root cause.

> *Ignoring the root cause of pain illustrates the problem with painkillers. They switch off an alarm that the body is using to warn of the damage that is occurring.*

Imagine the family woke up, saw the fire, turned off the alarm and went back to bed. Madness, right? But that is precisely the behaviour that can occur with painkillers and antidepressants. And precisely what I did for a decade.

An obvious reaction to this re-evaluating of pain is that it's 'easier said than done'. I couldn't agree more, which is one of the reasons why I included a section detailing my 10-year search. To show just how long it took me to reach this stage of learning. It took me a decade to start seeing pain as something that I could learn from.

One thing I openly admit is that, although I've learned to treat pain differently, this isn't solely based on inner strength. I wish I could say that this is the case, but it isn't. Necessity has always been a significant driver for me, and with no other choice but to try and figure out a different way to live with pain, I simply kept putting one foot in front of the other.

I also openly admit that had I found a way to switch off the alarm of pain, I would have done so immediately. However, I've never discovered the alarm. I still haven't. What I have found, though, is that by replacing a search for a cure with exploration for the meaning behind pain, my quality of life has improved. My time is now better spent.

The part of Daniela Sieff's definition I question, perhaps because my case is unique, is doing everything in our power to get away from pain because pain doesn't always reveal to us the source of damage. Whereas 'acute' pain is more easily identified, 'chronic' pain isn't. If we can't identify the source of damage, then it becomes impossible to get away from it, because we don't know what we are trying to get away from.

What I am proposing reflects my own experience with chronic physical pain, but I believe that it applies to all types of pain. Whether emotional, mental or spiritual, there is value in learning to perceive pain as a type of alarm. It is there to tell us that something is wrong, and that change is required. If we keep trying to turn off the alarm and avoiding change, then we will remain in danger. If we listen to the alarm and make the required changes, then our lives can be enhanced.

As much as I wouldn't have chosen my path with pain, I don't know what my life would have been like without it. Perhaps my wilder side would have been my undoing. Maybe my pain saved me.

## The Invisible Enemy

One of the most challenging parts of dealing with my pain has been its devastating effect on my relationships with other people. One by one, I have watched friends, family, colleagues, and the people closest to me leave my life. Although I've learned not to blame, this hasn't made the experience any more comfortable.

> **The struggle with pain is deepened when it's experienced in isolation.**

I couldn't understand why others had so little sympathy, empathy or patience with me. But a pain that can't be seen can't be understood. Neither by the person suffering or those around.

'Everyone has their breaking point' is an often-used phrase, and the point at which each person left my life was a sign they'd reached their breaking point with me. The toughest one was with D. We met in February 2009 and separated in January 2017.

She'd reached her breaking point.

Excluding roughly the first 18 months of my battle with pain, D was there with me all the way. Despite my own failings in our relationship, she stayed by my side and it's bizarre why I didn't appreciate this. It shows how much we are shaped by our past and how difficult it can be to authentically change. Because at the time I was unable to show love, despite being shown so much love.

Of all the people that left my life, D was the last to leave. She hung on and hung on, but ultimately my physical pain was causing her great emotional pain. It's a horrible reality of chronic pain and occasionally even worse than the pain itself. When you see how your own pain is causing pain to someone else you care about so deeply, it makes the whole situation even more painful.

The reality, though, is that when other people reach their breaking point with you, this is not something that your own pain will allow.

Even though people left my life to get away from my pain, I could never do so. I was a prisoner of my own pain.

The judge had struck his hammer, and I'd been given a life sentence.

*Until we learn to understand pain, we will all remain prisoners of our pain.*

For me, there was only one definition of my own breaking point – death. It genuinely seemed like the only way to end my pain would be to end my life. I came close to going through with suicide on several occasions and that may sound extreme, but there is a sense to it. I was never that emotional about it. I never sat about crying with a capsule of pills in one hand and a bottle of whisky in the other. I just thought about it objectively.

On one occasion when my pain was at an all-time high, I'd barely slept and was dozing in and out of sleep in the early hours of the morning. I was having a kind of waking dream – a lucid dream – about how much pain I was in. How it was inconceivable to be able to live a life like this.

When I fully woke up later in the morning, I'd practically decided that I would commit suicide. And at that moment, I didn't feel emotional. It just made sense to me that there was no point continuing with life if every day of life was to include so much pain. By this time, I was also a father, but even that just added more sense to it all for me.

By ending my own pain, I could stop inflicting pain on those closest to me. Not physical pain, but the pain that they experienced indirectly through my daily battle.

Getting so close to the end was reflective of not only the pain I endured, but also of the loneliness it brought. The invisibility of my pain was very influential on the total lack of support that I received. People couldn't see it. There was no name for it. It just burned away inside of me.

*All pain will fester until we find the root cause.*

Despite coming close to suicide, I didn't take that option. I never took the jump of despair. Instead, I made a discovery. A discovery about how this end represented an edge. And it was at this edge where authentic change would take place.

Instead of a jump of despair, I took a leap of faith.


## Pain in Perpetuity

As I've described, the invisibility of my pain has always been one of the most challenging things to deal with. But if I had to choose the single most challenging characteristic – beyond the sensation of the actual physical pain – it would be the eternal nature of it.

It just doesn't stop.

Minute after minute, hour after hour, day after day, month after month, year after year. It truly is relentless. But despite both the perpetual nature and the invisibility, I've never hidden my pain.

In fact, one of the main reasons that I eventually spoke about it less was because it started to be construed as some kind of desperate need for attention. It became heavily misinterpreted and caused me to feel resentment toward others, due to their lack of compassion and patience.

I tried to explain what it was like to be in pain 24 hours per day, but none of it ever had the desired impact. I would passionately talk about how it affected every part of life, but very quickly the conversation would shift to something else. It was hurtful, and I found it challenging to deal with, but I now have a higher sense of understanding and acceptance.

How can you show compassion for something you can't see?

I also learned of more value that could be derived from pain. My own experience of dealing with the invisibility of internal pain taught me to have greater compassion for others. Pain is an undesirable experience, but with experience comes knowledge. I know what it's like to live with perpetual pain and so I can, therefore, add value to the lives of others through what I've learned.

Even though the relentless nature of my physical pain is unique to me, I've become much more aware that many others have a similar experience. Whether it is physical, emotional, mental or spiritual.

For example, if someone who has lost a loved one to death isn't given the necessary support to help them deal with this loss, they may well live the rest of their life in perpetual emotional pain. Another example is a soldier returning from conflict not being provided with any support on how to deal with the potentially horrifying experience in their mind, so a life of perpetual mental pain may be endured.

Therefore, I know I'm not the only person facing endless pain. I have, however, found a way to work with it and learn from it.

What I believe needs to be recognized is that non-stop pain can cause a significant change to someone's personality. That is what happened to me. Aside from my promiscuous shenanigans throughout my teens and twenties, I had a larger-than-life personality. There was a guy who loved life and who, although lived his life more selfishly, was always surrounded by lots of friends. Pain changed this. It stopped me laughing, it stopped me smiling, it made me far less social.

For example, consider a migraine, or at least a bad headache because practically everyone has had one:

If someone has a migraine all day, then they will probably be grouchy by the evening. If the migraine lasts all week, then their patience would most likely have worn thin. If the migraine lasts all month, then other people would most likely do their best to avoid them. And if the migraine lasted all year . . . well . . . let's just say that not many Christmas cards would be forthcoming.

But even though the obvious reaction is to try and numb the pain with painkillers, the reality remains that this means turning off the alarm. It stops the body and/or mind alerting us that there is something of concern that needs to be attended to.

## Changing My Relationship with Pain

Since this all began in 2007, I've gained many lessons, but none more significant than this:

**I learned to change my relationship with pain.**

This is because by perceiving pain differently, it could become more of a teacher in my life than an enemy. It took me more than a decade to change my relationship with pain, but that is not meant to be discouraging – it should instead instil trust that I am authentic.

The reason it took me so long is that I didn't have the educational tools at hand – with the right information, a relationship change with pain can come much sooner.

The first time I considered possibly changing my relationship with pain was in 2015 when I was with my mentor. It took me years to believe that a relationship change could occur with the intangible, but that first discussion planted a seed in my mind. One which would eventually grow into a healthy oak tree of thought.

However, a seed can only grow if it's nurtured. If it's cared for. If it's persistently attended to.

**Each time a seed of personal growth is planted in our minds, it has potential only. It's our responsibility to help it grow.**

The seed he planted in 2015 really started to flourish when I attended a Cambodian yoga retreat in 2017. It was here I began to learn more about Buddhism. And it was through practical learning that I was able to gain a deeper understanding of words spoken by my mentor; I had to separate from pain and re-evaluate pain before changing my relationship with pain.

It was at this yoga retreat where I learned to meditate. When I first started, I could barely sit for 60 seconds. The pain was too severe. But I persevered, and with practice, I slowly improved. I was gradually able to meditate for longer.

The first part of the lesson between meditation and my pain was that around separation. It was far from easy at first – as I had endured thousands of days of pain by this point – but again, I persevered. Despite this, though, I found myself becoming frustrated. This is because I was getting confused with a separation from pain and a relinquishing of pain.

The problem was I had allowed myself to slip into an expectation that meditation would take away my pain. I needed to learn to delineate between separation and eradication. However, through more practice, I learned to try and just let my pain be. It was there, it was real, but it didn't need to dominate me. The separation wasn't profound, and it wasn't physical. It was happening in my mind. I was nurturing the seed my mentor had planted.

It's crucial to emphasize that this meditative experience didn't take away my pain. It didn't even reduce it. But my goal wasn't to eradicate or even reduce my pain, despite a powerful desire for this to happen, my goal was to change my relationship with pain. To accept that pain would remain with me, but that I could work with it in an alternative way.

This is where the seed planted in my mind by my mentor, was watered by the teachings of Buddhism.

The teachings of Buddhism are vast, but I learned one incredibly powerful lesson very quickly – 'Buddha' means 'teacher'. It was then that the seed really began to grow, and an astounding thought came to my mind: 'Was it possible my pain was a teacher in my life?'

The thought should have needed time to sink in, but it was as if my whole being had been waiting on this. Like it knew what was coming, and therefore prepared for it. I experienced an almost instantaneous moment of realization:

*My pain wasn't just a teacher. It was the ultimate teacher.*

This realization was extraordinary. But it was still only a realization. And realizing this didn't actually help to reduce my pain. Rather than let the usual disappointment take hold of me, I committed to more profound thought. I asked myself this question: 'If my pain was indeed the ultimate teacher in my life, then why would it be so relentless?'

My mind then went back to when I was captain of Stirling University football team. What were the characteristics that made me a successful coach and leader? As I wrote down those characteristics, a picture started to form – sacrifice, commitment, perseverance, persistence and a willingness to do what needed to be done. This provoked another question:

'What was the goal that my pain was trying to help me achieve?'

Although I couldn't answer this question at the time, it wasn't really the point. The point was that I continued to nurture this seed of thought, which had grown from an initial concept of changing my relationship with pain to seeing pain as a teacher in my life.

Once my mentor and I started to piece together more pieces of this puzzle around the meaning of my pain, a picture began to form. I considered that by perceiving my pain as a type of teacher in my life, I could more constructively work with it to achieve goals that, so far, had eluded me.

## The Glass Ceiling of Fear

Throughout my life, I'd often dared to aim for loftier goals, but when I reached a certain point, fear took over and I withdrew. I call this experience the 'glass ceiling of fear'. The trouble was I could see through it and had a vision of my loftier goals but couldn't break through. Extraordinarily, after all that I'd been through, perhaps it would be pain that pushed me through. Perhaps pain would help me reduce fear in my life, despite having lived with so much fear because of it.

As the picture became more transparent, further answers were forthcoming. For the first time, I was asking questions around my pain, and being provided with answers of depth. If my pain was indeed a type of teacher in my life, then I could adopt the mindset that this teacher was doing everything possible to keep me from being distracted.

*If we can learn to accept that the goal of pain is to push us to our potential, then we can use pain to our advantage.*

In other words, it was forcing me to stay away from the wilder side of life that I previously enjoyed which, although fun, was a significant distraction from reaching my true potential.

The analogy of the alarm became powerfully applicable. I started to accept my pain as an alarm in my life, alerting me how my lifestyle was causing me harm. Not just physically, but also mentally, as I became more frustrated by carrying the knowledge that I could do more than I was doing. I realized that I could live a life of purpose greater than my own.

It's crucial to note what I'm proposing here is all about perception. None of this was something that I could see and touch. But a change in mindset is one of the most powerful changes we can ever make. All of this was happening in my mind, but I still found it difficult to give up my social life. Adopting this new mindset helped me get past this in the same way that an athlete retains discipline when training for an event and has a purpose.

The seed my mentor planted in my mind has been one that I have been nurturing ever since. By learning to separate from pain, then re-evaluate pain, and finally change my relationship with it, I have been able to make significant progress in my mind.

This was progress in a much healthier definition. It was no longer about finding a cure. It was about learning to understand that pain can be the missing link to breaking through the glass ceiling of fear.

*Personal growth requires experiencing pain personally.*

43

# 5

# Purpose Through Pain

When I learned to change my relationship with pain, a door opened to something of significant meaning that added another dimension to my struggle. That something was finding purpose in my pain.

Not everybody asks the question, but the truth is that we'd all like to know why we're here. Each of us wants to know our purpose. We don't need to seek the meaning of life overall, but rather the meaning of our lives individually. This is an important discrepancy.

Consider why it's so demoralizing to be unappreciated or unnoticed at work or at home. It's because it makes us feel like we have no purpose. Conversely, when we see that we've made a difference, we feel valued. We feel that there was a reason for us to have put in so much time and effort. We feel we had a purpose.

What is important to remember is that feeling unappreciated is internal. If you were having a bad day at work but going on a dream holiday the next day, then that bad day wouldn't seem so bad. What was happening at work would be no different, but the difference would be in your mind.

The point is that if you are completely at peace with yourself, you can theoretically be happy in any job.

> *Primary change must come from within to allow for the true benefit of exterior change.*

Where purpose adds further value is that it can help find this inner peace. For me, this was incredibly important because I found it very difficult to be happy while in so much pain. There was an apparent correlation between happiness and pain in that more pain would always equate to less happiness. I was left to wonder whether I could ever be happy again if my pain were indeed perpetual.

As I pondered this, I read more by Daniela Sieff:

> *'Bolstered by modern media, we tend to believe that a normal life is happy, that anything other than happiness is abnormal and that there is something wrong with us when we feel depressed. The revelation that there is some evolutionary sense to our emotional suffering can help us quit blaming ourselves and other people, and concentrate on what we need to feel better.'*

I found these words insightful because they taught me to put less pressure on being happy. It was understandable that I was struggling to be happy because I was in so much pain every day – my chronic pain condition wasn't my fault, and neither was my unhappiness. This helped me achieve more self-acceptance.

## New Perspective

When we start to look more deeply at what we have the power to change in life, we realize that everything around us is out of our control. We can't control how other people behave or what happens, but we can change our perspective. Going back to the bad day at work example, the holiday didn't change anything at work, but instead provided a different way of thinking: 'Who cares about all the bad stuff today because I'm going on holiday tomorrow.'

Even though I couldn't change the reality of my chronic pain, despite 10 years of trying, I could adopt a new perspective. I could place less emphasis on achieving happiness and more on feeling fulfilled.

This book offers a perfect example of how I have achieved fulfilment but not necessarily happiness. There were periods when my pain was so bad that I had to write one-handed with the other hand holding my stomach. I'd be bent over in agony and writing on my knees sometimes. Of course, this wasn't a happy experience, but it was still fulfilling.

The explanation for this is that, whereas my happiness is all about me, my fulfilment is related to helping other people. Therefore, I believe that pain can't corrupt fulfilment in the same way that it can happiness. In fact, there can be an opposing relationship:

**More pain may decrease happiness but increase fulfilment.**

What I'm proposing here may be difficult to accept at first, but it is incredibly valuable. It also underlines the value of changing our relationship with pain. By seeing pain as a teacher, we can learn to perceive increased pain as a stricter lesson; it isn't something we want or enjoy, but we can't deny how valuable the education is.

Going back to writing this book as an example – I didn't create it because of being in pain, but because of the magnitude of pain.

When my pain started in 2007, it was nowhere near as bad as it would become years later. Yet, it was because the pain got so bad that I became more dedicated to finding the purpose behind it and helping others. This became my life's purpose.

I didn't discover the meaning of 'life'. I discovered the meaning of 'my life'.

Although my pain is unique to me, what I'm proposing here can apply to all pain. Whether in the form of trauma, loss, emotional distress, mental struggle or any other, if the painful experience endured can be used to help other people, then pain cannot stop fulfilment being achieved.

Our paths to fulfilment will vary, but we all share common ground in helping other people; it exists in all of us, regardless of how destructive humanity can be.

We may also find that our own pain starts to decrease as we become more selfless. Going back to my two previous examples in Chapter 4, someone who has lost a loved one will help themselves if they can reach out and share their experience with another person who has recently been bereaved. A soldier returning from conflict can find more inner peace by helping others who went through the same traumatic experience.

No matter what pain you are experiencing, you can find purpose.

**A life dedicated to helping others in pain cannot be anything else, but a life lived in less pain.**

Trying to help other people in pain hasn't directly reduced my own, but it has allowed me to find more inner peace. I am still in pain but suffer less. I am alive in pain rather than existing in pain.

Finding purpose in my pain has become so powerfully important to me, that it's difficult to put into words. However, the below paragraph encapsulates it most accurately. It is a word-for-word outpouring of emotion that was recorded during one occasion when I was with my mentor and opening up about living with chronic pain every day:

*. . . purpose is the difference between killing yourself and not. And I'm not embellishing that at all. Because it's the difference between just surviving . . . and living. And it's even worse than just surviving because if you only survive, it's like getting through each day, but this [chronic pain] is just hanging on. And then you get to the point of 'what is the point'? Why not just let go? If you know that every single day, you are going to have a migraine or be in such pain, it's just debilitating. Why hang on? Even if we find more depth, and we realize that we are all just specks of dust in the universe, then what does it matter if I live another year or another 35 years? Why hang on for another 35 years? The answer is purpose. If there is purpose behind my*

*pain, then it is worth hanging on for. It's worth fighting for. And when that purpose is about more than just me, it's a purpose that gains in potency. If my reason for being alive is to help others in pain, then I have found a reason for being alive . . .*

## Struggle Is Necessary

Finding purpose in our lives is extraordinary but doesn't guarantee a comfortable life. One of the reasons I felt a connection with my mentor from the moment we met was because of the life he'd lived. He had great wisdom, but it wasn't limited to his education in psychology or professional experience. It was also related to his own life. The pain and struggle he had endured in his life, led him to live a life dedicated to helping others. It was his pain and struggle that led him to his purpose. The struggle was therefore necessary.

My life has followed a similar path. I never wanted to live a life with chronic pain, and I still don't 'want' it. But it has provided the extreme push needed to take me to the only place in life where real and lasting change happens – at the edge.

What is essential to recognize is that struggle in life doesn't have to represent doom and gloom. Climbing a mountain includes strenuous challenge, but the view at the top can be beautifully rewarding. The struggle endured is, therefore, one of value. From a certain perspective, all struggle has some kind of value.

Finding my purpose in life helped me to become more at peace with my struggle. It helped reduce negative emotions, such as anger and frustration, and this made way for a more positive state of mind. One which invited a more open-minded way of thinking, such as perceiving my pain as a teacher or Buddha in my life. Suddenly I began to feel like I was working for the world, rather than working for myself.

*Whenever you are ready to tell the world that you are ready for service, the world will tell you, 'I am at your service.'*

Even though it's my pain that has caused a change in me, it doesn't mean that I've converted in some way. It's merely a recognition that there is an energy in the world which, when used in the right way, can lead to an expansion of our inner being. We can become more open-minded and more considerate of others.

## Being at Peace

When I look back at my past, I see how I was always trying to run up a mountain wearing ice skates. No matter how hard I tried, I just couldn't get anywhere. It was exhausting. Finding purpose in my life and becoming more at peace with struggle hasn't changed the elevation of the mountain, but did give me the chance to put on more appropriate footwear.

Recognizing the connection between purpose and struggle is essential. Because even if we haven't yet found our purpose, it's through our times of struggle that we might just find it. There is an example from my own life which, despite the obscure circumstance, helps illustrate this.

In spring 2016, I attended a friend's stag party in Budapest. I was used to missing social occasions by this point, but I decided to go and try. I knew I'd have to refrain from drinking alcohol, but I figured that it was a chance to see lots of old friends. Abstaining from alcohol bothered me less than not being able to truly join in with the old friendly banter. Everyone always says you don't need alcohol to have fun, but when the location of the fun is a pub with everybody getting drunk, you can't help but feel like a spare wheel.

On the second day, I came very close to caving in as the banter was flowing, and old stories were getting told. Would it really be so bad if I just had a few beers? I knew the answer, but I wondered if long-term pain was worth some short-term fun.

Just as I was about to grab a beer, a friend wandered over in a drunken state. He proceeded to tell me how his wife was having severe digestive issues. 'It doesn't matter what she eats,' he told me. A plight which I was more than familiar with.

He knew about my own battle with pain, so he just wanted to open up to somebody who could understand how she felt. And how he felt. He was totally lost as to what to do.

There at that exact moment in my own struggle of temptation, the world reminded me of my purpose. It told me that there were people everywhere that I could help, but only if I remained committed to 0 Days Off.

The reason that I've added this example is to highlight the point that struggle is very individual. Resisting drinking alcohol in a pub with friends may seem easy to others and not warrant the title of 'real struggle', but for me, it was. I desperately missed the camaraderie with old pals, and such experiences only served to make me feel more alone.

Being told that our struggles are not as bad as some others, offers very little value. Yes, people are starving in the world, but how does this help us with our own individual struggle? Our own individual pain?

It doesn't.

Struggle and pain are unique for every individual, and none of us should feel obligated to qualify either.

We don't even have to prove that our struggle has depth. My stag party example of struggle could not be farther away from finding a depth of meaning in life. But yet, it was through this experience I was reminded of the extent of my own life.

*In order to find peace, we must endure struggle.*

# 6

# Pain and Suffering – Relatives yet Strangers

Before I was able to change my relationship with pain, and really to start to learn from it, I was suffering a lot. The definition of suffering I always placed in close correlation with pain. I thought of them as much the same thing, and the *Oxford English Dictionary* definition of suffering served only to support me in my thinking: '[Suffering is] the state of undergoing pain, distress, or hardship.'

A useful way to try and more simply define suffering is to consider the grammatical context in which it is used. We can think of suffering as something that we 'do' and pain as something that we 'experience'.

For example, if you break your leg, you will undoubtedly feel physical pain. But your level of suffering, while the plaster is on, will depend on how you relate to pain. By linking to pain with an open mind, the sensation of pain will remain, but you'll suffer less. If you relate to the pain with a closed mind, then you'll compound the pain by suffering more.

Suffering and pain can, therefore, be deemed as different. Even though a close relationship exists.

## Do We Choose to Suffer?

As I learned more about suffering and this idea that we don't need to suffer even though we are in pain, I came across a thought-provoking question: 'Do we actually choose to suffer?'

At first, this concept seemed alien. Why would anyone choose to suffer? It almost aggravated me, as my own journey with chronic pain wasn't of my choosing. Therefore, all the suffering that accompanied it was also not of my choosing.

However, the deeper I dug in my exploration for knowledge, the more I learned.

Pain is unavoidable. It is a part of life. It is a part of all our lives. No matter who we are, where we are born, or what circumstances into which we are born, we will all experience pain as we make our way through life. My chronic physical pain is perpetual, so it never ends. But even if it did, it wouldn't mean I would never endure any other type of pain again. There will always be another type of pain to overcome. This applies to all of us. For example, just because we recover from the physical pain of a broken leg doesn't mean we will never again experience the emotional pain of losing someone we love.

When I was sitting by Mum's bedside in the hospital before she died, my chronic physical pain was extreme due to the amount of stress I was experiencing. Yet, this pain wasn't at the forefront of my mind. I can't even recall noticing it. The emotional pain I was experiencing in my mum's final moments was so intense that it took over every other sensation in my body and mind.

*We will all continue to have encounters with pain, which makes it unavoidable. Suffering, however, can be avoided. That is the theoretical thought and discrepancy.*

The explanation of this statement is that suffering isn't something that is caused upon us by external circumstances and influences. It's something that we choose to do inside of our being. Although I'm not putting this forward as definitive, it's an interesting concept that can be learned from. Because not everything has to be definitive for us to learn. That which is non-definitive can still have a definitive impact on our lives.

During my 10-year search, it could be said that I was choosing to suffer. Not because I had a desire to be in physical pain, but because I was trying to find a cure for it. I was trying to turn off the alarm that my pain represented, and the act of continually searching was a choice I was making.

Once I made a choice to stop searching for this cure, and accept my pain as part of my life, my suffering started to lessen.

My suffering lessened because I learned to change my relationship with pain.

This concept of choosing to suffer isn't easy to grasp. But it is one that can help us better understand how to deal with pain. A useful example is when someone mistreats us. Not in a physical sense, but rather hurting our feelings or betraying us.

The damage that occurs isn't something that's in the control of the person who is mistreating us. It's in our control because it's damage that is happening internally. If we let their harmful or negative behaviour continue to eat away inside of us, then we are continually choosing to suffer. If, however, we dismiss their actions as a waste of time and let them have little effect on us, then we are actively choosing to suffer less.

We suffer less because our suffering isn't taking place through the mistreatment of the other person. It's taking place in our mind. The event happened only once and is already in the past, but we keep it alive by replaying it over and again in our heads.

**Suffering takes place in our mind, not in our environment.**

Despite the sense of this, it isn't easy to practically execute in our daily lives. Not only do we need to educate the mind, but the state of modern society is entirely out of sync with how to deal with our own suffering. People continually collate more and more material things, thinking that these will somehow reduce their suffering.

They won't. They can't.

Material things – including money – don't address the source of our suffering.

We suffer in our minds.

During my 10-year search, I kept trying to reduce my suffering by making more money and finding more ways to cure my pain. This resulted in me suffering more. Years of my life were being committed to causes, which only ever led to disappointment and disheartenment.

Only when I looked inside myself, changed my relationship with pain and found purpose in my life, could I ease my own suffering.

## Inner Pain Requires Inner Change

The reality for most people in modern society is they place too little emphasis on internal change. This isn't a criticism because I was the same before learning more. They simply don't understand the futility of external change without internal consideration. My previous example of changing job illustrates this, but the principle applies to every area of life.

Relationships often fall apart because two partners blame each other rather than address the internal change that is required. This is what happened with D. Putting aside the significant impact of my pain, our problems as a couple had nothing to do with our external circumstances and everything to do with my inability to change internally.

It wouldn't have mattered where we lived, what holidays we went on or what actions we took, nothing would improve because I wasn't focusing on the internal. Or rather, I didn't know how to.

This is a personal example but the same applies to addiction, mental pain, loss or literally any other situation that can be thought of. Location changes, different things, new career, switching relationships or anything else externally driven will not solve the main problem. It's what is happening internally that matters.

> **What we need to remind ourselves of continually is that every-thing we need to be fulfilled is already inside of us.**

Another personal example is when my mum moved to Clydebank to escape the memories of my dad in Annan. The move made sense and helped temporarily but didn't resolve her inner turmoil. And in a turn of irony, my brother and I later got her a house back in Annan. I will always remember what she said when we were driving the removal van back to Annan: 'Let's go home, boys.'

But what is home? Is home bricks and mortar or a place where a feeling of peace resides? If you can live with less pain, does it matter whether you live in a castle or a caravan?

No matter where we go, we can't escape internal pain and no external action can change this. When I used to tell people that I couldn't escape my pain, I did so in the context that it was unique to me, but I've since learned that this is the case for everybody.

External actions which give a brief respite can be thought about as painkillers. Just like my mum's move to Clydebank provided temporary relief, it didn't get to the root of the problem. In fact, like any painkiller, it distracted from getting to the root cause and numbed the very thing that was trying to manifest itself as a change in her life.

## Painkillers Kill the Alarm

There have been many paradoxes in my journey with pain and one of these is how painkillers didn't work for me. I certainly understand why people take them, and there is no doubt that, during my 10-year search, I desperately wanted drugs to work. But outside of drowning myself in alcohol, nothing ever did.

*The problem with drugs is the problem with drugs.  Types may vary, but the damage is the same.*

Although I experienced endless disappointment during that decade, I now realize that it was not finding a drug that worked, which forced me to try and find a more natural way to deal with pain. Paradoxically, failure to reduce pain through medicinal means, led me to discover a more natural and fulfilling life.

This begs the question, 'Do painkillers offer an effective solution to dealing with pain?'

Consider this example: when we get a headache, we take a painkiller. We want a solution to the pain, and we want it fast. However, although a painkiller may address this single event of pain, it doesn't get to the cause. It can even create a damaging link between pain and drugs. These drugs can be medicinal or otherwise. Because whether a drug is legal or illegal has no bearing on the harmful link that can be created.

The reason that the link can be damaging is due to dependency. Every time we experience any kind of pain, we may end up looking to painkillers to solve this pain, because a connection between reduced pain and painkillers has been created.  When dependency occurs, it means that the body and/or mind has learned to recognize the importance of a drug. A physical need, as well as a need in the mind, develops, and if this need isn't met, withdrawal symptoms can occur.

Although getting a headache is unlikely to lead to drug dependency, the principle remains the same for any type of pain. Once we start to associate painkillers with pain relief, then we create a connection.

The vast majority of people who use medicinal means to ease their pain don't suddenly take the most potent form of drug available. There is a graduation process, which is often overlooked when someone is down and out. One which will most likely have started with a weaker drug.

The catalyst for this graduation through taking stronger drugs is that tolerance is created, which occurs when we no longer respond in the same way to a drug that once provided pain relief. This then leads to one of three possibilities:

1. the dosage of the same drug is increased; or
2. a new, and usually stronger, drug is taken; or
3. there is an exploration of the actual cause of the pain.

The unfortunate reality is that the third possibility is by far the most challenging road, because it involves experiencing more pain while the exploration is carried out. I've been exploring pain for more than a decade, and the whole journey has been fraught with failure and demoralization.

This is why I don't claim to have immediately found the courage to learn about my pain. I bounced between the first two possibilities for years. It was only when I didn't find a short-term or long-term solution that I then began to dig deeper through the third possibility. It's also why I have great compassion for anyone who has become dependent on strong painkillers such as opioids. Painkillers of which often do not provide the desired relief from pain and even when they do, only provide a very short-lived relief.

This point of short-term or long-term effect is vital in trying to answer the question I posed earlier. If painkillers are a short-term solution, then they can arguably be described as effective. However, the negative consequence of creating dependency and tolerance seem to far outweigh the short-term relief from pain.

The dangers of addiction and tolerance are dramatically emphasized by assessing statistical data around the number of deaths that are due to using painkillers, such as opioids. The data on the following pages relates to the UK and the US:

## Age-Standardized Deaths Drug Misuse, 1993 to 2016 (England & Wales)

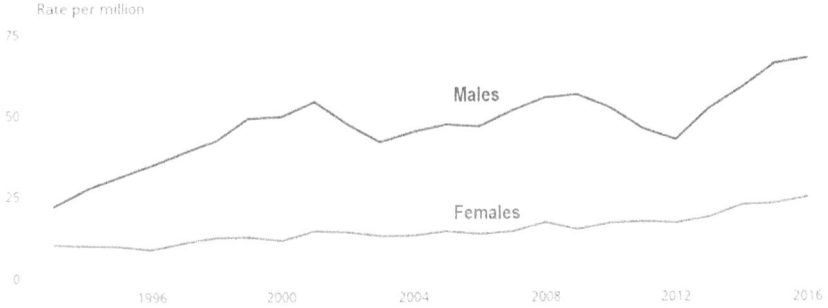

Source: Office for National Statistics, July 2019[1]

## National Drug Overdose Deaths, by Gender, 1999 to 2017 (US)

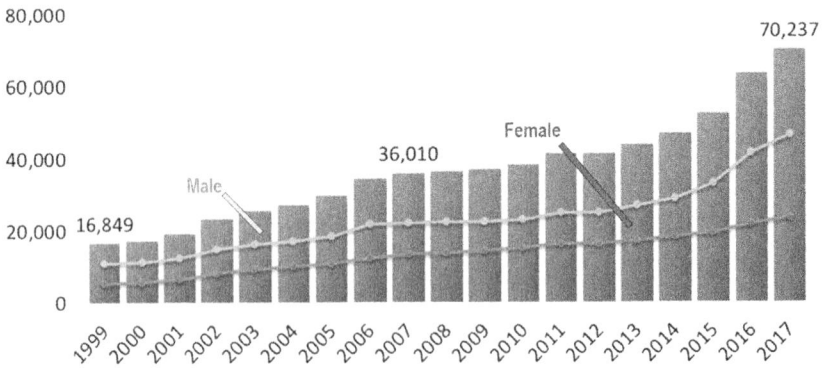

[1]  https://www.ons.gov.uk/peoplepopulationandcommunity/birthsdeathsandmar-
    riages/deaths/bulletins/deathsrelatedtodrugpoisoninginenglandandwales/2016reg-
    istrations

## Overdose Deaths Involving Prescription Opioids, 1999 to 2017 (US)

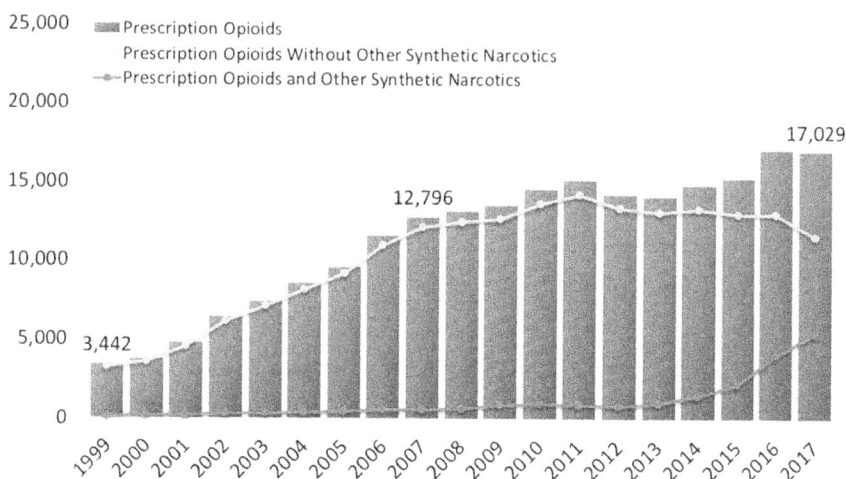

Source: National Institute on Drug Abuse, July 2019[2]

Without even closely analysing the statistical data, what is glaringly clear is the trend that more people are dying from either the 'use' or 'misuse' of painkillers. 'Use' relating to those drugs someone chooses to take of their own volition and 'misuse' relating to those drugs prescribed by a practitioner.

In the US, the scale of the prescription drug problem seems to have reached epidemic proportions. In 2016, more than 40 per cent of all US opioid overdose deaths involved a prescription.

The inclusion of this statistical analysis illustrates that the impact of painkillers on life overall is far more negative than positive. So much so, the eventuality of death can occur.

Death from painkiller use represents a tragic ending. Because not only has a life been lost, but the end usually comes after living in so much pain. The 'use' or 'misuse' of painkillers to the point of death often

---

[2]  https://www.drugabuse.gov/related-topics/trends-statistics/overdose-death-rates (also applies to previous table)

represents a person desperately reaching out for help and a means to reduce the pain they are experiencing. And who's to say my life wouldn't have ended the same way, had I found a painkiller that reduced my pain?

**Painkillers don't 'kill' pain. They temporarily 'numb' it.**

I now clearly understand that if I'd found an effective painkiller, I would have followed a very different path in life. One which would have encouraged me to cause more self-damage through alcohol consumption and one which would have led me away from finding my purpose.

I would never have written this book and I may well have ended up as another statistic on one of those charts. Therefore, to answer my earlier question, I don't believe painkillers offer an effective solution to dealing with pain. I believe we should focus on 'working' with pain rather than 'dealing' with pain. This will encourage a better quality of life long term.

## Short or Long Term

None of what I propose here is easy. This book isn't about having an easy life because I know the harsh reality of waking up in pain, going through every day in pain and going to bed in pain. I know this over thousands of days. It's very, very hard, which is why, as I said before, I don't judge anybody else for taking painkillers.

**2005**

**2015**

107 per cent increase

29.5 million antidepressant prescriptions

61 million antidepressant prescriptions

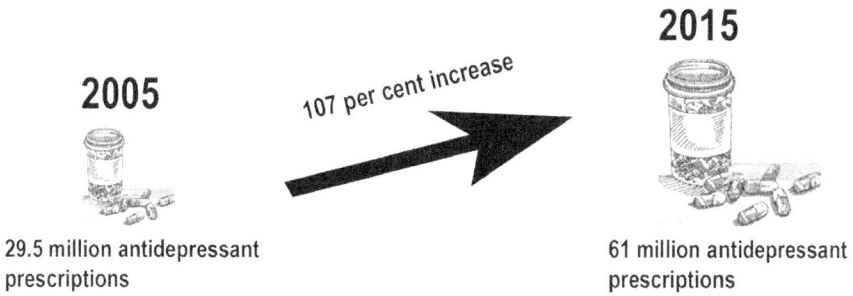

*Source: Mental Health Foundation, July 2019*[3]

Living with pain can be a living nightmare, but if we can start to see pain as something we can learn from, rather than something we need to hide from, then we may find an inner peace that we never had before the pain started.

We may even discover that it is pain that pushes us through the glass ceiling of fear and on towards our potential.

---

[3] https://www.mentalhealth.org.uk/publications/fundamental-facts-about-mental-health-2016

# III

# The Mind

*The mind is no different from the body. It won't develop unless we exercise it.*

# 7

# The Mind Is a Muscle

Developing the mind is the same as developing the physical body. Just like the muscles that make up our body, the mind can also be perceived as a muscle. To increase muscle strength, we need to work out the body. The mind needs a different type of exercise from say, our abs or quads, and a different environment exists, but the approach follows the same principles.

Practice, perseverance, consistency, discipline and doing repetitions, are all principles behind developing the physical body through exercise. The mind is no different; we need to practice, we need to persevere, we need to be consistent, we need to show discipline, and we need to train repeatedly.

As dull as repetitions may be, this is where the real value lies because if we don't train the body enough, it will be weak. If we don't train the body at all, it will deteriorate. This same principle applies to the mind.

It might be challenging to admit, but being weak-minded is more common than we think. That doesn't mean we're to blame and there's cause for offence. The reality is that most of us weren't educated in how to train the mind. If it isn't possible to strengthen the physical body without training, then how is it possible to strengthen the mind without an equivalent workout?

It isn't.

Once I accepted – without judgement and self-criticism – that my mind hadn't been adequately exercised, then it brought me into self-awareness. I committed to training my mind and subsequently started to move forward. But the first step was removing judgement because it led to self-criticism, with self-criticism leading to negative thinking, and then leading to fear. Fear can be debilitating.

**Fear is a dark room where negatives are developed.**

In the same way as going to the gym requires discipline, hard work and time, developing the mind isn't a quick fix and shouldn't be underestimated. Nobody works out once and expects to walk out of the gym looking like a professional bodybuilder. There are a sense and appreciation for the level of work needed, as well as the amount of time required.

The same sense and recognition are necessary for the mind.

I've learned that, like training the physical body, there will also be setbacks. Even when I started putting in real time and work, I kept taking steps backwards. I continued to let little things bother me and I continued to waste time worrying about things I couldn't change.

What helped me reduce self-judgement was recognizing that these setbacks reflected my mind's lack of education. I accepted it wasn't my fault because I learned to understand I hadn't received the necessary training. For example, consider a standard school curriculum. How much time is committed to educating the body? How much time is committed to developing the mind? A lot and none.

By recognizing this gap in our development, we effectively start to be more empathetic and compassionate towards ourselves and others so minimize judgement. We can commit to training the mind with more freedom, and we can grow as individuals. This is what I experienced personally.

Once I started to train my mind with commitment, I then recognized further synergy with my body. That of continual development. If I were to stop training my body, then it would weaken. The same occurs with the mind. Practice, perseverance, consistency, discipline and doing repetitions. The principles are the same.

And eventually, after all those repetitions, there is a particularly powerful reward: a reduction of fear in our lives.

## Understanding Stress

Stress is one of the biggest corrupters of life and remains profoundly misunderstood and underestimated. It is also one of the most significant obstacles in developing the mind muscle. If our minds are continually under a lot of pressure, then it makes it very difficult for us to grow this muscle. Like having a back injury prevents us from exercising, having stress in our minds prevents us from practising.

Stress is clever. Stress is ruthless. When the body has a weakness, stress will target this area. If this is left unattended, then stress will manifest. It can even compound whatever problem we have and worsen our situation. Stress can also be the root cause of illness or pain. I may not know what started my pain, but there is a direct correlation between my stress levels and the magnitude of pain that I experience. More stress has always equated to more pain for me.

Dealing with stress isn't easy. Even when we identify that we're feeling stressed, this doesn't mean we're automatically equipped to deal with it. In fact, without training the mind muscle, we don't have any tools at our disposal and too often our efforts to combat stress are ineffective or even self-destructive. By turning to drugs and alcohol, we can temporarily numb our senses, but when the effects wear off, the stress is still there and often worse. The condition of the mind is often worse. I believe the same applies to medicinal painkillers and anti-depressants.

> *The use of any mood-altering chemical, whether medicinal or recreational, denies us the opportunity of developing the mind.*

The only way to effectively manage stress is to shift our focus internally and address what it is inside of us that we need to change. If we don't then a vicious cycle can start, and my 10-year search is a perfect example of this. By searching for a cure, I was avoiding the need for change and continued to switch off the alarm that my body used to alert me of danger.

This led to more pain and, as a result, I felt trapped, exhausted and afraid.

## What Is Stress?

So, what is stress? Is it individually manufactured? Does it even exist? Why do some people experience stress more than others?

There isn't a simple answer to these questions because stress is a very complex phenomenon. But if I were pressed to give a definition of what stress has meant in my own life, it would be as follows: stress is an emotional reaction that takes control of the mind and body against our will, and in doing so, causes damage to our being.

Even though stress can be damaging to both the mind and body, we don't want to completely eradicate it because a certain amount can help us reach our goals and stay motivated. When stress is in balance, it could even be defined differently – rather than stress, it becomes focus. Our mind becomes sharp and we are in the moment – an example being athletes who perform at their peak when it counts the most.

> ***Our moment of truth can be defined by our understanding of stress.***

The way we turn stress into focus is the same way that we turn an unfit body into a fit body – we exercise the required muscles. When we exercise, we put the body under stress. We may even put it under so much stress, that we tear the muscles, which is what bodybuilders do. This is because when the tissue heals, it is more developed than it is was before. We don't want to tear our mind, but we do want to experience some stress to get the required practice. And the more we practice, the less stressful the same situation will seem as we become more focused.

The habit of most people is to blame the amount of stress they're experiencing on the situation that they're in. But consider who would endure more stress in this example – the president of a country addressing a nation, who has had extensive training on the mind, or an office worker speaking in front of a small team, who has had no training at all?

The point is that the level of stress we experience is far more related to what is happening inside of us than our external situation. And if we have put in the time to develop our mind muscle, then we'll be better equipped to deal with whatever external situation arises. We can stay in 'the zone', as it is often referred to, where we are not lethargic but also not panicking.

**The zone**

| Zero Stress | | | | | | | | | | Extreme Stress |
|---|---|---|---|---|---|---|---|---|---|---|
| laziness | | | | | | | | | | anxiety |
| lethargy | 1 | 2 | 3 | 4 | 5 | 6 | 7 | 8 | 9 | 10 | pain/illness |
| no drive | | | | | | | | | | panic |
| no motivation | | | | | The zone | | | | | no present mind |
| no positive pressure | | | | | | | | | | anger |

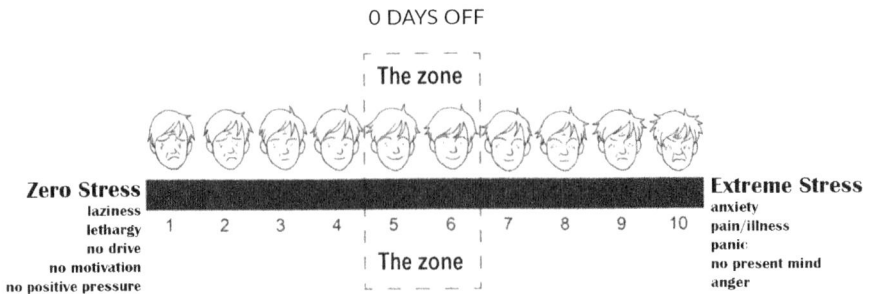

In the above illustration, being in the zone is 5 to 6 on the stress scale as this is where we find balance. What often prevents us from achieving balance is that we act so emotionally, but again, this isn't about judgement – human beings are emotional creatures. When someone is unkind or hurts us, or we receive bad news, then we have an emotional reaction. This is a natural response, but because we generally don't understand how the mind works, sometimes these emotional responses are out of kilter.

Emotional responses provide us with a signal to attend to what is happening so do have value. If we react with fear, we need to attend to what is making us frightened. If we respond with sadness, we need to attend to what is making us sad. If we react with shock, we need to attend to what has shocked us. However, rather than trying to eradicate emotional responses, we need to focus on what happens next.

By allowing an emotional reaction to take place and concentrating on what follows, we are better able to manage stress. We allow ourselves the opportunity to remain more focused and less stressed by staying around 5 or 6 on the scale.

*You don't need to change your situation to live with less stress. You need to change your mind.*

As my pain worsened over the years, my stress levels were constantly up at a 10 on this scale. I was ultimately out of balance. Stress was destroying me. No medicine, drug nor diet changed this. The only thing that has allowed me to bring it back towards a 5 or 6 was educating and training my mind.

As you will read throughout this book, all such lessons come back to my pain. Had I not started to experience chronic pain in 2007, I would never have learned about training my mind. My pain has therefore been a hardship in my life but has forced me down a path of learning that has taught me to reduce other forms of pain, such as mental stress. What follows in the next two chapters are the core lessons that have helped me achieve this.

# 8

# Desire, Intent and Process

One of the most significant causes of stress is when our expectations don't fit with the reality of a situation. When things don't work out the way we want them to, we can be left feeling disappointed, frustrated and even confused.

Without a better understanding of how to deal with this, an increase in stress can occur.

This is because whenever we set out to achieve a goal, we create mental images. We have a desire. A vision of how we want it to work out.

Once the desire is established, then we set our mind to achieve this goal. A mental plan is drawn out; an intent is created.

Most of us have fewer problems with desire and intent. Whether it is something trivial, like getting our chores done at home, or something more involved, such as setting up a viable business, creating a desire and setting an intention is usually straightforward. For example, if you have to clean a house, you plan; perhaps take out the rubbish, then vacuum, and finally put your clothes away. In doing so, you set an intent. If you desire to be your own boss and therefore decide to quit a full-time job and take out a loan, an intention is set.

What is less straightforward in our minds is how we deal with what happens next.

Once we are actively working toward a goal, we follow a process – the thing that comes after the desire and intent. The process of getting our chores done will most likely match the intent that we set. However, when the challenges are of a greater magnitude, then sometimes getting the desire, intention and process in sync is much more difficult.

Taking the other example, if we're setting up a business for the first time, then our process is likely to digress from our original intention. Because the higher the goal, the greater the number of variables. Finance, marketing, accounting, economic impact, customer behaviour, operational challenges, investor issues and management are all examples of the variables faced in setting up a new business.

So, where does stress occur in all of this?

Stress occurs in the gap between our intent and our process. This is the case across all aspects of life, and not just in the example of setting up a business. Becoming a first-time parent is another example. I don't know one parent who had their first child and a year later said that it had all worked out exactly how they expected.

Far from it!

I go back to this crucial point where stress occurs, which isn't in the external situation but rather internally in the mind. It is stressful setting up a business or being a first-time parent, but the degree of stress experienced will depend on the state of the mind muscle. This is why some people handle either experience better than others.

Therefore, developing the mind muscle is critical because it can be the difference between living a life of stress compared with living a life of focus.


## The Outcome

Once we become more focused than stressed, it's then important to understand where our focus should sit in relation to desire, intent and process. These are three crucial components, but there is a fourth – the outcome. This is where many of us become unstuck.

The problem isn't the actual outcome, regardless of whether it's what we might deem as a success or a failure, but placing our focus on the outcome because it isn't something that we have any control over.

The only control we have is internal in the mind. Here we can create a desire. We can set an intention. We can follow a process, but we cannot influence the outcome. It will ultimately be what it will be. And the outcome is completely out of our hands (and our minds).

By focusing on something that we have absolutely no influence over, we practically guarantee that we will increase our stress levels and slip out of balance. But why is this? If we know that we can't influence what will happen, then why when it happens do we experience stress?

It's because our focus lies with the outcome.

To explain further, think about an entrepreneur who tends to experience high levels of stress. This is because they focus on the outcome of getting rich quick. Many actors are subjected to high levels of stress because they focus on the outcome of getting that big break. Many first-time parents are subjected to high levels of stress because they focus on the added responsibility of a helpless child.

If the focus remained on their desire and their intent, and they enjoyed the process of being an entrepreneur, an actor or a parent, then they would stay more focused and more in balance. This would allow them to perform their tasks to a higher standard, creating a better result and less stress. I have experienced this personally and, although I'm not an actor, I am an entrepreneur and a father.

My dream was to become an entrepreneur, so I continually put myself in challenging situations, but something was still missing. I had a desire to be an entrepreneur, and I set an intention to achieve this. I also worked hard on the process, but I was fixated on the outcome.

Every time the outcome didn't match my intention, I was left with negative feelings of disappointment, frustration and confusion. As a result, I endured an incredible amount of stress.

The other negative impact I experienced by focusing on the outcome was to my confidence. I judged myself according to the outcome, when it didn't match my intention, and so deemed it to be a failure. In doing so, I considered myself a failure.

I ended up getting caught in a destructive loop: judgement led to self-criticism and self-criticism led to negative thoughts. Negative thoughts led to more fear and pushed my dream of becoming an entrepreneur farther and farther away.

A useful analogy, relating to my entrepreneurial journey, is scaling a mountain. I didn't have a problem signing up for the climb, but around halfway something would shift inside of me. It was as if the weather changed and I experienced more fear. I would retreat back down the mountain and judge the climb to be a failure.

I judged the climb to be a failure because I was focused on the outcome of reaching the top, rather than enjoying the actual climb. I was focusing on the future rather than the present and, as a result, experienced more stress. As Eckhart Tolle wrote:

> *'You can always cope with the present moment, but you cannot cope with something that is only a mind projection – you cannot cope with the future.'*

Shifting my focus to the journey itself has genuinely transformed my experience as an entrepreneur. The pressures remain the same, it's far from easy and taking risk requires a lot of self-belief, but my actual day-to-day life as an entrepreneur has become more about creativity.

If you're going to run out of money tomorrow, it won't serve you well to worry about it today. Again, I appreciate from experience that it's easier said than done, but by removing the worry, you can perform better today and give yourself a better chance of solving the impending financial pressure.

Whether it's starting a business, becoming a parent, competing in sport, or absolutely anything else in life, we simply can't control what will happen.

We can't control the outcome.

> *Life is a journey, not a destination.*

## Squaring Off

Although stress is more related to what's happening inside of us rather than what's going on around us, emotion is part of being human, and we will always react in some way to events of significance. For example, when a loved one dies, we may well find purpose in their death, but this will come later. We can't all be expected to react like Buddhist monks, and whether they show it or not, even they will feel sadness when they lose someone close to them.

Death creates a severe mental challenge, and a common suggestion is that we'll 'get over it' in time. This didn't work for me when my mum died in 2012 as I never wanted to 'get over' her – it felt too much like leaving her behind, and I needed an alternative way to deal with her death. One where I could keep her in my heart, but which also allowed me to move forward with my own life.

The alternative way I discovered was to 'square off' the loss.

Squaring off – like stress – is about finding balance. There is also a direct relationship between squaring off and stress, as squaring off a loss, can help us reduce stress. What squaring off means is allowing ourselves to maintain our memories, while finding a peaceful reconciliation to those thoughts with which we struggle. In other words, I learned to hold the memory of Mum in my heart, while peacefully accepting that she was dead and that I would never see her again.

My mum passed away when I was 32 years old. What I am incredibly thankful for is we never ever fell out to the extent that we weren't on speaking terms. We, of course, had our ups and downs, but there wasn't a single day that went by when we refused to talk with each other.

We had a special relationship and our close bond was exemplified dramatically at the exact point of her death. A moment which powerfully illustrated how deeply traumatic her loss was for me. My brother and I had been sitting by her bedside for three days, hanging on to a hope that she would somehow miraculously pull through again. Although this was a desperate hope, the fact that she clung on for three days was an incredible show of inner strength. One that summed her up entirely.

However, when her final moment came, and she took her last breath, I screamed out, 'No . . . Mummy . . . No.'

As a 32-year-old man, I hadn't called her 'mummy' in more than 25 years. But in that precise moment, I was just a little boy who wanted his mummy. It was a tragic and heartbreaking loss. One which, at the time, I had no idea how to deal with.

The major obstacle I experienced, as I grieved, was this aspect about 'getting over' her. I simply didn't want to. I couldn't. The saying 'time heals' did little for me, and I felt no willingness to leave her behind. But although this was all based on how much I loved her, my way of grieving was preventing me from moving forward with my own life.

I was effectively shackled to her death.

By squaring off her death, I slowly loosened the shackles. Until the point when the chains dropped away, which allowed me to treasure her memory and raise a smile when I thought about her.

Consider this useful analogy – squaring off is like balancing the books. It is a settlement of accounts with all debts paid and nothing outstanding. Whether dealing with profit, such as the beautiful memories of the person who passed away, or dealing with loss relating to the death – all accounts can be settled.

If we can't balance the books, which is what I experienced before I educated my mind, then the unsettled debts may manifest as guilt and shame. These are two words that are used regularly, but often without a simple understanding of the discrepancy that exists.

## Guilt vs Shame

Guilt occurs when we feel remorse for our mistakes. Guilt is a feeling of action. Shame occurs when we feel that we are the mistake. Shame is a feeling of being.

Following the loss of Mum, I thought I was experiencing guilt because I felt I hadn't been there for her enough. We had a special relationship, but my ambition had led me to pursue my own dreams of becoming an entrepreneur.

Mum never stood in my way. In fact, she always pushed me to chase my dreams and never stopped believing in me. However, even though I had her consent and encouragement to pursue my dreams, it didn't alleviate this feeling of what I thought was guilt. As I learned more about the meaning of guilt, however, I learned that it wasn't guilt I was experiencing – it was shame.

I thought I'd been beating myself up because of the mistakes I made by my mum, but rather I was beating myself up because I was the mistake.

This took the form of mental punishment. In believing I wasn't a good enough person and I was the mistake, I was causing myself mental torture. To the extent I started to develop thoughts that my pain may even be deserved: 'Well at least this makes up for me not being a good enough son,' I would think.

By repeating this cycle of beating myself up, I'd discovered a very damaging way of staying connected to her. As I couldn't find peace, I remained stuck in shame, and more shame resulted in more stress, which always led to more pain. But by learning to square off her death, I was able to escape this destructive cycle. I was able to keep her memory in my heart, but in a much less damaging way. I learned to address my shame and let go of the heavy burden I'd been carrying.

As my mind muscle kept developing, I also found a correlation between how I'd learned to address shame and where I put my focus. I had a desire to be a good son, and my intent always reflected this. My process wasn't flawless, but neither was Mum's. This is what made us human. But I was too focused on the outcome, which this time was a past outcome – her death. By shifting our focus to our desire, intent and process, while adopting a more present mind, we can alleviate guilt and shame. We can balance the books as we realize that the outcome of death was never something that we could control. We can also live with more freedom, which is what the loved one we lost would really want.

## Finding Your Own Way

When working with a mentor, the most valuable approach is for them to coax the best out of you. This is what all great coaches can do – bring it out of 'you' as opposed to dictating, demanding obedience, abusing authority or providing all the answers.

> *Personal growth comes from finding your own way. Not from being told which way to go.*

In a dialogue-based environment, this mentoring can create moments of enlightenment. Moments which, although few and far between, can feel like real breakthroughs as they are happening. It's often within these moments where the mind muscle gets the best workout and becomes more developed.

One such moment for me came when I was speaking in a free-flowing, unobstructed manner with my mentor. With my speech coming from deep within, I blurted out the words, 'I didn't create me.'

It wasn't planned, and there was no prepared thought behind it. I just said it and it turned out to be a moment of great significance because it would offer another mental aid in better managing stress.

How I came to realize the significance of 'I didn't create me', was related to the debt of shame regarding the loss of my mum, which I've just described. It was 2014 when I first said these words, so more than two years had passed by this stage, but time had not healed.

> *Time may not actually heal. A more educated mind almost certainly will.*

As always, I still had chronic pain as well as other sources of pain in life, such as grief. In 2014, I remained desperate to find a cure and D was also trying her best to help. She was also desperate to help me live with less pain so that we could try and embrace parenthood.

Earlier in the year, she'd taken our son to visit her family in Slovakia. Although I didn't go with her, she was still looking at ways to help me, even while she was out there and had a session with a tarot card reader. When she got home and prepared to tell me what the tarot card reader had told her, I could see she'd been affected by the reading.

There was various input, but the most poignant piece of the reading was, 'His pain is so profound because he also carries the pain of another. His mother.'

Simply put, she was saying that when Mum died, all the pain she had been dealing with in her life had been transferred on to me.

**Pain can be transgenerational.**

If there was any validity to this, then decades of pain had been passed on to me. Mum had endured more than 20 years of a confidence-destroying marriage, followed by abandonment, followed by a nervous breakdown. Despite the extremity of this prospect of the passing of pain, I was open to considering any possibility.

Whether the reading had any practical ground or not, the real question was, what could I actively do about it? If I was indeed carrying my mum's pain, what could I do to alleviate this pain? D had already asked the same question to the tarot reader, who responded by saying, 'He must go and kneel on his mother's grave and ask her to release him from her pain.'

And so, with desperation as my companion, I did.

Later in 2014, I found myself kneeling on my mum's grave, looking up at the sky and asking – out loud – for her to let me be free of her pain.

It may sound extreme, but it was just another day in the office with chronic pain. I'd already tried to pay cash to a Slovak surgeon and had someone else's shit transplanted up my bum, so this was just another long-shot attempt to live in less pain. I went with an open mind and wanted it to make some difference. It didn't.

Despite all my efforts and everything I tried, nothing ever worked. This was no different. This was just another failure.

Or was it?

My view upon my 10-year search is now dramatically different. During those 10 years, I saw all those attempts to reduce my pain as complete failures. Worthless and expensive – both in terms of time as well as financially. But my retrospective view is that all those failures were in fact not failures.

They were lessons. They were an education and reminded me of something Steve Jobs once said:

> **'You can't connect the dots looking forward, you can only connect them looking backwards.'**

This applied to how the words 'I didn't create me' came into awareness. They were brought out of me by this experience of kneeling on my mum's grave, as this highly emotional and frustrating experience was what I was speaking about with my mentor when the words came out.

I was looking back and connecting the dots.

In doing so, I realized that I wasn't deserving of so much pain every single day. I wasn't deserving of being burdened with my mum's pain on top of my own. I realized that I had many flaws, but I am not my own creator. My imperfections are part of my design as a human and not an imperfection of me as a being.

Coming to terms with not being my creator wasn't about avoiding responsibility but finally starting to move toward self-acceptance. Accepting that although I had made a lot of mistakes, they were an inherent part of my creation.

A playful analogy to think about this is in playing cards and how we can only play the hand we're dealt.

> **In life, we're not the dealer or the house, we're the player.**

As the player, our responsibility is simply to work out the best way to play our hand. It's not about continually changing cards, but rather about looking at what cards we have in life with honesty, responsibility and acceptance. All the extreme attempts I was making to try and get rid of pain represented me continually trying to change my cards.

Only through acceptance was I able to make progress.

Acceptance not only around my pain, but acceptance I wasn't my creator – self-acceptance. And it's through these various layers of acceptance where another tool to better manage stress can be found - I didn't create me.

We didn't create us.

# 9

# Letting Go

My journey with pain is unique to me, and the strength of my mind muscle is individual to me. But one thing that all of us universally share in our quest to manage stress is the considerable challenge related to letting go.

For me, hanging on to unhelpful thoughts and allowing them to continually swirl around in my head, has been one of the most challenging parts about learning to develop the mind muscle. Like going to the gym and finding a muscle that has never been worked before, I found a weak spot and knew I needed a lot of practice.

When we hang on to negative things in our mind, we are hanging on to the past. These things are gone and can't be changed, but our minds seem to play a trick on us – we constantly think about what happened and therefore bring the past into the present in our minds. Or more simply put, we're not living presently, we're living in the past.

*If we're living in the past or future, we're not living because we can only live in the present. Life is now.*

The more time we spend with our past thoughts, the more damaging they become and the more we get out of balance with stress. It's insane really – imagine if you got a knock on the head and forgot what had happened. You'd experience less stress.

When my dad walked out, and after my brother headed off to university later that year, it was just Mum and me at home. I was 16 years old. It remained like this for the next two years until I also went to university. My mum was in a bad way mentally as my dad leaving had devastated her, and she didn't know how to cope.

One of the habits Mum developed during this period was to go into the bathroom every night, sit on the toilet and talk to herself. Usually for a couple of hours. While she was there, she spoke out loudly, so I heard every word she was saying. Anger, frustration and confusion were reflected in her words. Lots of swearing, and lots directed toward my dad as well as lots of other stuff too. If I'd upset my mum that day, then I would also be on the hit list!

Just like my parents fighting so much during their marriage, it happened so often and eventually felt normal.

What was causing my mum so much pain was clinging on to the past. She couldn't let go of the painful feelings which had built up internally. Her mind was entirely dominated by negative thoughts, which kept swirling around and around.

Each lap caused more damage and led to more pain.

The repetitiveness of this, however, wasn't due to my dad. He only walked out once. Yet, my mum relived it every day, through hanging on to what was a past event. An event she couldn't change, but also one she couldn't let go of.

With no exit for all these negative thoughts, stress crippled her mind.

What Mum didn't realize, or she wasn't educated to realize, was that she was inadvertently choosing to relive the trauma of her abandonment, daily. This wasn't a rational choice. It was a choice borne out of a lack of authentic information on the mind. Every evening when she went to the toilet, to verbalize profoundly negative feelings towards my dad, she was recycling the trauma.

By replaying the event of my dad walking out, she let him damage her every day. Her trauma kept compounding because she was going over it again and again. She had 0 days off and was in perpetual pain.

**If we don't learn to let go of the past, we throw away the key to our own prison cell.**

Had her mind muscle been more developed, she would have been able to see her abandonment as a single event. And with the correct process, she could have let it go. As a result, her path in life would have followed a dramatically different direction.

As I now look back on this with a more developed mind muscle of my own, I can see how my life was following a similar pattern. This wasn't due to Mum's experience, but rather my own lack of education of the mind.

I now admit with an open heart just how difficult I've found it to let go of things in the past. Without an exit, whatever negative occurrence happened in my mind just kept doing lap after lap of damage.

Chronic pain changed this for me, and this is undoubtedly where pain can add value to our lives – it can force change. I still need to practise and accept this as a lifelong practice, but I am now much better at letting go. What this has allowed me to do is create more space in my mind.

## Clearing Out the Clutter

Creating more space in our minds should be a universal goal. We want to get rid of the old and make way for the new – we want to get rid of the clutter. Like a hoarder who has accrued a vast number of useless objects over a long period, the only way to create space is by having a clear-out.

But how do we go about doing this?

Sticking with the example of a hoarder, imagine you were asked to provide some advice on how to create more space in this hoarder's house. If you saw a pile of newspapers in the corner of the room, would you suggest never buying another newspaper? No, of course not, you would suggest the old ones be thrown out to make way for the new ones.

In this way, we can apply this principle of 'out with the old, and in with the new' to the mind. We don't need to avoid collecting new experiences in life, we just need to make space for them by getting rid of the old stuff. By creating more space, we open ourselves up to collecting new experiences as well as trying new things.

**By removing clutter, we also remove fear from our minds.**

Dealing with the future is no different. Worrying about what the future may or may not bring just takes up space in our minds. It creates more of this clutter, which is of little value as it's literally yesterday's news.

If we can learn to live more presently, not only will our lives be enriched, but so will those around us. I am a far more present father than I used to be, and this has helped improve my relationship with my son – something of which has provided me with some truly priceless moments.

During one of our forest walks, I was telling him how much I loved being there with him. He looked up at me and said, 'That's why I choose the longer walks, Daddy, so that we can be together longer.' He was only four years old at the time.

Perhaps that's one newspaper I won't throw away!

## Detaching from More Than Just 'Things'

During my adolescent years, I never thought I'd take such an interest in Buddhism, but my pain pushed me to learn. Buddhism is a non-judgemental philosophy, as opposed to religion, and can provide many valuable lessons on how to deal with stress. One is the three clinical poisons in life: attachment, anger and confusion.

Anger and confusion are more evident in meaning, but it's through a deeper understanding of attachment which helped me in my own efforts to keep stress more in balance.

**The more attached we are, the more we will struggle to let go.**

When we think about being attached, we most often think about material things. Inanimate objects that exist outside of ourselves. But on digging deeper, we discover we're also attached to living things. We're attached to people.

The thought of letting go of people, especially those closest to us, is a daunting prospect, but there is sense to it.

One of the most significant forms of attachment is between a parent and a child. This is mainly because a child is dependent upon a parent for survival. Natural responses occur between parent and child, with almost animal-like instincts taking place. A mother fiercely protecting her young being an example.

As a single father, the prominent form of attachment is with my son. Until I started to develop my mind muscle, I never saw any fault in this. And even as my mind muscle developed, it still took me some persuading that letting go of my son made any sense at all. I had such a special 'bond' with him, so why on earth would I want to change this?

When I allowed my mind to become more open, I gained a deeper understanding of the difference between 'bond' and 'attachment', and I learned it is possible to have one without the other.

In fact, I learned it is even possible to have a better 'bond' without being 'attached'.

Although this may not be initially easy to understand, the following example helps to explain.

Consider the various childhood stages which are challenging for a parent: crying as a baby, tantrums as a toddler, complaining as a young child and mood swings as a teenager. Follow this with a whole load of other potential issues such as drugs, alcohol and crime, and it becomes easy to see how a whole world of parenting stress is created.

What is significant is that the level of stress experienced by the parent is directly related to the depth of attachment that exists with the child. The more attached the parent is, the more stress that will occur.

The more stress the parent experiences, the more stress the child will experience.

*By discriminating between 'bond' and 'attachment', we find another way to keep stress in balance.*

Where a critical difference in the relationship exists is that unlike children, adults can learn to independently manage stress. They can learn about the difference between a 'bond' and 'attachment', and they can learn that they can have one without the other.

What has helped in my own understanding of this difference is exploring a deeper understanding of 'love'.

When we think about what 'love' means, we often think about finding it through someone else making us happy. Romantic movies often quote the line, 'Does he/she make you happy?' The sweet romance is that if so, this is all that matters.

When we bring this back into our own real lives, though, we discover a problem. By trying to find our happiness through someone else, we are effectively putting the responsibility of our happiness in their hands. Husband, wife, son, daughter, or friend. Relationships vary, but the principle remains the same. We hand over the responsibility of our happiness to another.

By doing so, we create a dependency.

Dependency guarantees, at some point, that someone else will cause us to become unhappy. We have put the fate of our happiness in their hands, so their actions will directly affect our happiness.

No matter how stable and positive we are, if the other half of the relationship is volatile, we will be drastically affected. Even if the other side of the relationship is stable and positive, then, at some point, the other person will act in a way that upsets us. And even if the other side of the relationship is unrealistically flawless, they can't avoid sickness and death.

If we are so attached to them, losing them may be unbearable. The stronger the dependency, the more upset we will be.

So, does this mean we need to love others less? Does this mean I need to love my son less? No.

It simply means we need to genuinely take responsibility for our own happiness. Or in my case, the pursuit of fulfilment (see Chapter 5). We need to try our best to avoid letting the actions of others dictate the happiness and fulfilment in our own lives.

As challenging as it first seemed, the more I learned, the more I became persuaded that there was real merit in applying this to my relationship with my son. If every time he got in the slightest bit of trouble in his life, I let it profoundly affect me, then I would have to accept I'd be in for a life of considerable stress.

A life completely out of balance.

By learning to understand the difference between 'bond' and 'attachment' – with a deeper understanding of 'love' – we take responsibility for our own happiness and fulfilment. This can help us improve our relationships with the loved ones in our lives. So, what can initially seem like distancing from these loved ones can end up creating a better environment.

A less stressful environment.

## Belief and Faith

Figuring out stress is like trying to solve a jigsaw puzzle. When starting out, all the pieces are a jumbled mess. But with patience and perseverance, a picture can start to develop with more and more pieces eventually fitting together. A very important piece in my own jigsaw of stress was discovering faith.

Faith not with religious reference, but rather faith that everything that's happening is happening as it should, even if I don't completely understand it.

At least not until after I can look back and connect the dots.

The starting point for my learning about faith was being able to understand the discrepancy in the meaning of belief. Both faith and belief are crucial to our lives, but – just like guilt and shame – a significant difference exists.

When we have belief, there is a reality that something will turn out to be the way we expect it to be. There is an outcome we expect to be commensurate with our own expectations. When applied to something we are trying to achieve, belief occurs when the expected outcome matches our desire.

When we have faith, we let go of the outcome. We accept that what will evolve will do so through natural means and that any eventuality is out of our control. By learning to have faith, we learn to have a more open mind.

> **The practice of being more open-minded is a valuable exercise in developing the mind muscle.**

When we have faith, we place focus on our desire and our intent, and we follow a process. Because we don't shift our attention to the outcome, we avoid getting out of balance with stress.

Faith is a powerful stress management tool.

When I look at my life in the rear-view mirror, I can see just how much my lack of faith prevented me from achieving real progress. Not only with my pain. With my life. I was always far too focused on the outcome and deemed myself as a failure if things didn't transpire the way I wanted. This prevented me from living presently and enjoying the journey.

My journey with chronic pain exemplifies the lack of faith in my life. During my 10-year search, I had the belief that I would find a cure. But when I continually failed to achieve this year after year, it waned. With a lack of belief and no understanding of faith, I reached my breaking point. I reached my edge and considered suicide.

But that is also where I found faith. When I felt like I couldn't take any more and it mattered most, faith replaced belief in my mind.

Having faith has taught me a considerable amount. And as I learned more about faith, I found synergy with other lessons I'd learned. The jigsaw was starting to take shape.

I learned to let go of outcomes in my life. I learned to let go of finding a cure. I began to accept whatever is meant to be in my life will, in fact, be. I had no control over this. I had no control over whether I would ever find a cure or ever again live a day without my pain.

As difficult as this was to accept, it was through acceptance that I discovered my purpose in life. My purpose in pain. To help others in pain.

To create 0 Days Off.

## 0 Failures with 0 Days Off

When faith entered my life, it made me think about this concept of failures. I'd learned to reframe those failures from my 10-year search as lessons, but I wanted to go deeper. I wanted to understand what failure had meant throughout my life.

> *If all that has happened in our lives was meant to happen, then how can anything that has happened in our lives be a failure?*

Through deep thought, I started to consider whether failures existed. Or whether it was just a misunderstanding of what they represented.

If failure does exist, then arguably, this book is a failure. Because it is a book of failures. If counting the number of 'times' which I tried to cure my pain and failed, the number is in the hundreds. If counting the number of 'days' which I tried to cure my pain and failed, the number is in the thousands. If counting the number of 'minutes' which I tried to cure my pain and failed, the number is in the millions.

As true as this is, had I found a cure for my pain on day one, then I would never have written this book. I would never have reached out to others in pain, and I would never have found my purpose in life.

So how can all those events which led to the creation of *0 Days Off* be failures? They can't.

As this realization sunk in, I adopted a new perspective around failure.

Rather than just see failures as lessons, I redefined them as 'necessary diversions'.

Diversions not only there to teach me, but also there to guide me. With necessity.

Redefining failures as necessary diversions helped me alleviate more negative feelings about the decade I spent searching for a cure. It made me even more accepting that, despite how torturous the decade was, it was an absolute necessity in my life. It could have been no other way.

## Perception

Redefining failures as necessary diversions hasn't made my journey more manageable. But this book isn't about finding a cure, nor is it about finding an easy path through life. It's about how to achieve progress when it seems impossible to move forward.

One area I previously struggled with was isolation. My journey became a very lonely one, but this is often part of the package with pain – you must make it on your own.

My understanding around this loneliness, only improved when I redefined failures as necessary diversions. The necessity of all my failures made me realize that my isolation was mandatory. Despite the hardship of loneliness, it was the lack of people around me that created a much more optimal environment to focus on o *Days Off*.

Fewer people also meant fewer distractions.

**Isolation can force us to seek more from within ourselves.**

The reality is that had I received more support – emotionally, financially or otherwise – I would almost certainly have fallen back on this. Only when the safety harness is taken off can any of us truly grow.

As I had no other options, I needed to find a way and do the hard yards. Like a blacksmith's forge, I had to be heated, tested and hammered to become stronger.

Accepting the necessity of this isolation helped me accept that everything in my life was as it should be, and this represented another mind tool for keeping stress in balance. Pain, loneliness, struggle. All were necessary, and everything was as it was meant to be. What's critical to all of this is perception.

As I approached 40, perception became critical in my life.

No family home, no pension, and none of the other material luxuries that all my old friends seemed to have. With such a strong work ethic and so many educational qualifications, I questioned how my life had turned out. How could it be that I'd ended up in the middle lane driving a mini metro pedalling my legs like Fred Flintstone? While everyone else breezed past me in their Ferraris and Lamborghinis?

How I answered this depended solely upon my perception. And what I perceive affects what stress I experience. If my perception reflects there is no meaning behind what takes place in the world, then my life forms a miserable shape.

By thinking negatively that things haven't worked out and drawing the conclusion I'm simply not good enough, as well as believing my pain is just an unfortunate affliction, then my life reflects total doom and gloom - sleepless nights, stress ravaging through me, no self-worth and most likely drunk at the bottom of a bottle each evening.

If, however, my perception reflects everything is as it should be – even if the outcome is not as I expected – then my life can take on a whole new complexion.

By believing there is a purpose behind what happens in the world, I can start to see things in a different light. I can even slowly begin to figure out what the world is trying to tell me. I can learn from my pain instead of hiding from it, and I can develop much more self-compassion. This can, in turn, allow me to stop defining myself by my mistakes, avoid worrying about the future, leave the past behind and be far more present. I can even give myself a good shot at achieving my potential.

Most valuable of all, I can find the continued motivation to help others, even when living my own life with chronic pain.

*What we often need in life is not a change of circumstances, it is a change of perception.*

People frequently talk about transformations in life, but the way they go about trying to achieve a transformation is often flawed. Changing job, changing the location and even changing the people around can't compete with the power of altered perception.

The fantastic thing is that there's no exclusivity. We can all change our perception.

We can all wake up with a new set of eyes. And when we do, then we find an effective way to rebalance stress.

# 10

# Changing Our Relationship with Stress

There are many references to relationship changes with the non-tangible in this book, but the first will always be with pain. This is what pushed me to develop my mind muscle, and this is how I learned to change my relationship with stress.

To add some illustration, the following diagram has been created:

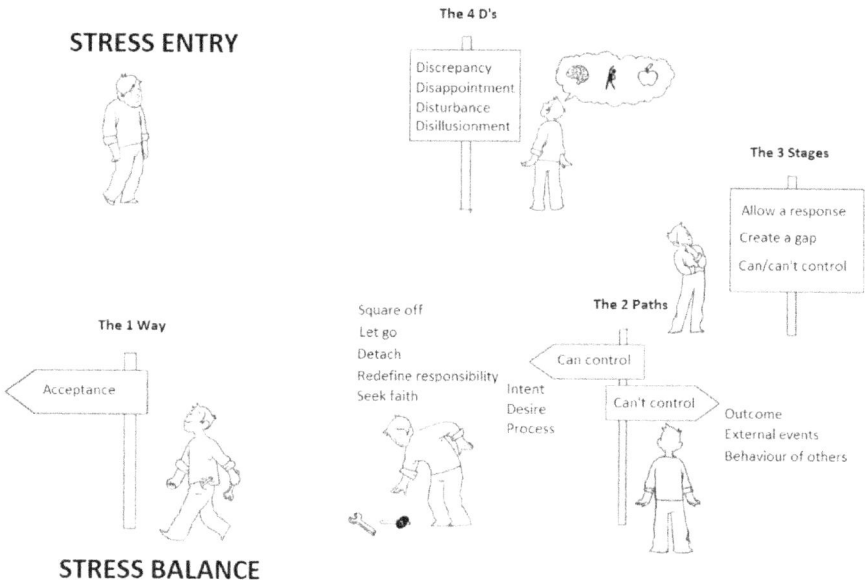

This shows a simple four-stage journey and brings together all the lessons I've referenced in the two previous chapters, including the stress management tools which can offer great value to the mind.

Imagine you're the character at the stress entry point and you're experiencing one of the four D's. Perhaps a discrepancy has occurred in what you expected to happen and what did happen, or you're disappointed, or you're disturbed and upset by a situation, or you're disillusioned because things haven't turned out the way you wanted.

When you reach the next signpost, you learn that it's absolutely fine to allow an emotional response when a stressful event occurs. Even though stress occurs in the mind, we are emotional creatures, and showing emotion is healthy if expressed correctly.

At the next juncture, you are provided with one of two directions. You either focus on what's happening inside of you, which you can control, or on everything that's happening around you, which you can't control. By choosing the path to look inside yourself, you then access valuable tools that can help you greatly in managing stress.

Finally, you make it through to acceptance and no longer question what has taken place. You have faith that everything has happened for a reason, and you're at peace with the knowledge that you can't connect the dots looking forward.

You understand that you can only connect the dots looking backwards and that the story of whatever has happened hasn't had a chance to play out in full yet.

> *We're obsessed with judging events as good or bad. But if we let these events play out, we may find that the bad becomes the good and the good becomes the bad.*

## Acceptance

Acceptance isn't one-dimensional and can be applied across many facets of our lives. Even to the extent that this becomes one of the foundations upon which we live. Although each of us is unique, we all have an innate 'ability' to accept the things that have happened to us in the past. And each of us has a natural 'ability' to accept everything that is happening in the present.

*The more we accept in life, the more we gain in life.*

However, many of us haven't exercised the mind muscle, specifically in this area of acceptance. Just like a muscle on the physical body that's been left neglected, it needs training to turn this innate 'ability' into a 'reality'.

During any human life, challenges occur. Some are very painful, such as illness, loss, and heartbreak. The pain varies, but the principles behind acceptance remain the same. The more we practise acceptance, the more precious time we can give ourselves to positively embrace life. The more we avoid acceptance, the more time we stand to lose and the more we open ourselves up to suffering.

When my journey with pain began in 2007, I had an undeveloped mind muscle. Therefore, I didn't understand how powerfully influential acceptance could be. The moment I was told that I had a 50-50 chance of getting oesophageal cancer, I started to physically tremble. I felt myself turning ghostly white, and my desperate need for reassurance caused me to respond by saying:

'But I'll be OK, won't I?'

I was literally on the other end of the spectrum of acceptance, and my reaction was a frightened plea. Begging to be told that things weren't that bad.

At that point, I desperately needed reassurance. My stress levels were off the scale. The news – and the way it was delivered – were fundamentally traumatizing.

The vast distance that existed between acceptance and my state of mind in 2007 is illustrated by how long it took me to integrate the information into my life. Why did it take me so long to give up alcohol, despite being given such ominous odds of cancer? Why did it take me so long to let go of my old life, even though my life was clearly misaligned with my health? Why did I remain in the same damaging situations, despite these situations making me sicker?

**We often become sick in our lives, because we become sick of the lives we're living.**

Denial? Fear? A lack of education?

Perhaps all the above. I can't provide a definitive answer, but what I can say is I was full of fear and devoid of acceptance.

Had my mind muscle been more developed, allowing me to truly understand the power of acceptance, then the influence on my life over the following decade would have been staggeringly different.

By being able to accept what I was being told, I could have remained in a calmer state – physically and mentally. I could have avoided being dominated by fear and begging the doctor to tell me – with no basis in reality – that everything would be OK. Acceptance may not have completely removed my initial reaction to tremble – allowing this emotional reaction is vitally important – but it would have allowed me to stabilize the ship more quickly.

A more stable ship would have allowed me to steer myself towards the discovery of purpose more quickly. Instead of asking 'why' from a position of feeling sorry for myself and drowning in fear, I could have asked 'why' with a view towards the horizon.

To think of what this news could mean for my life as a whole.

Acceptance – or the lack of it – truly was a dictator of my life. My lack of acceptance on that one day influenced my life for the next 3,650 days. But although this may have been the case, those 10 years became my training days. They represented thousands of days of training my mind muscle. Including this neglected area of acceptance.

My innate 'ability' became a 'reality'.

By thinking about days as repetitions, it took me thousands of repetitions to achieve this. I developed my mind muscle on the same principle of repetitions as I developed my physical body. The result of all these repetitions was the creation of a process. This is the process included in the previous illustration and is still one that I follow today.

I admit my progress was slow. It took me many years before I could efficiently move through to acceptance. But this is an admittance that I make without judgement. I am accepting of the time that it took, which illustrates how I have also achieved another type of acceptance: self-acceptance.

Self-acceptance gives us the power to move forward with freedom. To use our valuable time more wisely by reducing fear and truly accepting ourselves for who we are. By letting go of these unrealistic expectations that we need to strive for the impossibility of perfection. Or that we need to strive to please others.

Self-acceptance allows us to embrace our flaws. Not hide from them.

Self-acceptance doesn't, however, mean that we need to stubbornly avoid change. 'A leopard never changes its spots' is a phrase often used as an excuse. But if we avoid change, we avoid improvement. And if we avoid development, we avoid growth.

My pain has been the source of my growth.

## Awareness

Certain words play a vital role throughout this book and hold a particularly special meaning to me. **Purpose**, **faith** and **the mind is a muscle** are examples of these. **Awareness** is another.

Awareness is closely connected to the mind is a muscle. To become more aware, we need to do repetitions and give the mind a workout. These repetitions may come in the form of practising the stress management tools I've just discussed – squaring off, letting go, detaching, redefining responsibility, having faith, being present minded – and making our way through to acceptance.

The more practice we put in, the more aware we become, and what this simply means is becoming more open minded.

Even though my journey has taken a spiritual turn, as I have learned to change my relationship with pain and seek deeper meaning, I don't describe myself as spiritual. I prefer to think of myself as being more aware. Spirituality can often be misconstrued as converting to a religion.

*We don't need to convert to spirituality to become more spiritual.*
*We just need to become more aware.*

Growing up in Annan, there was a religious influence, as we attended church, but this didn't mean we were taught to discover more depth in our own lives. Just like my point about the mind muscle being neglected, no education was provided on mental health or how to develop inner strength.

Perhaps that is changing now, as we become more aware, but a new curriculum that teaches children how to manage stress, be more present minded and find happiness within themselves would go a long way in better preparing them for life. Rigidly educating our children and sending them off into high-pressure careers without teaching them how to deal with stress is like putting them through boot camp and sending them into battle without a rifle.

They're doomed.

Improving my awareness has helped me to authentically change my life. Not just make external changes around me – such as quitting alcohol, altering what I eat and spending my time differently – but achieve a profound internal transformation.

Whether we choose to reference awareness or spirituality, though, all that really matters is how our own lives are affected and how we affect the lives of others.

In my experience, better awareness has always led to an improvement in both sets of lives.

## Visions and Voices

One of the reasons I've personally leaned away from the word 'spiritu-ality' is because I seemed to be associating it with 'bolts of lightning'. Or 'having visions' and 'hearing voices'. What I found along my own journey was that when such experiences didn't occur, I was left disappointed. Feeling that I'd failed. Even more, I felt like I was the failure.

I questioned what I was missing. Whether I wasn't committing enough to spiritual growth.

But it was nothing to do with my state of spirituality. What was missing was access to authentic information. I didn't have a deep enough understanding of what spirituality meant, and I hadn't yet simplified it as becoming more aware.

I remained undeterred, though, and I continued to undergo repe-titions with my mind muscle. I had learned of the genuine synergy between the mind muscle and muscles in my body, and I knew that if I continued to train, then my mind muscle would become more developed.

What helped with training my mind muscle was changing my percep-tion. The subtle difference between perception and perspective is that perception is how we think about or understand someone or something and perspective is our point of view. You could say that by changing your perception, you develop a new perspective on life.

*We can't control what is happening around us, but we can influence how we perceive it.*

I learned that being able to 'see' with more awareness didn't have to be about having actual visions. It can be about being in a situation that remains unchanged but seeing it from a different perspective. Through a different set of eyes. Seeing failures as necessary diversions is a perfect example of this.

I also learned that being able to 'hear' with more awareness didn't need to be about hearing actual voices. It can be about listening to our own inner voice, which simply means becoming more in tune with our intuition. Everyone has moments in their life where they make decisions that they can't entirely explain.

A hunch. A gut feeling. A natural reaction. These all come intuitively from within.

Each time I was given a new medicine by a doctor, something inside told me that it was wrong. But I took it. Because, at that point in my life, fear was more potent than awareness.

This gut feeling wasn't definitive. I couldn't base it on factual evidence. It was something that simply came from within. It was my inner knowledge. The knowledge stored inside my body.

**Our inner voice often represents the connection between our mind and body.**

The role of intuition in my life became apparent during a two-month stay at a yoga retreat I visited in Cambodia in 2017. It was a wonderful experience and I met some inspirational people, but once again, it didn't provide a solution to my pain. About halfway through my stay I expressed a little disappointment to another guest, and she suggested I ask for help from above.

I thought, 'Why not?' After all, I'd already knelt on Mum's grave. I desperately wanted some help. From anywhere.

Soon after, I swam out into the sea, sat on a rock and asked for confirmation, 'If I do the right thing, my pain will ease?' These words weren't prepared and I seemed to have an intuitive recognition that my pain was linked to how I lived my life.

Then . . . nothing.

No sign, no vision, no voice, no anything. Just me. Sitting on a rock. Looking up at the sky. Talking to myself. I jumped back into the sea and swam back to shore. I was disappointed. So much pain and so much change and nobody listening. It just seemed so unfair. I desperately wanted some help. From anywhere!

When I made it back to shore, I sat on the beach and noticed a storm passing on the horizon. It was a stunning sight, and I found it quite calming. I started to think about my choice of words and why I'd chosen those exact words. Why didn't I just say, 'Help me'? But as I sat there, I became aware that the answer was in my original question. It was not in the choice of words, but how they were being used. By removing the question mark, the question became an answer:

'If I do the right thing, my pain will ease.'

It's at this point where perception becomes so essential because there are several ways to perceive this experience. There is the perception that I was just telling myself this because I wanted to find an answer. That these were just the utterings of a desperate man who had been in pain for more than a decade. However, what value can I extract from this perception?

None.

Alternatively, there is the perception that I was being provided with an answer. That my improved awareness had genuinely allowed me to tap into something more profound in my mind. What value can I extract from this perception?

A huge amount.

I can dedicate myself to doing the right thing, which I intuitively define as helping other people in pain. By doing this, I can improve the quality of my own life by finding purpose in my pain and try to improve the quality of others by sharing what I've learned.

Just like with my improved understanding of awareness, all that really matters with perception is how our lives are affected and how we affect the lives of others.

When we raise our awareness, the onus is not on the tangible. It's about looking beyond the physical. It's about searching within ourselves. My 10-year search was a decade spent searching through physical means and provided no alleviation of pain. In fact, my pain got worse. So, while I didn't find a cure on that beach – I did find an answer. Whether the storm replied or I told myself what I wanted to hear makes no difference because there was a positive influence on my life which, through this book, I am trying to share with others.

When I look back on this experience, I wonder what it is that made me turn around and sit down. I was frustrated and upset, but I was compelled to sit and calm down. Why did I do this? The truth is that I don't know. But I spent no time trying to figure that out.

I now spend my time applying the words that I spoke.

I simply wake up every day and try to do what I believe to be the right thing, in a challenging world with the heavy baggage of chronic pain. My daily efforts can be summed up by what is frequently documented as the Buddha's last words: 'Do your best'.

That's all any of us can do.

# 11

# Changing Our Relationship with Death

The time I spent in Cambodia and how I ended up there is just another example of my journey with pain. Although it has been – and still is – a difficult journey, it is through pain that I've become more enlightened in life – even on subjects we often avoid discussing, such as death.

I've already explored how death can bring us pain, but why are we so afraid of it? One answer is that death represents an ending, after which there is no second chance.

Even with spiritual or religious recognition, such as believing in an afterlife, there is no disputing that a physical ending does occur. Spirituality and religion, therefore, don't necessarily take away the fear of death.

Like any other person, I feared death. But I now perceive death to have two very distinctive sides.

On the one hand, I don't want to die. Despite my references in this book relating to how close I came to committing suicide, this has solely been due to the magnitude and consistency of physical pain that I have endured. The pain was forced upon on me but doesn't mean I want to die.

I want to live.

I really want to live!

On the other hand, there is the harsh reality of what living with physical pain every single day means for me. It significantly reduces the quality of life that I can live. And this is where acceptance plays an integral role. I have accepted that although death represents an ending to my life, it also represents an ending to my pain. I can't deny that there is some appeal in this to me.

When my pain reached extreme levels in the past, I would sometimes sit and think that an end to all of this wouldn't be such a bad thing. Yes, it's a sad thought, but so is the idea of living with physical pain every day. The way I've learned to manage this thought is the same way I've learned to work with my pain – to find purpose.

**Finding purpose in our pain can be the difference between living and dying.**

By waking up each day in pain, and believing that my pain has a purpose, I can find the will to make it through another day. Or even more than that, commit to creating value for others by recognizing that my pain forces me to lead a less selfish life.

This is precisely why money and financial riches mean nothing to me anymore. I continue to recognize them as necessary, but they don't hold a depth of meaning to me. They won't change my pain and won't provide fulfilment. My dedication to helping other people in pain also doesn't change my pain, but it does provide fulfilment.

**Living an authentic fulfilling life can be our saviour.**

Once again, perspective is crucial.

Due to the enormity of my physical pain for so long, I was pushed close to death. Although this seems like an obviously negative position to arrive in, there was something positive that came from it – I became much more aware of my own mortality, and I learned to fear it less.

Being able to extract such a positive from getting so close to death was reflective of my mind muscle, which had become more developed. I'd learned to find correlation in my learnings, and I connected death with faith. If what was going to happen was meant to happen, including the timing of my death, then why fear what I can't control?

Having more faith resulted in less fear. This applies to everyone.

Dying represents an ending, but by changing our relationship with death, we can progress more in life. If we can learn to live in less fear of death, then we can learn to live in less fear of so many other things in our lives. For example, the fear of losing money. The fear of what others may think. The fear of rejection. The fear of failure. The list goes on and on.

All fears pale into insignificance when compared with the fear of death. Death is the only one that causes a finite ending. We can fail, but we can get back up. When we are dead, however, we are completely out of time.

Changing our relationship with death is a serious workout for the mind muscle. It's one of those workouts which is very tough at the time, but highly rewarding afterwards. And there are many rewards to be gained. First, detachment from people can start to come more easily. Second, letting go of the past and stopping worrying about the future can happen more frequently. Finally, taking risks and pursuing your dreams can become less stressful.

*Through the pressure of finite time, death is a great motivator. It motivates us to live with more freedom.*

## The Value of Death

As death provides an ending for all of us, it heightens the pressure on time. With a less developed mind muscle and without changing our relationship with death, this pressure is often ignored. By becoming aware of this pressure, we get motivated to really live.

We can start to live without regret and really take a gamble on life. Not betting in a casino but betting on ourselves. And if the bets don't pay off? Then perceiving failures as necessary diversions helps us overcome this and learn.

Consider the regrets of some people when they're on their deathbed. There is very little reference to people wishing they'd made more money or spent more time working or worrying about the opinions of others. Regrets are based on not having the courage to follow their own dreams or wasting time trying to please others or not spending enough time with those they love.

**If you think fear is bad, wait until regret kicks in.**

My pain may well have been torturous to live with, but it has meant that I will be more at peace when I die. It has taught me to reassess my values and what my goals are in life. It has also made me aware of the futility of chasing material gain. No matter how much money I was ever going to make, it would never have gotten close to the fulfilment I have achieved through writing this book.

There is a modern-day obsession with material gain, and our definition of success has become so heavily based on how much money we have in the bank that it has completely lost its value of definition.

A much more meaningful definition of success is reaching the point in life where you have nothing to prove to yourself and nothing to prove to anyone else. It should also be remembered that success is another matter of the internal – if you feel successful, then you are successful. You don't need anybody else's affirmation.

Consider this book – how should it be defined as a success? I read somewhere that a book is deemed successful if it sells 10,000 copies. Is this how I should judge what I've written? Or should I rather consider the words I noted earlier in the book:

**To save one person is to save the whole world.**

Is one life positively affected not far more valuable than a million books sold which end up as coffee mats and make no impact?

Success, when it is defined as numbers, means worrying about the future and placing our focus on the outcome. That only ever results in less fulfilment and more stress. By focusing on my desire, intent and process, I keep my stress levels more in balance and I remind myself that I can't fail. I created a desire to help other people, I set an intention to write a book and I followed a process to create it. What happens next is out of my hands.

Pain in life is undesirable, but it can help you achieve more peace in death. You're dead far longer than you're alive, so it's worth exploring this and thinking about how it is you're spending your time. It's ticking away as you read this.

> **Death is not what we should fear. Not truly living is much more frightening.**

If you can stop living with regrets, it means you won't die with them. You will be free in life, and you will be free in death.

## Changing Our Relationship with Love

Changing my relationship with death may sound extreme, but every intangible relationship change that I've included in this book has had a positive impact on my life. They are all changes that occur in the mind, and they are all reflective of a developing mind muscle.

> **We can make endless changes around our lives, but until the change occurs within, our lives will not authentically change.**

Another example is how I learned to change my relationship with love. Once again it involved authentic change, and once again, this change happened when I reached an edge in life.

When D and I separated, it caused my pain to spike significantly. The emotional distress of us no longer being together, plus me moving out of the family home with our son, plus suddenly living alone in pain, was as close to my breaking point as I think I ever got.

Looking back, I think this was my edge of all edges as I'd just been betrayed in business and everything was collapsing around me at the same time. With the loss of work and family accompanying the loss of my health, along with a social life long gone, I was at an all-time low.

Even though separating from D caused me more pain, I instigated it. Whether she believed it or not, I simply didn't want her to live a life of pain. It didn't have to be her destiny, even if it was to be mine.

What I didn't show enough compassion for was her own pain – not only had she lived with my chronic pain for years, but our separation meant being alone in London as a single mum. She'd taken a gamble on our relationship by moving to London, and it hadn't paid off. I let her down badly.

One night, months after our separation, we sat together and discussed how we could improve what had become an overbearing situation for both of us. My health wasn't getting any better, and she'd also reached an edge in life – she was at her wits' end. It was during this evening when I finally developed an awareness of her pain.

*0 Days Off* was not only my journey in pain. It was also hers.

She'd never had a day off.

**Without resolving our inner pain, 0 Days Off may become every-one's story.**

Feeling her pain was too much for me to bear, and with a completely present mind, I tabled the possibility of my suicide. As dramatic as it sounded, there was sense to it.

The option to commit suicide had crossed my mind on several occasions, but as I said earlier, I was never that emotional about it. Anyone who lives every single day of their life in pain will know that making a conscious decision not to live anymore isn't about emotional collapse. It's about objective thinking. Because even with purpose, the raw nature of pain can make the journey of life incredibly difficult.

D's knee-jerk reaction was, of course, to tell me not to talk in such a way, and that the idea was ridiculous. But as I gave her my reasoning, we entered a sensible discussion. I genuinely felt that my suicide would be what was best for all three of us. It would bring an end to my own pain, and truly release D to pursue a new life. A life she deserved.

Even when I thought about our son, my mind created images of the two of them travelling the world together, having adventures and creating beautiful memories. Although I wouldn't be there, this was still my preference because for me to go too would mean bringing my pain. I just didn't want that for them.

As we sat there and pondered such an extreme possibility, I blurted out the question of whether she'd like to go back to Slovakia. It was a question without thought as if I was just asking it to try and comfort her without really expecting that she'd say 'yes'.

She didn't say this word, but her reaction said it all.

It had to happen.

It did happen.

Taking my five-year old son to live in a different country and leaving him there would be enough to write another book about pain. Not only mine, but also D's. It's not that I never see him, but the repetitive act of leaving never gets any easier – any parent will understand this and for those who aren't parents, it's like breaking up with somebody and getting back together with them repeatedly. The heartache never ends.

As always, though, I've learned a lot from my pain and done my best to apply the principles of this book. I try to have faith that everything will work out as it should and remind myself that things haven't yet had a chance to play out in full – we haven't yet been able to connect enough dots.

> *If we judge a situation as soon as it happens, we only see the trailer. Only once we've seen the full movie can we decide whether it was good or bad.*

When my mentor and I discussed this sacrifice, he described it as 'an incredible show of love'. He was right. Not for our son, as that love was never in question, but love for D. After so many years of us both questioning whether I loved her, we found an answer. I did. I really did. I loved D, which was why I was finally able to put her first.

She had put me first for years – because she truly loved me – and I had always put myself first. Finally, I was able to act with true love.

Finally, I was able to change my relationship with love and understand what love truly meant – putting someone before yourself, no matter the cost.

The two biggest sources of shame that I carried with me were about Mum and D. Although I'd learned to square off the loss of my mum and accepted her passing, this didn't change the fact that she was dead. The finiteness of death meant I never got the chance to express my love for her in the depth that I would have liked.

With D, I did.

My act of love toward D, allowed me to settle an enormous emotional debt. It was a debt that had been building up for years and had been left outstanding for a long time. But here I was, with cheque in hand, making payment.

The debt was settled, and I alleviated a source of significant shame in my life.

It doesn't, however, mean that my show of love reflected how I acted when it came to going through with the move. I found it far more difficult than I was prepared for and failed to apply the process I'd imagined. But in perceiving failures as necessary diversions, I would like to share those failings with you.


## True Heroes Need No Reward

When I agreed to support D's move back to Slovakia, my desire and intent were intact, but I fell short when it came to the process because I focused too much on the outcome. The main problem was that I created expectations – I expected her to be immediately happy and show gratitude towards me.

I had played the part of the hero and I wanted a hero's reward, but the truth is that true heroes don't need gratitude of any kind. They simply act.

The expectation of seeing immediate happiness was based on a viable question I asked D several times after the move, 'Why increase my pain tenfold if it's only going to marginally decrease yours?' This was, however, an extremely unfair question to ask and goes against everything I propose in this book about how to address inner pain. In the same way that moving location was never going to solve my mum's inner pain, the same applied to D. The same applies to all of us.

External changes will only ever cover up the cracks of inner pain. What we always require is inner change, and sometimes the only way to achieve this is to be given time and space. Sometimes in life we need to just let people be.

We often forget that the act of doing nothing – or not reacting – can be as powerful as any action taken. D needed space to develop her own mind muscle and time to find her own inner resolution. Something that I wish this book helps her with. As Alan Watts said:

**'Muddy water is best cleared by leaving it alone.'**

Although these lessons are directed towards how I could have done better, there is also an important consideration that adds some further insight into why I struggled with the process of this move to Slovakia. Not only do I now live with chronic pain and without my son, but the nature of my health condition is in direct conflict to travel and emotional upheaval.

Any chronic pain expert – if there is one – would tell me straightaway to stop travelling and any nutritionist would tell me to stay in the UK and eat the food I know works better for me. Therefore, the depth of my sacrifice goes beyond the move of my son as I also compromise my health, which clearly is hard enough to deal with.

The truth is that I don't have the answers, and I accept that. I don't know if I can physically keep flying to Slovakia, and I don't know what lies ahead. All I know is that, in the moment when I became aware of someone else's pain other than my own, I acted with love. As Viktor E. Frankl wrote in *Man's Search for Meaning:*

**'Love is the ultimate and highest goal to which man can aspire.'**

# IV

# Nutrition

*To accept what we're taught without question may well become the biggest nutritional mistake we ever make.*

# 12

# Nature's Building Blocks: Macronutrients

To cover the broad spectrum of nutrition would take more than this book. But understanding the basics is essential before the bigger picture can become more apparent. To gain this understanding, however, there is a crucial need for access to authentic information. I read through endless amounts of information that lacked authenticity, which resulted in a significant loss of time.

Even with the facts to hand, it's still not enough to tell how we react to food. The only source that can reveal this information is our own body. In other words, we need to know what food is doing to our unique body, because each of us is individual.

This is something which is now more underestimated than ever before, with convenience food being mass produced.

> *Deciding to learn about our body's requirements is a significant life decision.*

Regardless of what anyone else tells us, or what others tout as being 'good food' or 'bad food', we must listen to our body. Outside of processed junk food, there is arguably no 'good food' or 'bad food' in a universal sense. There is only what food works for us individually.

Just like getting spiritually in tune with our inner voice holds significant value for the mind, getting nutritionally in tune with what we eat holds significant value for the body. If we continue to solely follow the guidance of others, then knowing what to eat can be very difficult.

Even those with the best intentions can only provide input according to experience with 'their' own body. And even those who are qualified therapists can only provide input according to the reactions that they see on 'other' bodies.

*I am not 'their', I am not 'other', I am 'me'* is a valuable mantra to adopt.

Consider this – even if every other person on the planet reacts to a particular food in the same way doesn't mean that you or I will. We are truly heterogeneous.

I avoided treating myself like an individual for many years. I would eat what was promoted as being generically healthy and listen to advertising hype over the messages from my body. What this meant was that I was avoiding taking responsibility for my own nutritional health. I was creating a dependency on others as I followed the nutritional information they provided.

This dependency on others created a major obstacle to my progress.

In hindsight, I can see just how much of an obstacle this dependency was throughout my 10-year search. I relied on doctors, nutritionists and therapists in a desperate attempt to try and find a cure.

> **By eating without question and taking medicines without question . . . without question, we become like zombies.**

Where I didn't create a dependency was in relation to my physical fitness. I always took full responsibility for this. Why? Because this is the education I received when I was growing up. I understood how to get physically fit because I was taught through coaching and gained plenty of experience by frequently exercising.

Like everyone else of my generation and previous generations, I was provided with 'physical' education, but not 'nutritional' education. Nor any self-development of my 'mind'.

It's no coincidence that, despite the pain I have endured since 2007,

I have managed to remain physically fit. I had a desire and an intent to stay physically fit, but I also had the desire and intention to eat the types of food that may allow me to live in less pain. As a result, I stayed fit, but couldn't figure out what to eat because there seemed to be a critical discrepancy in the process that I was following.

In physical fitness, I had been provided with authentic information and education. I could, therefore, follow an effective process to get and stay fit. In nutrition, however, much of the information that I accessed lacked authenticity.

My zombie's face was on as I followed without question, and my process was not only ineffective, but also demoralizing and damaging.

At the core of this flawed process in nutrition was this issue of dependency. There was also considerable naivety based on hope. And hope was based on my undeveloped mind muscle. I hoped that whatever diet I was following would work, and I believed the promises of miracle cures and magic formula.

**The vulnerability of illness can make us the most vulnerable of all.**

In writing this book, I make absolutely no claim of miracle cures. In fact, I do not make a claim of any cure at all. My commitment is based on authenticity. I know exactly how it feels to be lost and alone with a hopeless reliance on hope. I also know exactly how it feels to go through the same flawed process of following guidance and information that drastically overpromises and damagingly underdelivers.

It can be a living nightmare.

It can be a lonely, living nightmare.

I lived this lonely living nightmare for many years.

So, do I write about nutrition with good news or bad news? Neither. I am providing real news in the form of authentic information, while retaining that this authenticity is based on my experience. Therefore, there is no guarantee that what I suggest will work for anyone else –

there is simply no substitute for committing the time required to get to know what food suits each of us better.

> *Just like a tailor-made suit fits our body best, we need a tailor-made diet to be the best fit.*

Although this may seem like I'm being pessimistic, I'm not. I am honest and realistic. It should not be forgotten that in every section of this book, I show progress. This section is no different. Despite the odds stacked against me, the thousands of necessary diversions and the extremity of a digestive health condition that can be provoked by sipping water, I have been able to make progress with food.

So much so, that I've managed to achieve yet another change – I've changed my relationship with food.

Of all our relationships, food is one of the most important. An entire life can be spent battling food, following failed diet after failed diet, and feeling guilty every time a sweet treat is consumed. This represents a negative relationship with food – one so influential that it can unbalance our whole life and cause us constant misery.

If, however, we can create a more positive relationship, then we can thrive each day. We can feel energized and eat the foods that work better with our unique body. We can also avoid wasting so much time fighting temptation.

This isn't about following a new diet. It's once again about a change of mind.

> *Food can be the provider of life or food can be the detractor of life. It's that powerful.*

## Simply Uncomplicated

The world of nutrition can be complicated, but such complication is often created by others, in an attempt to persuade us that we need to pay for knowledge we can't figure out on our own. It's essential not to be naive and expect to understand the full world of nutrition, but a basic knowledge can be helpful and is certainly something we can all learn. And an excellent place to start with the basics of nutrition is with macronutrients:

- Carbohydrates
- Fat
- Protein

Although these macronutrients are widely known, what is often missing is an understanding of the role of each. An understanding of which need not be complicated.

### Carbohydrates

These are one of the two primary sources of energy for the body. Fat being the other one. When we eat foods containing carbohydrates, they are converted and then absorbed into the blood as glucose (blood sugar), which gives us energy.

There are three main types of carbohydrates:

- Starches
- Sugars
- Dietary fibre

The body can digest starches and sugars, but fibre isn't fully digestible. Fibre comes in two forms:

- Soluble – such as vegetables, seeds and the peel or skin
- Insoluble – such as oatmeal, beans and fruits

Soluble fibre attracts water and helps soften stools. Insoluble fibre doesn't dissolve in water and adds bulk to stools. Both soluble and insoluble fibre can appear in the same food, such as in avocados.

There are lots of technical terms used to describe carbohydrates - complex carbohydrates, simple carbohydrates, good carbohydrates, bad carbohydrates, glycaemic index and many others, but it's your preference which terms you use.

My process, however, is much simpler and based on listening to my body rather than getting bogged down in technical terms.

The energy we get from carbohydrates can be thought about like building a campfire. We use both paper and wooden logs to get the fire up and running. The paper represents what is known as 'fast-burning carbohydrates', with example foods being white bread, cereals and sugars. Just like paper on the campfire, they set alight quickly but soon burn out.

The wooden logs represent what is known as 'slow-burning carbohy-drates', with example foods being rolled oats, tree nuts and beans. Just like logs on the campfire, they set alight more slowly but don't burn out as quickly. They are therefore deemed as having more value in a diet.

*Of the three macronutrients, carbohydrates stay in the stomach for the least amount of time.*

## Fat

The secondary macronutrient source of energy is fat. As fat isn't soluble in water, unlike carbohydrates, it's thought this makes it more difficult to digest. I now question this because digesting quicker doesn't mean digesting better. Ease of digestion is a very individual concept, and people may discover they can more easily digest fats than carbohydrates.

This is because fat plays a critical role in digestion. It aids with the absorption of vitamins such as A, D, E and K and diets that are too low in fat can cause health issues.

There is much debate over which fats are healthy and which are unhealthy, especially when it comes to animal products. It is a considerable task to find truly impartial information, which is why it's so important to listen to our own body. What is becoming clearer now is that we may have been mistaken to demonize natural fat as the source of ill health.

**Of the three macronutrients, fat stays in the stomach the longest.**

## Protein

This is the third macronutrient and, although it also provides energy, it isn't a primary source of energy. It's only called upon in extreme circumstances, such as starvation. Gym users who look to protein for their energy hit are therefore misinformed because it's the fat and carbohydrates that provide the primary energy in a protein bar rather than the actual protein.

Protein is the 'muscle' word, and those in the fitness industry obsess about it. But although protein does help to both maintain and develop muscle, the body can only use so much. It's not just a case of eating more protein and building more muscle without limit.

Once we eat more protein than the body can use, it gets wasted.

The strange thing about the three macronutrients is that protein is known as the good guy. This is the one that helps us stay thin and build muscle. Fat historically plays the role of the bad guy because it makes us fat. And carbohydrates seem to represent the neutral role – there appear to be as many supporters as there are critics.

But here's the reality:

Fat doesn't necessarily make us fat, carbohydrates don't inevitably pile on the pounds, and protein doesn't necessarily keep us thin.

Eating *too much* fat can result in more body fat.

Eating *too many* carbohydrates can result in more body fat.

Eating *too much* protein can result in more body fat.

Put simply – if we eat too much of anything, we gain fat.

**Protein stays in the stomach for a shorter time than fat but a longer time than carbohydrates.**

What is important to note about what I've written here as a grounding for nutritional knowledge is that it's not fact. People often like to use the term 'scientific fact' when trying to win an argument about nutrition, but there is really no such thing.

It is all 'scientific theory'.

There is debate over whether excess protein does cause body fat to increase, and there is debate over whether carbohydrates cause obesity, contributing to a dire state of global health. There is also debate over whether fat causes more body fat, even when consumed in large quantities, if carbohydrates are completely excluded. We shouldn't, therefore, expect to find definitive answers but rather continue to explore and test on our own bodies.

Other people may mislead us, but the body won't lie.

## The Digestive Process

When we eat food, we often do so with an 'out of sight, out of mind' mentality. We lack awareness of what's going on when we eat. But again, it isn't a necessity to gain an advanced technical understanding to achieve progress within our diet.

Even having an overview of the digestive process can benefit our health, so let's look at what happens when we eat.

The first part of physical digestion starts in the mouth. Saliva is created. This saliva is the first attempt of the body to break down food. It's often underestimated, but it's certainly not unimportant. As one of the main goals of digestion is to break down food, each part of this breaking-down process is essential. This includes what happens in the mouth when we chew.

Once food leaves the mouth, via swallowing, it travels down the oesophagus – the long tube that connects the mouth to the stomach. A body part which I am, of course, intimately familiar with due to my adventures in Slovakia and my 'toss of the coin' chance of getting oesophageal cancer.

When food reaches the bottom of the oesophagus, which is also the top of the stomach, it reaches a door-type mechanism. Following a series of contractions, this door then opens and allows food to pass through into the stomach. Once the food is clear, then the door closes again.

Or at least it should unless, as in my case, there is a faulty door.

Once food enters the stomach, then it proceeds to mix with corrosive stomach acid. There is a constant mixing of food and stomach acid together. If the stomach acid is out of balance, then it can rise up into the oesophagus, causing damage. This being especially the case if the door is faulty. As a result, people can experience acid reflux.

Stomach acid is corrosive, but the corrosiveness is critical. It continues this breaking-down process of food and further contributes to the release of nutrients. Energy is also released. The more technical description is that food is continually broken down by gastric juices containing hydrochloric acid and pepsin, which is a digestive enzyme that converts proteins into simpler, more easily absorbed substances. This is assisted by hydrochloric acid, which – when in balance – creates the right acidic environment. Too much acid in the stomach can cause acid reflux. Too little acid in the stomach can cause acid reflux.

As an example, from my own experience when I was taking acid-suppressing medicines, I had my zombie face on and didn't ask questions. I just held out my hand and swallowed the medicinal drugs that were given to me. Eventually, I awoke from my slumber and decided to stop taking medicine and start changing my life.

*No medicine is as potent as a change of life.*

As food continues to mix with stomach acid, a liquid type paste is produced. This is called chyme. It's in this form that food is then passed into the small intestine. The breaking down of food continues in the small intestine, and peristaltic waves occur that shift the chyme back and forth. There is a continual mixing with digestive enzymes and fluids.

The pancreas is responsible for continually breaking down starches (carbohydrates), and bile from the liver emulsifies fat. Bile is a fluid that is made in the liver and stored in the gallbladder. Understanding this can help those who struggle with fat digestion.

If we don't have enough bile, or there is an issue with the liver or gallbladder, then it can be more problematic to digest fat.

Most nutrients are absorbed in the small intestine, which is also where most of the energy is released. Not everything can be used, and waste occurs. This waste is then passed through into the large intestine, which is also known as the colon and has four basic parts:

- The ascending colon on the right side of the body
- The transverse colon across the middle of the body
- The descending colon on the left side of the body
- The sigmoid colon at the end of the descending colon, with a curvature shape, and connected to the rectum

Waste passes through each part of the colon, in the order above, via muscles which squeeze it along slowly.

If all is working well, the waste passes through the colon. Water is removed from the chyme in the colon, allowing a more solid form to be created. This solid form sits in the sigmoid colon until significant movements cause it to be emptied into the rectum. The rectum connects the colon to the anus, and the anus is the last stop before the waste is finally excreted. Lastly, provided constipation is avoided, we pass stool.

It took me more than 10 years to understand this process. Yet it took less than two hours to document it. Basic and 'less' information, doesn't necessarily mean use'less' information. If the information is authentic, then basic information may sometimes be all that we need.

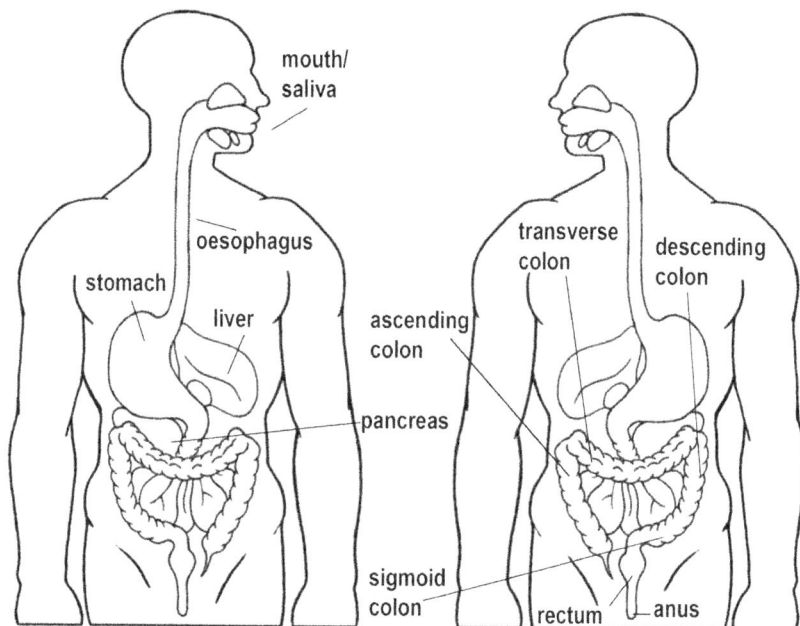

## Clean Living, Clean Diet, Clear Mind

Understanding what happens to our food when it enters the digestive system can help us make much better decisions towards our health. If we eat food that is misaligned with what our body wants and needs, then repercussions may occur.

Bad food choices can negatively affect the mind, and these can be categorized into two types - 'physically mindful' and 'emotional'.

A physically mindful effect occurs when we eat something that makes us groggy and fuzzy-headed – it's unpleasant and can make us feel unwell. It can even affect our self-confidence and ability to perform as it can knock us completely off our game.

An emotional effect occurs when we associate food with memories and feelings. If, for example, we remember eating food that tasted delicious during a wonderful time with family, then this can provoke strong emotion.

Whether physically mindful or emotional, each can have a powerful effect on us, and there have been plenty of occasions when I've experienced both. An example is Chinese takeaways, which is a food I miss due to both the taste and the memories of when I was younger. During one visit to Annan, I walked past a popular Chinese restaurant and the smell just seemed to carry me in. I knew that there would be repercussions, but it was a long time since I'd enjoyed a meal, so my discipline collapsed. The experience of eating the meal was emotional, and the after-effect was physically mindful as I felt awful.

**_Eating is a very emotional experience. This will always be the case until we change our relationship with food._**

This doesn't mean the occasional takeaway is bad for everybody, but rather that through better awareness of our own body we can make better decisions. The more time we commit to getting to know our body, and what it prefers and dislikes, the better we'll feel.

If, however, we just chuck anything down our gullet without question, then when things start to go wrong, we'll have no idea what to do. We'll immediately run to the doctor, put our zombie face on and take whatever medicine helps to reduce the feeling of pain and discomfort. We'll switch off the alarm of pain and let the fire spread through us like a burning house.

Taking responsibility for our own health includes taking responsibility for what we eat. If we want to feel good, have more energy and live with a clearer head, then we need to take it upon ourselves to make individual nutritional decisions based on our unique design.

# 13

# Sugar – Sweet Poison

It's often said that a little sugar won't do us any harm, but we can no longer deny that sugar isn't good for our health. Especially when it's refined. It may indeed be true that a little sugar won't kill us, but when we consider how we used to think about something like smoking, then it can massively change the context. This may seem like an obscure comparison, but there was a time when we saw smoking as far less dangerous to our health than we do now.

How will we view sugar 30 years from now?

Consider how different our awareness was towards smoking 30 years ago. Cigarettes were openly advertised, and there was still debate over just how damaging tobacco was. What has changed today isn't that cigarettes have become healthier, it's that our understanding behind the harmful effects of smoking has improved.

Now consider how different our awareness will be toward sugar 30 years from now. Just as with smoking, there will be a gradual evolution in our understanding of just how destructive sugar can be. The financial power of companies that create sugary products is still far from being overcome, but there was a time when cigarettes could be freely advertised, without any health warnings attached.

Even now, more and more companies are being forced to show the sugar content of their products, and a sugar tax has been introduced in the UK.

Before I truly understood how badly sugar provoked my pain, I still had sweet products in my diet. This didn't necessarily mean chocolate bars and confectionary, because such foods were prominent provocateurs, but rather foods like gluten-free cereal. But gluten-free doesn't mean sugar-free. As I sadly discovered when I also had to begrudgingly say goodbye to gluten-free beer.

I now know that refined sugar is very bad for my pain. That is unmistakable. That is also a specific reflection of my own unique health condition. However, the negative effect of sugar on health is a universal consideration.

Each us has an individual design, but I pose the challenge for anyone to show me that eating refined sugar – in any amount – is healthy.

## Sweet Experiments

As I became more passionate about this subject, I decided to test out the dramatic effect of refined sugar for this book on a body that had been cleansed of sugary foods. My own. I knew I was in for a rough ride, but being human, I certainly embraced the opportunity to devour some ice cream and chocolate. So, here's what happened.

It was Wednesday evening when I ate the foods that went down a treat. My pain had always been about delayed reactions, so actually eating the food wasn't problematic. I savoured every sweet mouthful and then braced myself for carnage when I woke up on Thursday morning. Surprisingly, it wasn't that bad, and I wondered, 'Have I somehow improved my condition through all my discipline?'

The answer to that question came like a wrecking ball around 4 p.m. when things turned very bad.

What I experienced was much more extreme than I could have imagined. I was shivering for more than 24 hours, developed a fever, couldn't get off the sofa and felt abysmal. I looked horrific, was completely white and had a thumping headache. It was like having the world's worst hangover. And I've had some hangovers!

In fact, I was so beaten up by it that it was Saturday evening before I could even function.

The whole experience made me think of sugar as a drug. It can provoke addiction, and the body can build up a tolerance to it. This can cause us to eat more of it, with its potency seemingly weakening. Like medicine or drugs, though, the potency isn't weakening. Our body is becoming more used to it and reacting less profoundly.

**Food-related tolerance can even be as powerful as drug-related tolerance.**

Comparing refined sugar with smoking and taking drugs may sound dramatic, but these are seeds of thought that I'm planting. If what I'm saying encourages someone to cut down on sugar, rather than cut out sugar, then I will still have provided a positive influence.

Also, for anyone who does doubt the impact of sugar, I recommend trying what I did to see for themselves. Try going through a period of eating no refined sugar – and this does need to be done diligently – then reintroduce sugary products. There is no greater persuader than personal experience.

## Digestive Design

My exploration into the impact of refined sugar on my body was informative, but it didn't take me any closer to figuring out what foods I could eat to live in less pain. Cutting out sugary junk was something I'd already figured out. What it did make me think, though, is whether my body was reacting badly to sugar in any form.

This was when I started to consider whether my body was reacting negatively to carbohydrates because they convert to blood glucose (sugar). So, even though eating a bowl of porridge sounds healthier than a bowl of sugary cereal, if it all ends up converting to sugar in the body, then was this a clue?

The argument against this is that different types of sugar should be defined differently from a health perspective. So naturally occurring sugars, especially found in fruits and vegetables, are deemed as healthier than refined sugars found in sweets.

What I am highlighting, however, is the possibility that the human digestive system – at least in some of us – is less efficient at breaking down carbohydrates. Therefore, whether the carbohydrates come in the form of fresh fruits and vegetables or candy bars, if the problem is carbohydrates, then choosing the healthier option isn't going to aid digestive issues.

What is once again so essential to keep in mind is that every 'body' is unique. Every 'body' is different. Despite all the supporters and critics of carbohydrates and fat – and even the nature of how my own diet has ended up – I don't believe that one size fits all.

Regardless of which way of eating works best, I wholeheartedly believe that every 'body' would benefit by focusing on eating simple, natural foods against complicated, processed rubbish.

Consider the incidence of digestive conditions such as irritable bowel syndrome and irritable bowel disease in less developed countries. Those who don't have access to processed and unnatural foods experience fewer digestive conditions, despite the lower standard of living.

**We can learn more from people who have much less.**

So, does this mean that there's a call to panic? Does this mean that we have to organize rallies waving banners and shouting, 'No more sugar!' I don't believe so.

For me, it comes back to awareness. Even with all my pain and the extreme experiences with sugar, D and I don't ban sugar of any kind from our son's diet. This may sound hypocritical, considering my smoking and drug comparisons, but the point really is about awareness. We both accept the world we live in, and we are educating our son so that he can make informed decisions around his own health.

I also believe that it's better to be a role model than a preacher. That attraction is a better attitude than promotion.

By seeing how I do my best every day to avoid eating sugar, it provides a positive influence on my son. He sees what I eat, and we talk a lot about food. We talk about what is good for his tummy, and what food makes his body happy.

I tell him that sugar makes his body sad but also place a lot of emphasis on independence. His decisions eventually will be his own. And already, many of them are. He has a choice of what he eats at school, and all D and I do is encourage him to make better choices. We keep an eye on it but still let him make his own decisions.

I will never forget when he came home after visiting D's family around his fifth birthday and was so proud to tell me that he only ate a small piece of his birthday cake.

I haven't dictated to him. I have planted seeds of thought. As he grows up, it will be up to him to nurture these seeds, and I have faith that he will.

Although what I'm writing here doesn't sound like great news for those who have a sweet tooth, I'm confident that even the sweetest tooth can learn to have a better sense of appreciation for whole and natural foods.

### *The better our food, the greater our appreciation.*

Trying to find balance in our body is not about denying food but appreciating it more. Why not aim to feel good when finishing a meal, instead of stuffed? Why not try and feel lighter after a meal, instead of bloated? Why not avoid guilt around foods that are obviously unhealthy, and feel at peace when we finish eating?

There is often a misconception that by eating more healthily, there is a trade-off. That healthy foods don't taste as good. But this isn't true. Especially where the appreciation of food is considered.

The more we appreciate our food, the better it will taste.

What I pose here is something that applies to all of us. If we live on a diet of junk food, then our appreciation for food will diminish. If we eat fresh, natural food, which makes us feel good and provides us with clean fuel and lots of energy, then we'll appreciate it much more.

> *If we can eat well and not overindulge, then our appreciation for food can be significantly improved.*

I have a health condition that is unique to me, but the questions around sugar are worth asking universally. By asking such questions, we can not only positively influence our own body, but also the bodies of those around us.

Just ask my son.

# 14

# A Smooth Operating System

When I think about my body, I think of it as a business. There is a head office and a gut office, and we want everything running like a 'smooth operating system'. We want the body to be well managed with minimal disruption.

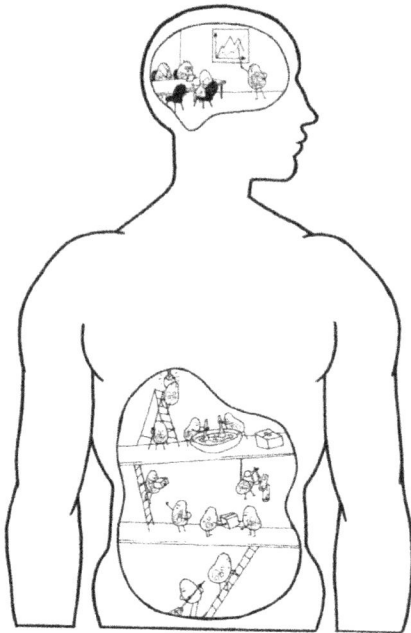

If both offices are managed well, then my mind and body are in good shape. If either office is being mismanaged, however, then disruption can occur. If both offices are being mismanaged, then a breakdown can occur.

If both offices are being mismanaged for an extended period, then a form of bankruptcy can take place.

**Health bankruptcy is much worse than financial bankruptcy and takes far longer to remedy.**

What's important to understand is that, although the body can experience bankruptcy, it's in the head office where all the decisions are made. This is where we decide what we eat, and it's often our dietary choices that dictate our state of health.

Even when we think about digestion, it too starts in the head office.

Physiologically, the digestive process begins in the mouth with saliva. But the first part – and perhaps the most influential part – of how well food is going to digest, is the decision made on what type of food is eaten. If the head office sends down junk food, or even foods touted as generically healthy but are misaligned with our individual design, then there will be complaints from the gut office.

If this happens continuously, then a breakdown may eventually occur.

To achieve a smooth operating system in the body, we need the mind and body working in harmony. We need the head office to send foods down to the gut office, that fit with our own unique digestive systems. Foods that do not cause a build-up of clutter.

Again, we want to create space in both the mind and the body. For example, we don't want worries, fears and the past dominating our thoughts because it causes a build-up of mental clutter. In the same way, we don't want food building up in our body and getting stuck because this causes another form of clutter to build up.

When there is too much clutter in the mind, we can experience stress. When there is too much clutter in the body, we can experience constipation. Clutter can lead to constipation and constipation can lead to a breakdown in the body.

This type of breakdown occurs because the body can't efficiently expel food that has become waste. With nutrients already extracted through the digestive process, this leftover waste needs to be taken out. Just like a garbage bin at home, if we take out the waste regularly, our home will remain fresh.

Constipation isn't something I believe should be taken lightly. Not only can it have a negative impact on the quality of daily life, but it's a sign that something isn't working in the body. Every 'body' is different, but no 'body' should be full of clutter.

> *Just like pain is an alarm alerting us to a problem, constipation is a sign that an issue needs attending to.*

In my opinion, constipation is a serious health 'consideration'. I truly believe that. I choose my words carefully here because it isn't necessarily a health 'risk'. It's instead a 'consideration'. It's a way for the body to tell the mind that it doesn't like what food is being sent down. Or that there is a problem in the body.

My health condition may be unique to me, but the distressing effects of constipation are not. In the US alone, it's estimated that more than 60 million people are afflicted by chronic constipation (US Department of Health and Human Services, 2018). Yet, it remains massively underestimated.

Achieving a smooth operating system is about putting in the time towards creating a more harmonious relationship between the two offices.

> *The body is naturally designed and prefers the natural way.*

If the head office can understand what provides the best working environment for the gut office, then the gut office has a better chance of minimizing disruption and performing to a higher standard. In my experience, this is a far more effective approach than avoiding responsibility and running to buy laxative medicine.

## Water – Nature's Nectar

One of the first decisions we make when waking up each day is what we're going to eat and/or drink. I've tried and tested many approaches, and the winner every time is water.

I drink about half a litre of room temperature water upon waking each morning. Room temperature may sound like a small issue, but I've found it to be of importance. If the water is too cold, it can provide a 'shock' to the system, and this isn't what we want, especially when we first wake up. We want the head office to gently start the working day and give the gut office time to get going.

By starting off my day with nothing but water, I immediately create good relations between my two offices. To clear out clutter and get my digestive system up, running and operating smoothly, my gut office wants for nothing more than water. It's the only tool it needs at that time of the day – almost like a sweeping brush to just brush away the old clutter and get ready for the new day.

If drinking water doesn't help me go to the toilet a few mornings in a row, then my head office knows that there's a problem. So, there is no drawback. If it allows me to pass stool, then great, and if not, then it acts as a signal that a blockage has occurred, and more than a sweeping brush is needed.

In all the money I've spent on nutritionists and therapies, I honestly believe that water is one of the most fantastic health products out there. My morning ritual of drinking water when I wake up has also taught me about more health benefits of drinking water earlier in the day.

## Feeling Fuller

Feeling fuller encourages better dietary habits in the morning because we don't need to eat straight away. This isn't about starving but rather considering that giving the body water and letting it settle can be used as a replacement to sugary breakfast foods and drinks. Perhaps also as an alternative to coffee as my section on coffee will elaborate on.

**Small differences remain small, but accumulative effects occur.**

## Rehydrate the Body

By drinking more water earlier in the day, we also put a huge tick in the box of our daily target of water intake. It's well known that many people don't consume enough water every day because they simply forget. Drinking more in the morning, therefore, takes away the burden of having to continually remember to drink more.

What's important to remember is that we want to achieve balance. Drinking excessive water can not only be an annoyance as we run to the toilet too often, but can potentially result in a loss of electrolytes, which is why it can make sense to drink more in the morning but rather just sip throughout the day.

## Better Sleep

Another benefit of drinking more water in the morning is that it encourages better sleep. This is because by drinking less in the evening, we need to urinate less frequently while we sleep.

The more undisturbed our sleep, the better.

I am as passionate about water intake as I am about constipation. These are areas where proper attention can make significant differences in our lives. Therefore, it's worth paying attention to the colour of your urine.

None of this is about being obsessive, it's about being sensible. How much effort does it really take to look down at the toilet and check your urine colour? It's easy to recognize that cloudier urine is another alert in the body, telling us that we are dehydrated. In modern society, we should simply feel lucky that we can quickly react to this alert through access to clean drinking water.

By developing this habit and checking our urine colour, we may also find that we have a positive influence on others. Almost every day when my son has the toilet, he runs to me with great pride and tells me that he has had a clear wee. He sees it as an achievement and feels so proud of himself when he does this.

The smile on my face when he tells me this, however, reflects more than just a sweet moment between father and son. I also smile because I've successfully planted another valuable seed of thought in his mind. As he grows up, this seed will be easy to nurture.

He will always know to keep an eye on the colour of his urine, and what to do about it when it starts to become less clear.

Water truly is nature's nectar.

## The Coffee Conflict

All areas of nutrition cause debate, and one of particular interest is coffee. Across the globe, we are huge coffee drinkers, and it's perhaps been in and out of my diet more than any other food or drink because it invites so much conflict between my two offices. So, is it good or bad?

As always, 'good' and 'bad' are not useful referential terms. It's about education. It's about understanding. It's about achieving balance. But before going into my perspective with more depth, I would like to simplify what I've experienced as the major conflicts that occur in the body with coffee.

## Bowel Movements

On the plus side, coffee can cause a relaxation of the bowels, allowing stools to pass and therefore more waste to be expelled from the body. On the negative side, coffee has a dehydrative effect. Along with relaxing the bowels, coffee is also a diuretic, so it makes us urinate more. The loss of fluid can lead to a dehydrated colon, which encourages constipation.

## The Kick

On the plus side, coffee can give us a kick when we feel tired. I personally believe the 'sharpened mind' argument is heavily embellished by coffee promoters, but there is no doubt that coffee can provide a boost if we're feeling sluggish. On the negative side, coffee causes anxiety. This I know all too well. And if we dig a little deeper, one of the things that we all need to accept is that caffeine is a drug, and a cup of coffee does contain chemicals.

Although I'm not going to make the argument that having a cup of coffee is the same as taking cocaine, having experienced both, I can genuinely confirm that certain similarities exist. The high is always followed by a low. The body creates a dependency on caffeine and the effect weakens as more is taken, so there is a need to take more or a stronger version. When the more elated feeling wears off, anxiety can set in.

I'm not calling coffee drinkers drug addicts, but it's important to be honest with ourselves. Coffee is a stimulant and can affect both our mind and body.

One of the main drawbacks with coffee and one that is often underestimated is that which relates to anxiety. I've had panic attacks caused by drinking too much coffee, and some of them have been extreme.

On one occasion, it felt like I was dying as I just couldn't calm down. This was even at a point when I'd developed my mind muscle, so I knew how to calm my mind and body, but this time I couldn't get on top of it. My hands went numb, my legs started to feel like jelly, my right eye started to close, I couldn't move my neck, and my lips were so dry that when I looked in the mirror, they were curled up inside my mouth.

I honestly thought that I was about to have a heart attack.

**In simple terms, a panic attack is an imbalance in the mind and body.**

When I look back on this experience, although it was far from pleasant, I'm now able to do so with a better understanding of what was taking place. The more coffee I drank, the more electrolytes I lost and the more out of balance my body and mind became.

The reason I wanted to share this personal story isn't to scaremonger coffee drinkers, but to instead suggest that those who suffer from anxiety may find some benefit in reducing caffeine intake.

Once again, I'm simply sharing my experience – I no longer drink coffee, but each of us must find our own way. What I believe is universally essential is to develop an understanding and awareness of what coffee does to our own unique body. As long as we are honest with ourselves, then our head office can make the best decisions for our gut office.

For me, as always, there is the crucial consideration of digestion. And from my experience, coffee is counterproductive to keeping my digestive system operating smoothly. It seems to cause my gut office to work in a more anxious state and rush the process of breaking food down. It can also worsen acid reflux and make it more difficult to keep my body optimally hydrated.

Once I reduced caffeine, and then eventually eliminated it, I found that my stomach had an improved environment for digestion. It was a crucially important dietary adjustment for me.

This doesn't mean that a cup of coffee per day will upset everyone's digestion, and I retain my belief that every 'body' is different. For example, as much as caffeine is acidic, the subject of acidity should not be misconstrued. Not everyone will experience acid reflux from drinking coffee as I do. The stomach needs acid, and digestion can only occur with efficiency if an acidic environment is present.

To sum up coffee, it's neither good nor bad in my opinion, and these terms are very subjective in any case. What I believe to be important is that if it is consumed, it's done so with education as well as improved awareness of hydration and electrolytes.

# 15

# Chew on It

Once the head office makes that first decision of the day, the next part of keeping our digestive system operating smoothly comes into play. The decision of what to eat is accompanied by a very important action that is often underestimated in the digestive process – chewing.

Despite the lack of progress that I've been able to achieve with professional nutritionists, every one of those I visited told me to chew more often before swallowing. But I didn't listen. This was because the therapy being provided was ineffective at reducing my pain. Therefore, I let judgement and disappointment cloud potentially useful information.

*One of the keys to unlocking progress with our health is knowing what information to use and what information to discard.*

Chewing food properly is not only important to those with digestive issues, but it also represents a vital role in the process of digestion for everyone. When food is sent down into the body, we want it to be in the most broken-down form possible.

The more our food is broken-down when it arrives in the body, the more grateful the gut office will be. Chewing, therefore, helps contribute to a more harmonious relationship between our two offices.

If the body can't properly break food down, then undigested food passes from the stomach to the colon and is a cause of constipation. It can also lead to acid reflux, as this undigested food sits in the stomach longer than it should.

> *Of all the expensive digestive supplements available, the most effective is the one that's free . . . chewing!*

To enable proper digestion, we want our head office to make the decision to chew food more times before swallowing, and we want our gut office to pass food from the stomach into the colon in a more broken-down state.

However, one of the challenges with modern society is that it's misaligned with good digestion. This is because people are often in a rush, which therefore usually equates to eating quickly and chewing less.

> *Chewing food 5 to 10 times feels sufficient. Chewing food 20 to 30 times is efficient.*

Although it may seem unnatural to chew food so many times before swallowing, it really is just a case of practice. There was a time when chewing food a few times and swallowing was second nature to me. Nowadays, every time a mouthful of food enters my mouth, it's second nature to me to chew 20 to 30 times and break down food to mush before swallowing.

Just like developing the mind muscle requires repetitions, improving our digestion through better chewing is no different. The more we practice, the better we get.

An effective way that I found to practise chewing in the past was to take a very ripe banana and try to chew each bite at least 30 times before swallowing. The reason that I chose a very ripe banana (and it does need to be very ripe) is because it's a food that could easily slip down after only a few chews.

It may seem like a very minor part of digestion, but like so many suggestions I make in this book, subtle changes can genuinely make a difference. Especially when combined. By simply chewing more, we create another way to get our two offices working more efficiently together.

Once again, we may also find that developing such a healthy habit positively influences others.

## Eating Calmly, Digesting Smoothly

Another challenge we face in modern life, and the misalignment with good digestion, is that it creates an unhealthy type of environment for us to eat in. The rushing around causes an increase in stress, and eating in a more stressed state of mind does equate to eating with a more stressed condition in the body.

What we need to be aware of is that the working environment of our head office will directly affect the working environment of our gut office. And vice versa. The two offices are always connected, and when one is struggling, so will the other.

When we first sit down to eat, the state of our mind and body will directly affect our digestion. In my experience, there is just no debating this. If we eat when our stress is out of balance, then this can cause our digestive system to get out of balance.

The longer this goes on, the more difficult it becomes to sort out.

Even though I thought it to be of little significance at first, I've come to learn just how important it is to eat in a calm state. Whenever I've eaten in a more stressed state, there have always been negative repercussions. I also end up chewing my food less when I'm stressed, because my mind is so distracted and thinking about what is bothering me.

My body is also tenser, and the gut office doesn't work well under pressure.

The way I now address this is by committing to dropping down the gears and calming down before I start to eat. This can be described as 'mindful eating'.

As the aim with stress isn't eradication, and rather to keep it more in balance, we want to be in a more balanced state when we start to eat. If our stress has jumped up to a 9 out of 10 because we're having a bad day – which can happen with even the most developed mind muscle – we want to show awareness of this and try and bring it back between a 5 and 6.

The process that I follow to achieve this is to briefly meditate before each meal. I also internally express gratitude for the food that I'm about to eat.

When people think about meditation, they usually conjure up the image of a Buddhist monk sitting cross-legged on a mat. But this isn't what meditation is about. Meditation does play an integral role in the life of a Buddhist monk, but the practice of meditation can be done anywhere. Standing on a train, flying on a plane, sitting in a restaurant. We can practise focusing our mind and shutting out the noise in any situation.

**The most wonderful thing about the freedom of meditation is that we are free to do it anywhere.**

One of the biggest misconceptions I believe that exists with meditation, which is a misconception I had before starting the practice, is that it's thought of as only being done well if we can empty our minds. Then I learned this invaluable lesson: meditation isn't about emptying the mind. Meditation is about calming the mind.

When we think about it this way, it fits seamlessly with the idea of 'mindful eating'.

Another misconception with meditation is that it takes a considerable amount of time. But meditation carries no official time frame, and I've genuinely found value in meditating for 60 seconds. Consider how many people use the saying, 'Take 10 deep breaths', when asking someone to calm down, yet they have little awareness of meditation.

Breathing is a core part of meditation, and it's all geared towards calming the mind. A calmer state of mind will result in a calmer condition in the body.

My meditation practice before eating, therefore, takes only a few minutes. Sometimes only one minute. A valuable 60 seconds. By breathing deeply, putting aside whatever is bothering me in my mind, and literally letting my shoulders drop, my whole conditioning changes in preparation to eat. Therefore, I often found that eating after I practised yoga was a more optimal time.

With a calmer mind and body, I can focus on two very important elements that contribute to better digestion and a smoother operating system. The first one being chewing, and the second one being to eat slowly.

Identifying these two elements may start to sound impractical, but when considered in the greater context of our health, our life and the fact that there are 1,440 minutes available each day, the possibility to achieving both becomes much more realistic.

If we are used to wolfing down our lunch in 10 minutes, it's worth asking ourselves whether we really can't somehow schedule our day slightly differently and increase this to 30 minutes.

If making this happen meant we got paid more money, would we somehow find a way? Most likely, yes. Most likely, the financial reward would motivate us to come in to work slightly earlier, to create this bonus-paying lunch challenge.

And yet, if we do this, we are getting paid a bonus in our lives. One far more valuable than money.

We are getting paid a bonus for better health.

## Finish a Meal

The last consideration in this practice of eating more calmly is what happens when we finish eating. If we've done all that great work around meditative preparation for food, eating calmly, eating slowly, and even providing a positive influence on others, the last thing we want is to then undo all this good work at the final hurdle. We want to retain this state of calmness when we finish our meal, so the best thing to do is . . . to do nothing.

Before we start eating, the hard work is with the head office – decisions that we make around what we eat and how we prepare to eat are crucial. Then when we start eating, the two offices need to work in sync; the head office oversees chewing and eating slowly, and the gut office is doing all the manual labour of digestion as the food gets sent down.

Afterwards, when we finish eating, the work is all in the body.

We don't want to overwork our digestive system by adding more food and overeating.

What I've learned about my own body is that it doesn't like to work on too many things at one time. So, once I finish a meal, my body wants to focus on breaking that meal down and processing it as smoothly as possible.

Therefore, the start, the middle and the end of eating a meal are all important. The principle of staying in a more balanced and calm state applies to every stage.

> *A stressed mind when we start eating will mean a stressed body when we start eating. A stressed body when we finish eating will mean a stressed mind when we finish eating.*

## The Mixing Bowl

Once digestion is underway, what takes place is out of sight, which can cause misunderstanding around what happens to food when it arrives in the stomach. There are two opposing viewpoints that I've come across: the more holistic opinion, and that usually propounded by medical and scientific fields.

When food enters the stomach, it takes time to digest. The time that food takes to digest depends on its type. There are plenty of sources of information about how long different types of food take to digest; fruit and vegetables are thought to take around 45 minutes, grains and rice around two hours, fish three to four hours, and meat four hours plus.

This is a sensible guideline only, however, and excludes individual application. Every person is different, and digestion times will vary according to not only the food but also digestive health.

For example, there have been times when I've eaten a large bowl of grain-based food and experienced it taking far longer than these average figures to digest. Even though this may have been skewed by bloating and other factors, the principle of individuality remains.

Where most debate exists, however, is in what happens to food when it enters the stomach.

Those in the holistic corner tend to support the view that meat stays in the body for longer than fruit and vegetables. Up to seven days for meat, with fruit and vegetables passing through in 24 to 36 hours. One belief being that because meat stays in the body for so long, it starts to rot. Like a piece of meat that has been left out of the fridge to fester.

The opposing view is the more scientific view. The argument is that the body can't segregate different types of food once they enter the stomach. There aren't compartments where each food drops in to, so there isn't one for fruit, one for vegetables, one for fish and one for meat. It all just gets mixed together.

It is like a type of 'mixing bowl' in the digestive system, where all the ingredients are mixed together.

Opposing viewpoints always make it difficult to find definitive answers, but on this occasion, I lean more toward the scientific viewpoint. I don't believe that the body segregates food types, and I do believe that the physiological explanation around all food turning into chyme as part of the digestive process makes the most sense.

However, although I believe that food isn't segregated during digestion, this doesn't mean I believe that the body treats all food the same way. I'm not saying that an apple takes as long as a piece of steak to digest. What I am saying is that, through learning more about nutrition, my mind is more in sync with my body.

My suggestion to others, therefore, is to learn about how long each food takes to digest in their own unique body. For example, I find milk very difficult to digest – even plant-based milk. When I drank almond milk in the past, it just sat in my stomach and didn't seem to move. When I ate salmon, however, then I intuitively felt it slip through my stomach with less disruption.

The nice thing about the mixing bowl analogy is that it's easy to understand. The way of thinking about it is transferable to an actual bowl used for mixing food in a kitchen. We only mix certain foods together in a bowl because they match according to taste and texture.

If foods don't fit together, we don't mix them.

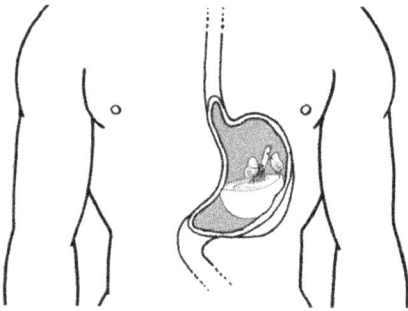

We can think about the mixing bowl relating to digestion in the same way. Any time I ate salmon, I just grilled it. No sauces, no additions, no anything. Just plain grilled salmon. However, that didn't mean that it was the only food that appeared on my plate. I may have had it with some avocado, for example.

If I was to take the salmon and avocado and mix them together in an actual mixing bowl in a kitchen, how would it taste? It would taste quite good. One would not corrupt the other and, in fact, dipping some salmon in a bowl of mashed avocado can be particularly tasty.

However, how would this dramatically change if I threw a piece of chocolate cake in the mixing bowl? The salmon would be ruined, and the cake would not be able to be enjoyed. It doesn't fit together.

By following the mixing bowl analogy, this is what's essentially happening when we have dessert. As much as we would not appreciate mixing it all together in a kitchen bowl, our body doesn't appreciate mixing it all together in the mixing bowl of the digestive system.

I found so much merit in this analogy that my head office started to see no distinction between the bowl in the kitchen and the mixing bowl in the digestive system. Decisions began to get based on what would mix well together, as well as what could potentially make my gut office's working day easier.

**_When food becomes confusing, the body gets confused._**

The more types of food that I added to my bowl in the kitchen, the more complicated it got for my body to break down. If it's too complicated for my mind, it's too complicated for my body.

Complication doesn't encourage good digestion.

# 16

# A 12-Inch Stomach and a 30-Foot Digestive System

Many of the lessons I've learned about digestion have related to the stomach. Probably because my pain occurs towards the top of my stomach. But as I kept developing my mind muscle, I discovered that by focusing so much on my stomach, I was excluding a large portion of the digestive system. By doing that I was, in fact, excluding most of it.

The average size of the adult human stomach is around 12 inches (30cm) and, despite how much food we eat, it stays remarkably the same size.

The average length of the human digestive system, however, is around 30 feet (9m). Therefore, by focusing on my stomach, I calculated that I was ignoring about 97 per cent of my digestive system.

A jaw-dropping realization.

Despite all my efforts to stay hydrated, chewing, eating calmly, taking into account the mixing bowl analogy and working hard to create a better working relationship between my two offices, I realized that I still wasn't paying enough attention to an area of huge importance – my colon.

Perhaps the biggest lesson I learned about the colon is just how important it is to keep it hydrated. Without hydration, clutter can build up and constipation can occur, which is why my morning ritual of drinking half a litre of water is usually enough for me to go to the toilet and empty my bowels. If not, then I know that there's another problem.

What I also learned, however, is that it is possible to drink too much water. If I drank water excessively, then electrolytes seemed to be flushed out of my body, causing me to feel anxious and out of balance. I even became more constipated, which taught me that overhydrating is counterproductive.

In continuing to explore my colon, I learned more about how my body was reacting and started to figure out something which had confused me for so long – red rashes appearing on my body after I ate or drank. Once again, there are two opposing explanations for this from the more holistic side and the more scientific side.

The holistic argument is that this is a good sign because it shows that the body is eliminating unwanted toxins. I never fully bought into this because I went for long periods (years) when these red rashes continually appeared. Either I was the world's most toxic person or there was another explanation. The other reason for my scepticism is that this theory creates an opportunity for all sorts of detox programs and leads to propaganda.

The scientific argument is that the body is perfectly capable of excreting toxins through sweat and urine, and that if toxins were retained in the body then it would die. Again, I lean toward this viewpoint because it makes more sense to me and is aligned with my experience. Once I finally found a way of eating that was more aligned with my individual design, no more rashes appeared.

Learning about the colon has been another piece of the digestive jigsaw puzzle. There were many more pieces of knowledge required, but each one put in place created a clearer picture.

## Poo Analysis – Dirty Work, But Worth Its Weight

If we can improve the health of our colon, then we create more space. We get rid of the clutter and dump waste. Literally. Although this clutter is waste, however, it doesn't mean that we can't learn from the very thing that we're trying to flush away.

**The condition of our stools can teach us a lot about the state of our health.**

Just like chewing my food more times is now a habit for me, so is checking my stool when I finish on the toilet. The main reason to check our stools is to try and gain some insight into what is happening in the body and the gut.

There are so many different viewpoints around what represents a healthy-looking stool, and the type of diet being followed is massively influential, but this need not detract from the value that can be gained from taking a few short moments to assess what has left the body.

I can only go by my own experience as well as take into account the information that I've read, but it seems that more formed and darker coloured stools represent those in better condition. Dark coloured of course excluding blood, and any blood in the stool should prompt a swift visit to your medical practitioner.

My understanding of what a healthy stool should look like highlights another reason why a plant-based diet didn't work for me. It is, however, important to emphasize that I was on a narrow plant-based diet, and a broader plant-based diet may well have provided a different result. What I found was that the colour of my stool was very light and seemed to be lacking in nourishment.

I now know that this was a powerful signal from my body that, due to following such a narrow plant-based diet, I was nutritionally deficient.

**Following any diet should be done with nutritional education.**

155

As soon as I introduced salmon back into my diet, it helped me produce what I saw to be a healthier stool – more formed and with better colour.

As always, so much can be learned from simplicity. And a simple analysis of the nutrients included in salmon highlighted to me just how much nutritional value can be provided by a single food. Especially if that food is aligned with individual design, which makes nutrient extraction more efficient.

Although it may not be the most appealing thing to do, checking your stools can be a healthy habit. With a slightly adjusted mindset, it also doesn't need to be one that grosses us out. It can just be a quick part of our process when we go to the toilet:

We finish, we look, we flush.

The reason that checking your stools can be so valuable is that it is like a free test result. It can show which foods your body has struggled to digest and even help provide a dietary guide. This is where it's once again important to treat yourself as an individual – regardless of how other people digest certain foods, your body may react differently.

It takes courage to be individual, but this courage may drastically improve your health.

A good example for me is nuts. No matter whether I steeped nuts in water with salt or followed any other method to try and help them germinate and be easier to digest, eating nuts (and seeds) is one of the worst ways to provoke my pain. It's excruciating. And this excruciating pain is accompanied by visual evidence when checking my stool.

Every time I ate nuts, they appeared in my stool as if they'd barely been chewed. This despite me going into overdrive to chew the nuts before swallowing. Because nuts offer such nutritional value and importance to a plant-based diet, I persevered and persevered. I did the same with seeds.

What this showed was that I had my zombie face back on. I was letting external information around the potential benefits of eating nuts and seeds take priority over listening to my body.

*One of the hardest disciplines about not letting people influence us is related to those who mean us well.*

Looking down into the toilet at this free test result can be an incredibly powerful way for our gut office to communicate with our head office. When we eat, the process of digestion becomes invisible to our eyes, but by briefly checking the waste that has left our body, we find a distinct and hugely informative way of seeing what's going on.

In my life, I've also once again experienced a positive consideration of influence on others. Along with feeling great pride for having a clear wee, my son also loves telling me if he has had a good poo. I know that it sounds like a downright bizarre father-and-son pastime, but checking his poo together is something that we habitually do.

Stool analysis may be dirty, but it truly is worth its weight in gold.

## Electrifying Electrolytes and the Probiotic Myth

Having been through the digestive system from those first moments of drinking water and deciding what to eat, to poking around in the toilet pan (not literally) and checking our stools, what then becomes important is maintenance. We want to maintain the operating system in our body and keep it running as smoothly as possible, which brings us to electrolytes and probiotics.

The role of electrolytes is to keep the body in balance, which is always what we want to aim for. In terms of the more technical definition, electrolytes are ionic minerals, with a positive or negative electrical charge, and help provide balance in the body in several ways:

- Allow cells to create energy
- Move water and fluids around the body
- Move nutrients and waste in and out of cells
- Balance cellular water levels
- Ensure that our organs and body overall are working effectively

The following is a useful summary of five critical electrolytes along with some core functions of each:

- **Calcium:** helps muscles to contract, aids blood clotting and maintains healthy bones and teeth
- **Potassium:** helps keep blood pressure levels stable and connects with the rhythm of the heart
- **Magnesium:** helps to retain bone strength, reduce anxiety, and promote good digestion
- **Sodium:** regulates fluid in the body and helps maintain the nervous system
- **Chloride:** helps maintain fluid balance

One area of nutritional education that would have served me well during my 10-year search is that of electrolytes. Not about gaining an advanced understanding or technical expertise with the intricate detail of what electrolytes do, but instead, to just be informed of their importance.

If we don't get enough electrolytes in our body, as well as retain them, then a whole suite of health issues can occur. My panic attack was an example of this. It also showed that I had a limited understanding of the relationship between electrolytes and hydration.

When we think about hydration, we think about water. But as I described in the section about the colon, drinking too much water can dehydrate the body. It's the same with salt. Salt can provide hydration to the body in the form of the electrolyte 'sodium', but too much can have the opposite effect. In other words, we want to find the sweet spot, and this is only possible with authentic information and a deeper understanding.

*Electrolytes provide balance in the body. Balance in the body allows balance in the mind. Balance in the mind and body is the definition of balance in life.*

Dehydration is not the only thing we need to be aware of. We also need to make sure we're giving the body enough electrolytes. A problem of which seems to be getting worse with more nutrient-weak processed foods.

The following table includes a list of example foods, which offer good sources of electrolytes. Iron has also been included, as I've learned of its great importance and its role around blood production. Without enough iron, the body can't make enough healthy oxygen-carrying red blood cells.

| FOOD | CALCIUM (MG) | POTASSIUM (MG) | MAGNESIUM (MG) | SODIUM (MG) | CHLORIDE (MG) | IRON (MG) |
|---|---|---|---|---|---|---|
| Avocado | 11 | 450 | 25 | 6 | 6 | 0.40 |
| Mango | 12 | 180 | 13 | 2 | 0 | 0.70 |
| Bananas | 6 | 330 | 27 | Trace | 109 | 0.27 |
| Spinach | 119 | 682 | 80 | 30 | 112 | 1.89 |
| Broccoli | 44 | 373 | 21 | 7 | 70 | 0.75 |
| Mushrooms | 3 | 378 | 10 | 4 | 125 | 0.21 |
| Almonds | 240 | 780 | 270 | 14 | 18 | 3.00 |
| Sunflower seeds | 110 | 710 | 390 | 3 | 0 | 6.40 |
| Yoghurt (Greek style) | 126 | 184 | 13 | 66 | 159 | 0.11 |
| Cocoa powder | 130 | 1500 | 520 | 0 | 0 | 10.50 |
| Coconut | 13 | 370 | 41 | 17 | 110 | 2.10 |
| Salmon | 11 | 412 | 30 | 49 | 86 | 0.45 |
| Mussels | 38 | 90 | 23 | 290 | 460 | 2.53 |
| Scallops | 29 | 240 | 38 | 180 | 410 | 1.10 |
| Beef steak (sirloin) | 6 | 370 | 25 | 63 | 53 | 2.10 |

*Source: McCance and Widdowson, July 2019*[4]

As always, we don't need to become technical experts to make progress, we just need access to authentic information to help us stay more in balance.

Taking in enough electrolytes can play an important role in helping us achieve this.

## Are You 'Pro' Probiotics?

The second of the two elements in keeping our digestive systems operating smoothly is probiotics. Probiotics are less of a cut-and-dried story for me than electrolytes, due to the significant influence of the supplement industry. The idea behind spreading good bacteria

---

[4] https://www.gov.uk/government/publications/composition-of-foods-integrated-dataset-cofid

throughout our body makes total sense, which is what probiotics are thought to do, but this has created a huge commercial opportunity that many companies have capitalized on.

The problem is that because health information provided by companies is typically motivated by their balance sheet, as opposed to what is genuinely good for us, we are forced to rely on our own knowledge.

Regarding probiotics, I've done my best to learn as much as possible, but even in my own mind, it remains a subject of much debate.

The only supplements that I ended up taking an interest in were those relating to electrolytes and probiotics. Although I have a keener interest in the former, the problem that I've always found with electrolyte supplements is that they provoke my pain. Probiotic supplements, however, do not do this and seem to have a milder effect.

The main reason that I buy into the potentially positive effects of probiotics is because of my experience with higher probiotic foods such as kimchi.

Kimchi is a Korean side dish that's eaten as an accompaniment to almost every meal. I first came across it when I was living and teaching in South Korea. Due to its spicy and very particular taste, I didn't care for it much, but as I wanted to become more embedded in the culture, I persevered to the point that I started to like it. Then ended up loving it.

Kimchi is a combination of cabbage, spring onion, garlic, ginger, chilli and glutinous rice powder. The mix of ingredients offers a fascinating insight into the influence of how food is prepared. Garlic is a good example. Usually, in the past, this food had worsened my acid reflux, but when included in kimchi, I found the effect to be quite different.

It seems that the fermentation process involved in preparing kimchi changed the impact that certain ingredients had on my body. When my acid reflux was bad in the past, I found that kimchi could even be a food that helped.

***How a food is prepared can be as influential to digestion as the food itself.***

160

Diets in the West could benefit by including more fermented foods such as kimchi. Considering the degree of my own digestive condition, the fact that I found kimchi to be much less provocative to my pain was a good enough sign that it carried some benefits to digestion. And it was also a way to get some more electrolytes in.

The second probiotic food that I did reasonably well with, in the past, was raw goat's yoghurt. The goat's yoghurt choice being simply because I seemed to do better with goat's milk than with cow's milk, but it's the raw element where most of the value lies. Raw meaning that it isn't treated or heated in any way and is eaten straight from the goat.

It should be noted that this does carry risk because heating reduces the risk of infection, but I've personally never had any issues due to the sources from which I buy. I go direct to a farm. On the flip side, it should also be noted that it's in the process of heating that there's a significant loss of nutritional value. Hence the benefit of raw.

As always, it's tough to be definitive about what is genuinely making a positive difference to our digestion. But with raw goat's yoghurt, I found it to be more apparent. Whenever I ate commercially bought goat's yoghurt, it caused a spike in my pain. Whenever I ate raw goat's yoghurt, though, the pain was less.

For me, that is my gut office telling my head office that, in no uncertain terms, the raw option is a much better tool for digestion. This also persuaded me that there is some depth to the beneficial effects of probiotics and the spreading of good bacteria in the gut.

### Food can represent a journey of awareness.

My experience with probiotics is similar to so much of my journey with health and nutrition. It's all about small benefits adding up to larger leaps of progress. Kimchi, raw goat's yoghurt or any other food that has a higher probiotic content has in no way cured my pain or solved my own digestive issues, but sharing my experience with these foods may be useful for others.

Lastly, there is a word of caution. The effects of probiotics are heavily embellished in my opinion, especially when in supplement form. I've personally achieved more progress by focusing on electrolytes.

Being aware of both, though, has been beneficial.

# 17

# Fasting – The Non-miraculous Miracle

Our focus so far has been on what we eat, but the decision of what not to eat can be just as important. We want the head office to give the gut office food that helps it function better, but we also want the head office to restrict those foods which cause damage and lack in nutritional value. The only way to achieve this is to take the time to learn. As L. Frank Baum said:

> *'No thief, however skillful, can rob one of knowledge, and that is why knowledge is the best and safest treasure to acquire.'*

When we start following a new diet, there can sometimes be considerable confusion in the head office, because we believe the new foods we're eating are solely responsible for health gains. We forget that what we've removed from our diet is also significant.

For example, if someone who eats enormous amounts of junk food suddenly starts following a juicing diet, then they may experience an improvement in health. Consuming nothing but blended fruits for a period may genuinely make this person feel better.

However, as much as I would undoubtedly advocate eating more fruits than junk food, what must be considered is the effect of removing what was causing damage and lacking in nutritional value. Which is why the stories of miraculous improvements in the marketing campaigns of diet promoters are flawed. Because they often include those who previously had unhealthy diets lacking in nutrient density.

Had the person simply removed the junk food, then a significant improvement would have occurred in any case.

Therefore, I reaffirm this point - we can achieve significant health benefits by deciding what not to eat as well as what to eat. There is no need to be dragged into following prescriptive diets, which are fuelled by industry and profit.

## The Benefits of Fasting

Before I became persuaded of the potential benefits of fasting, I had come across this idea many times before. The problem I found, as was so often the case, was being unable to find authentic information. I'd tried cutting out solid foods on various occasions but because I didn't understand what was going on, I misjudged the potential value.

The other issue was that I let myself be led by those who stood to gain from my need. So, when I followed a fruit juicing diet, I did so with my zombie face back on and followed the sales pitch that came with whatever product I was buying.

Just like the idea that rashes across the body can represent toxins being excreted, I bought into the propaganda that an increase in my pain – which occurred continuously on a fruit juicing diet – was part of a healing process due to the goodness of fruit.

It wasn't. The high level of sugar in fruit was the cause of more pain.

Imagine just how tightly glued my zombie face had to have been stuck on for me to follow a juicing diet and stick to it. I can't express with any more passion how you must develop the courage to be individual and listen to your own body. I'm not attacking fruit, despite growing concerns of sugar consumption in all forms, but rather encouraging people to learn for themselves.

**Don't expect others to know a lot. Learn for yourself.**

When most people think about fasting, they believe it's something they'd struggle to do. Yet, we all fast at some point during the day or night. Mostly at night. For example, if we eat our last meal at 7 p.m., avoid any evening snacks, and then have breakfast at 7 a.m. the next morning, then we have successfully completed a 12-hour fast.

We don't usually feel the need to get up at 1 a.m. because six hours have passed since our last meal. If we had to do this every night, we would find it a real struggle. So, from this perspective, the concept of fasting is not so unusual.

A lot of people mistakenly think about fasting as a type of starvation. That isn't the case. It's about going through a limited period without food, which the human body is more than capable of coping with. This isn't to say that fasting should be taken lightly, and where any pre-existing health conditions exist, medical guidance should be sought. So, in a very elementary sense, a fast is just about eating less to try and help the body.

### A healthy, hydrated human body can go 30 to 60 days without food.

The main challenge in understanding fasting, which is the same as practically all areas of nutrition, is that there are so many varying viewpoints.

There are those who support it and believe the body benefits from regular, as well as extended, periods of not eating. They think fasting gives the body time to heal. Then there are those who oppose it and alternatively, believe the body doesn't need a break from digesting food.

A common argument I've heard from the opposing side is that the digestive system is like an organ in the body, such as the heart. The design is based on never needing to take a break and stop working. A counterargument from supporters of fasts is that if the digestive system replicated the heart, then we would need to continually feed it while we slept. However, when we sleep, the heart can't stop beating, but the digestive system can effectively shut down for the night and go into a rest and repair process.

Throughout my journey with pain, I've been persuaded by arguments of both sides. This has so often been the case for me, as I wanted to believe that what I was being told – or sold – was the answer to all my problems. I now know that this was simply a reflection of the previously less developed condition of my mind.

*An undeveloped mind muscle relies on hope. A developed mind muscle is built on faith.*

With so many negative experiences around the subject of fasting, by the time I started the fast, my scepticism had reached its peak. What made me at least try it was the authenticity of those who guided me at the Cambodian yoga retreat.

They lived what they taught, and they did so every day of their lives. This, to me, is what inspiration really is. It isn't about having the best motivational music with the biggest-budget video, but rather in how the person behind the cause lives their own life each day. Even when the curtain is drawn.

This is also why my mentor and D are inspirations to me, and my mum was an inspiration to me.

*Inspiration is about how we live our lives, not what we acquire in our lives.*

The person who led me in my fast at the Cambodian yoga retreat was not someone who was proposing a fast because he'd heard it was a good idea. He underwent fasts regularly and did so for periods of between one and 21 days.

It was mind-blowing. How could someone not eat for 21 days?

The guidance that he was able to provide was based on real personal experience, and as I have repeatedly said; this is the greatest knowledge that any of us can share with others. Therefore, I went in to my fast with an open mind and an open heart.

**When we reopen our minds, we can reopen our hearts.**

I had nothing to lose and education to gain. As long as I didn't look to fasting as a cure and rather appreciated that it was just another way in which I was taking responsibility for my own health, then I gave my mind muscle the correct warm-up for what would be a very different type of training.

## My Fasting Journey

When I was discussing the length of fast with my guide at the yoga retreat, we decided that three days was the right time frame. It was long enough to give my body a chance to experience the prospective power of self-healing but short enough that it wasn't going to be too much for me during what was my first official fast with the correct guidance.

One of things he said to me in preparation for my fast was, 'A fast should end when the body tells us it's time.'

This made perfect sense with the way of thinking that I'd adopted around my two offices, so I made sure that I placed emphasis on clear lines of communication between my head office and my gut office.

What this prompted me to do was remove rigidity from the fasting process. I would commit to the three days but would keep these words in mind. What transpired as a result of this was quite extraordinary – my fast lasted for eight straight days. If the three days of only eating fruits and vegetables as a follow-up are then included, what started out as a three-day plan became an 11-day journey.

As always, I had *0 Days Off* in mind, so I documented each day of my fasting experience in the table on the next page.

| | | ↔ | ↑ | ↓ |
|---|---|---|---|---|
| | | **Neutral** | **Positive** | **Negative** |
| | | Feeling neither up nor down | Feeling an improvement and more positive | Feeling worse and more negative |
| **Day** | **Notes** | **Energy** | **Mood** | **Hunger** | **Pain** |
| Monday [Day 1] | Straightforward and no ups and downs. Exercise as normal with my morning swim and two yoga classes. | ↔ | ↔ | ↔ | ↔ |
| Tuesday [Day 2] | Sleep fine but feel sick throughout the day. Pain worsens but still swim and practise yoga. | ↓ | ↓ | ↓ | ↓ |
| Wednesday [Day 3] | Bad sleep but feel better in the morning. Feel even more positive in the evening. | ↑ | ↑ | ↔ | ↑ |
| Thursday [Day 4] | Good sleep and reasonable morning but feel very sick in the afternoon. Plus start to feel new pain on my right side. | ↔ | ↔ | ↓ | ↓ |
| Friday [Day 5] | Day starts off rough and I expect to start eating again today, but something tells me to persevere and the day gets better. | ↔ | ↑ | ↔ | ↓ |
| Saturday [Day 6] | Spend two hours in the gym with good energy, which is extraordinary. Things turn bad in the evening, though. | ↑ | ↓ | ↓ | ↓ |
| Sunday [Day 7] | Water only but pain is bad. I do pass stool, though, which alleviates new pain on my right side. | ↔ | ↑ | ↔ | ↓ |
| Monday [Day 8] | First day that I don't exercise and rather just go for a calm walk. Feel like it's time to break the fast. | ↓ | ↑ | ↑ | ↔ |
| Tuesday [Day 9] | Start eating slowly and in small amounts - just have some fresh fruit and experience incredible appreciation for food. | ↔ | ↑ | ↑ | ↔ |
| Wednesday [Day 10] | After a good night's sleep, I completely empty my bowels. Less energy but I expected this as energy needed for digestion. | ↓ | ↑ | ↔ | ↑ |
| Thursday [Day 11] | Final day of my journey and looking forward to eating. Energy is still lacking but my mood is good and I learned a lot. | ↓ | ↑ | ↔ | ↔ |

Although the fast didn't provide a cure for my pain, the experience was incredibly educational. My mind muscle was given a major workout and continued beyond the end of the fast. There was so much more to learn when analysing the experience in more detail.

One of the greatest lessons being related to sugar.

Both coconut water and sugar cane juice are high in sugar content. I drank a lot of both during the first period of the fast, although decided to reduce sugar cane juice and focus on coconut water out of personal choice. I then ended up on only water for days 7 and 8.

My sugar intake during the fast, albeit natural, highlighted another conflict between the more medicinal viewpoint and the holistic world. At specific points during the fast, my pain was awful, but because I was in an extremely calm environment, my stress was more in balance. I was also not eating food.

With stress and food being two of the main protagonists of my pain, and both significantly lowered, then why would I still experience so much pain?

The medicinal perspective would argue that it was because I was consuming too much sugar in the coconut water and sugar cane juice, which makes sense. However, my pain was also bad during the last two days of the fast when I was only drinking water, which implies that self-healing was occurring, which is the holistic perspective.

One of the holistic beliefs of fasting is that as the body uses up energy in the digestion of food, this energy can instead be reallocated to healing parts of the body which are damaged or injured when a fast is undertaken. This also made sense, and I believe it's possible to extract value from conflicting viewpoints if done so with an open mind.

### *An open mind has unlimited potential.*

My individual design didn't fit precisely with either viewpoint, but by learning from both sides, I gained the most benefit. I now believe that my body did benefit from this period of fasting, but I also believe that the sugar intake was counterproductive in working with my pain.

This exemplifies how removing foods from my diet helped me, but also how individuality must remain at the core of our thinking.

Although it may seem obvious that the better option for me would have been to pursue a water-only fast, this then brings up the crucial subject of electrolytes. One which I believe every person pursuing longer fasts should consider.

As electrolytes keep the body in balance, when we restrict electrolyte intake, we risk getting out of balance. So, although I was drinking a lot of sugary juice, it was natural and high in electrolytes. This played no small part in my continued ability to exercise throughout my fast.

The problem with drinking too much of these drinks is the diuretic effect. On top of drinking coconut water and sugar cane juice, I was also drinking too much water. My kidneys were, therefore, flushing out electrolytes, and my colon became dehydrated. I now realize that this was the reason for the pain on the right side of my body.

However, just to throw a spanner in the works, the fact that I did pass stool on day 7 after not eating any food for a week does heavily support the more holistic beliefs. Then to throw another spanner in the works, the fact that I passed stool after eating a plant-based diet for more than a month by this stage shows that any type of food can get stuck.

Not just meat.

There is so much conflicting information, which makes our nutritional journey much more difficult, and that's why we'd be far better served by removing judgement and simply sharing what we learn.

What influenced my way of thinking was the state of my mind muscle. With a weaker mind muscle, I would have submitted to blaming others and feeling disappointed because I had again failed to find a cure for my pain. With a more developed mind muscle, however, I just saw the whole experience as a source of learning.

One which I gained a better understanding of as more time passed.

What I was again reminded of was just how tough it can be to consistently act with individuality. Those who influenced me at the yoga retreat did so with pure hearts and the absolute best of intentions for me, but what I needed to do was allow this influence – so commit to a fast – but not prioritize it over listening to my own body.

It truly does take real discipline and great courage to act with individuality in all situations.

**_Authenticity provided by others cannot replace authenticity provided within._**

I learned an incredible amount from my fasting experience in Cambodia, and despite the evolution in my understanding, I am eternally thankful for meeting the kind, passionate and dedicated people who guided me and remain inspirational figures in my life. However, the reality we must all learn to accept is that no one has all the answers to human health, and it is of little value to blame others when they don't provide the solutions we so desperately seek.

## Alternative Energy Sources

When we think about powering the body, we usually think about food as being our only source of energy, but this is a limited perspective. Although food is undoubtedly a primary source, several others became apparent during my 11-day fast.

My usual day at the retreat, including yoga two or three times a day, started at 5:30 a.m. and finished around 9:30 p.m. But because I was so used to fighting pain, exercising, working and being a dad, to have this reduced to just needing to focus on my pain and exercise was something of a luxury.

However, when I started the fast, one of my thoughts was that I needed to be careful about conserving energy, so I decided to draw back on the amount of exercise I was doing. Even though I only had to focus on healing and exercise, I still adopted the mindset that I should take it easy while fasting. But then, something changed in my mind.

During my morning swim on that first day of fasting, I questioned why I was forcing myself to conserve energy if I felt like I had the energy to swim as usual. I was going against one of my primary aims, which was to get my two offices communicating more clearly and my mind and body working as one.

If my body was not sending any messages to my mind that it was tired, then why was I making the decision to exercise with less intensity? This is what prompted me to just exercise and practise as usual, and let my body be a guide for my mind.

The real education around energy, however, took place on the second day. I hadn't eaten for 24 hours, and it was a tough day. I didn't feel like going for my usual morning swim but pushed through and made it down to the sea. Once there, I began to feel like I did any other morning. My energy levels seemed the same, and I swam for my usual time and distance. When I thought about why this was, I again considered the two different perspectives.

From the medicinal perspective, the salt and nutrients gave me energy. From a holistic perspective, the life of the sea was giving me energy. The world was energizing me through its most natural means. Through learning to not get caught up in rights and wrongs of varying viewpoints, I simply learned from both sides.

**Opposing beliefs may be worth following if each provides value.**

My own belief is a combination of the two perspectives. There is something special about swimming in the sea that I believe goes beyond the physiological, but there is no doubt that the salt and other nutrients provided by the sea were of great value to my body.

In fact, following many more dietary adjustments since arriving back from the yoga retreat, I am now profoundly convinced of the abundant health benefits provided by spending time in the sea.

I also believe this to be the case with the sun. I found that on the days when I was feeling very low on the fast, I benefitted from spending time in the sun. Getting vitamin D in abundance provided me with a more uplifted feeling and gave me energy.

Beyond the sea and the sun, there was also one more natural source of energy that I tapped into – nature. The trees, the plants and those living things around us that contribute to fresh air and create a healthy environment. One day during my fast, when my energy was particularly low, I went to a forest and literally just jumped around on rocks, climbed trees and swung from branches.

It was tremendous and brought out the little kid from Annan in me. I felt uplifted by exercising 'in' nature 'with' nature.

I'm not writing anything groundbreaking here, but the experience taught me of the significant amount of energy that is available from natural sources. It had such an effect on me that I now make a consistent effort to exercise more often in nature.

When I came back from Cambodia, I started to take my son for forest or nature walks and camping trips. What I saw in him was fantastic, and I noticed his mood would lift as soon as we arrived. This, for me, is really where the holistic perspective holds more prominence. I believe there to be something undeniably special about spending time in nature.

Particularly about our health.

## Fat Fasting

Despite not personally fasting to lose weight, I appreciate that weight loss is an important subject to many, so I would like to share my thoughts on this.

As ever with nutrition, there are conflicting views. I have come across as many critics of fasting being used as an approach to weight loss as I have those who advocate it. The critical view is that when a fast comes to an end, the weight that was lost during the fast will very quickly be regained. This being especially true with shorter fasts, due to a lot of lost weight being fluid or water weight.

Switch over to those who support fasts, and there is some sense to the argument that if we consume less food, then we will lose more weight.

The debate also exists around muscle loss and whether fasting results in fat and muscle being lost simultaneously or fat being lost first.

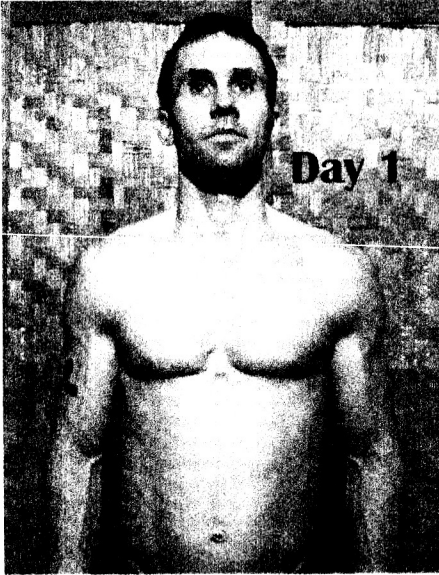

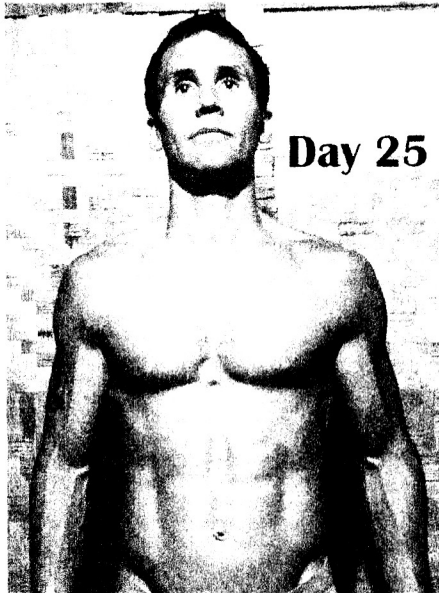

So, is fasting effective for losing weight? Can it result in a genuine reduction in body fat? All I can provide as a way of answering these questions is what I've learned through my own experience. To illustrate this, I kept a photo record of my changing body shape while at the yoga retreat. This is demonstrated by four images on the previous page, which tell an interesting story.

The Day 1 image was taken as soon as I arrived at the yoga retreat. I had just endured an incredible amount of stress in business, and this is reflected in the dark circles around my eyes. My diet at this time was based on eating a lot of salmon, gluten-free oats, vegetables and raw goat's yoghurt.

Looking at the Day 1 image and the Day 10 image, there is a notable difference. As I lacked any education on plant-based diets, I thought that the weight would drop off me as I excluded animal products and would be able to eat as much as I like. But once again, that just reflected my uneducated mind on the subject of nutrition.

The fact that I was eating so many carbohydrates – even though they were all deemed as the healthier kind of fruits, vegetables and grains – resulted in me gaining body fat. Even exercising for three to four hours per day didn't prevent this.

Following the tenth day and recognizing that my body fat was increasing, which was misaligned with working with my pain, I then started to be more disciplined. I couldn't change the type of food because everything was served as a buffet in the yoga retreat, so I rather changed the volume of food I ate. I also reduced the number of my meals from three to two per day by cutting out lunch.

As a result, another significant change in shape occurred. This is shown by the difference between the Day 10 image and the Day 25 image. There is a notable reduction in body fat, despite there being no change in my exercise schedule, which was always very consistent.

Simply put, I was ingesting less energy, so I needed to expel less energy to lose weight.

Despite the changes in the first three images, it's in the fourth image that the most significant change occurs – Day 38. It probably comes as no surprise that this image was taken at the end of my eight-day period with no food. The weight loss is considerable, and there appears to be a significant reduction in body fat. So, it would seem like fasting is an effective way to lose weight, but several lessons are important to consider.

One lesson is that the loss of water weight should not be underestimated. I didn't have any means of measuring my body fat percentage when I was in Cambodia, but the reduction would have been less than the perception of the images. A genuine loss of actual body fat is different from the body just dropping fluid due to a dietary change.

What is interesting, though, is that there is a clear retaining of muscle even though I did far less gym work in Cambodia – my exercise was predominantly yoga and swimming. Fasting didn't cause a drastic loss of muscle mass, which makes sense, because when we really think about it, for the muscle to deteriorate is a significant bodily shift.

Therefore, I think that missing a few meals or the mandatory requirement to eat within a two-hour window following a workout is embellished to the point of being flawed. I believe that muscle building, as well as maintenance, is far more related to the overall quality of a diet.

Another lesson I've learned more about since my return from Cambodia is the medicinal perspective about what is happening in the body when we fast.

## Insulin

Of all the endless sources of information about nutrition and the body, learning about insulin when combined with the ultimate teachings of your own body is useful.

Insulin is a hormone produced in the pancreas, which regulates the glucose (blood sugar) levels in our blood. If there is a lack of insulin, then this can result in diabetes. Diabetes is a disease that occurs when the body's ability to produce or use insulin is impaired.

When we fast, we don't consume any food. As such, our insulin levels drop. This isn't necessarily a bad thing, and some modern research supports the view that this can be beneficial to our health. During the first 24 hours of fasting, blood sugar levels drop due to the limited intake of carbohydrates, so the body switches to burning fat.

The technical name for this switch is ketosis.

Once blood sugar levels have dropped – therefore meaning that there has been a reduction in insulin – the body starts to burn through fat. This correlates with the images of my changing body shape.

When food is reintroduced, and especially following an extended fast, then insulin levels are very low. Granted, I was intaking sugar calories from coconut water and sugar cane juice, but these were easily burned off through the exercise I was doing and daily movement. Also, the last two days of my fast were water only, so this caused a further drop in blood sugar.

The exciting part happens when food is reintroduced to the body. If the food is high in carbohydrates, this causes a rapid increase in glucose (otherwise known as blood sugar) and a spike in insulin.

As insulin is often nicknamed the 'fat storage hormone', the body suddenly starts to regain fat. There is also a renewed retention of water, which can cause a change in physical appearance.

Because I was on a plant-based diet and the foods I ate following my fast were very high in carbohydrates, I noticed a significant and rapid regaining of weight. This is therefore where the crux of the real answer lies, in terms of whether fasting can be effective for losing weight.

For me, the role of the mind is just as important as the role of the body. If fasting causes a change of mind and results in a lower intake of junk food consistently, then I believe that it can be effective for weight loss. If, however it doesn't, then upon returning to the diet which was followed before the fast, the body will very quickly return to the same shape as before the fast. And I do mean very quickly.

*There is no greater change than a change of mind.*

Therefore, it may be more useful to just concentrate on eating fewer junk foods than going to the extreme of an extended fast. This is because consistency can be defined as an authentic change - a change that is lasting.

If a fast can, however, be followed by a change of mind, then I do believe this to be an even more effective way to lose weight and reduce body fat.

Because the purpose of my fast was self-healing and not weight loss, I ate foods that were aligned with the beliefs of the plant-based diet and cleansing the body. My swift weight gain following the end of my fast was therefore not necessarily related to the fact that I'd started eating again. It was associated with eating a huge amount of carbohydrates and sugar.

Even if I'd started to eat foods that were lower in carbohydrates, I'd still have experienced weight gain because eating any food causes an insulin reaction. But I would not have regained as much body fat.

In summary, fasting is worth trying and insulin is worth learning about in my opinion.

## 'Break'fast

When I finished the fast, I wasn't thinking about what I should eat in relation to my body weight or shape. I was just thinking about whether any self-healing had taken place, which could help me live with less pain.

When a fast comes to an end, whether it's for detox reasons or weight loss, what we eat and in what volume is important. In fact, how we break a fast is as important as the fast itself.

Of all the fasts that I've now completed since returning from Cambodia – which has usually been for between one and three days – it's always the end of the fast where retaining discipline is the most difficult.

There is a natural urge to gorge on everything that we can get our hands on.

When I finished my fast in Cambodia, and I had done my three-day follow-up of only fruits and vegetables, I felt like I was ready to eat a mountain. Therefore, I went to a local vegan café and ordered half the menu. Or perhaps it would be more accurate to say I ordered the whole menu.

It was as if my mind had been hijacked, and I desperately wanted to pig out.

One of the most important considerations with a fast is that we fast mindfully. We need to decide why it is that we are doing a fast. If we fast to try and lose weight, this is very different from fasting to try and attend to a digestive issue.

Our reason, therefore, should heavily determine what we eat when it comes to ending the fast.

When I was in the yoga retreat, I was fasting to try and heal my pain and improve digestion. As I was on a plant-based diet, I had little choice but to eat fruits and vegetables when my fast ended. However, I've since learned about the subject of ketosis, which makes many types of fruits and vegetables an inappropriate choice for those who want to keep their bodies in a ketogenic state.

The physiological state of ketosis is an important point to expand on. When glucose (blood sugar) levels drop to a certain level, and the body switches to fat as a source of energy, then if no food is being consumed, the body starts to utilize fat. Therefore, promoters of ketogenic diets talk about this diet turning the body into a 'fat-burning machine'.

We don't want to get caught up in all the marketing exaggeration, but I do believe there to be some useful depth in the information that explains how the body can get used to burning more fat more efficiently. That being if it is only dealing with fat.

To put it more simply, the body may find it easier to burn body fat if we make fat a primary source of energy over carbohydrates.

If weight loss is the primary motivation for fasting, I would suggest opting for lower carbohydrate foods when breaking a fast. This is because I believe in the more physiological perspective regarding insulin response in the body. It can be a great disappointment to go through a fast – which can be tough – only to see all the hard work vanish in no time at all.

Most important, whether a fast is undertaken for reasons of self-healing or weight loss, is to try and eat as cleanly as possible. The way that I like to think about this is in the example of setting aside time to clean our car.

When we clean our car, we do so because it's dirty. It usually takes some elbow grease to get it shiny, so we do have to put in time and effort. Although it may not be the most enjoyable thing to do, when it's done, we feel a sense of accomplishment.

Imagine, however, if immediately after the cleaning is finished, we take a bag full of rubbish and pour it into the car. This would be deemed as madness. Yet, this is precisely what we do if we finish a fast and then stuff ourselves full of junk food. We're not necessarily undoing all the good work, but we've certainly devalued the effort that we put in.

When we fast, we clean up our body, so it's a real pity to lose the shine so quickly.

### Fasting is a practice and practise leads to improvement.

My final suggestion around fasting is perhaps not to get too caught up in it. My life has become so serious because of my pain, but I found more value in trying to fast in a relaxed way. I just try to see a fasting day as a peaceful day, when I don't need to think about my pain being provoked by food.

What fasting isn't about is damaging our relationship with food. We don't want to end up hating food so that we eat less and restrict our intake of nutrients. We want to improve our relationship with food so that we can make better decisions and improve our health.

Ultimately, we want to change our relationship with food.

# 18

# Changing Our Relationship with Food

Before my pain started, I didn't pay any attention to food volume or in-depth nutritional information. I just ate what I wanted, with taste being a driving factor in my decision-making. I loved food, I loved to eat, and it was a source of pleasure in my life. I think it's because our relationship with food is so deeply important that it can be compared to the relationships with our loved ones. During the time with my mentor, I was discussing the loss of my mum and how to deal with it when he planted another seed of thought in my mind:

### *Relationships don't end. Relationships change.*

Along with being able to square off the loss of someone, as described in Chapter 8, I think that this is a wonderfully beautiful way to deal with bereavement. To think that I still have a relationship with my mum hasn't represented a negative clinging on, but rather a positive way to think that I simply have a different relationship with her now. Even though she is dead.

Changing our relationship with food can be as profound as changing our relationship with another person – a negative relationship will serve only to hurt our health, and this is the same with food. As much as we want to take pleasure from eating, once we start to rely on it for pleasure, then we become ignorant of what is good for our body.

Although we naturally associate food with the body, it's the mind which plays the most pivotal role because we must change our mind before we are able to change our relationship with food. Whether we're trying to improve our relationship with a person or improve our relationship with food, there needs to be an authentic change that occurs inside. The kind of change that is lasting and cannot be easily reversed.

I once read somewhere that the average US woman spends around 17 years of her life on diets. What a frightening waste of time. There is no authentic change occurring, with changes limited to which diet will be followed next.

> *It can be more difficult to change an addiction to food than it can be to change an addiction to drugs or alcohol.*

Imagine the difference between authentically wanting to eat fresh, natural food against always fighting temptation for food that harms our health. The time saved cannot be put into words.

What is crucial on the path to changing our relationship with food is to exclude self-judgement. My journey started in 2007, and it was 2018 before I started seeing food as more about sustenance than pleasure. It therefore took 11 years to stop letting food control me.

There's no place for self-judgement because of the same reason I keep coming back to – we weren't provided with proper education about nutrition or the mind. Therefore, we should not blame ourselves for struggling to make such a significant change in the mind. My fasting guide at the yoga retreat said it well:

> *Think about how long your mind has been a mess – it's naturally going to take time to tidy up.*

By removing self-judgement, I was able to take an objective view and realize that I'd been developing habits around food since childhood.

## The Habit(s) of a Lifetime

When my pain began in 2007, I was holding on to my old life. I worked a lot, I partied a lot, I drank a lot, and I ate a lot. But I also exercised a lot. Even though I had unhealthy hangover meals, multiple-course social meals, and plentiful food at home, I didn't gain weight. Playing sport and regular exercise took care of this.

As my pain worsened, I eventually moved away from alcohol and socializing. My diet stayed much the same, though, and I continued to eat takeaways and anything else I wanted. Even when I cooked at home, I made a lot of food and ate a lot.

But still, I avoided weight gain through exercise.

As my pain got much worse, and I began to recognize it as a serious disorder, I was forced to stop eating certain foods. Takeaways went out the window, as did things like Sunday roasts, cereals, pasta and a whole host of other foods that I enjoyed. The number of food types that I ate reduced, but what didn't change was the volume. I still devoured monstrous platefuls of whatever I was eating.

But once again, my commitment to exercise prevented noticeable weight gain.

When my pain reached peak levels, I was pushed to trying extreme diets. But whichever diet I followed, I still ate a lot. The type of food was different, but the amount remained the same. More food resulted in more pain, and being in so much pain was a serious hardship.

I continued to treat food as a source of comfort, despite it being a source of pain. My balance between pleasure and pain was heavily weighted in the wrong direction – towards pain.

From one perspective, I was in denial because it was becoming more and more evident as time passed that overeating conflicted with managing my pain. But the struggle of dealing with illness every single day meant that I turned to whatever would bring me some sort of pleasure. With practically every socially related activity gone from my life, I was left with food.

My story is my own, but this idea of turning to food for comfort is something I think is shared with almost everyone. Life can be very tough, and when it is, food can often be the only friend we have. The unfortunate reality, however, is that when we eat with stress and eat for comfort, we most often don't eat with awareness for our health.

In this respect, food is no different to drinking alcohol or taking drugs; it can offer a temporary release from the harshness of life.

Once I started to better understand just how deep our relationship with food went, it allowed me to take a less emotional viewpoint. It urged me to look into my past and see if I could find any clues as to why changing my relationship with food was so incredibly difficult.

After all, even though I'd been in pain since 2007, I'd been alive since 1979.

## Looking Back

As I started to look back through my childhood, I identified two very interesting habits: one around exercise and the other around food. Since literally being able to walk, I'd always loved exercising, and since literally being able to eat, I'd always loved food. So, these two habits were deeply embedded from infancy.

They truly were habits of a lifetime.

When I started to look at different stages of my life, these two habits cropped up again and again. It didn't matter which period of life I chose, there was a pattern. For example, when I looked at a typical day in my life at secondary school, it painted a profound picture.

**On the dietary side:** My breakfast at home in the morning consisted of sugary cereal, full fat milk, white toast with butter and jam, and a cup of (caffeinated) tea with two teaspoons of refined sugar and more full fat milk. My morning snack at school usually included a huge sugary milkshake, a chocolate bar and a packet of crisps. My lunch at school was chips in a buttered roll, a can of fizzy pop, an ice cream or chocolate bar and another bag of crisps. Then later in the evening at home, I would have a sandwich with white bread, biscuits and even more crisps. This would finally all be topped off by more white bread toast, butter and yet another cup of sugary, caffeinated tea.

The only meal that held any semblance of being healthy was what my mum cooked for dinner early evening. And although she always made a great effort, her knowledge about nutrition was limited. She'd grown up with food in such scarcity that, let's just say 'nutritional value' and 'balanced diet' weren't exactly buzzwords at the time.

**On the exercise side:** Each day I did my paper round in the morning, played playground footy with my pals at lunchtime (after wolfing down our food), then went to physical education class a few times a week. I also played football and other sports in the evening and was always outside doing something on the weekend.

No matter how many calories or how much energy I consumed, I always burned it off. And with no physical evidence that my diet was doing any damage, due to no visual weight gain, I never gave a second thought to what I was eating. Also, I was a boy growing up in Scotland as part of a working-class family. I wasn't exactly interested in flying the organic vegetable flag.

Beyond this lack of awareness around my unhealthy diet, I also lacked awareness about the two very powerful habits that were developing. Ones I would find tremendously difficult to change when I really needed to.

By piecing this all together, I further developed my mind muscle. I gained a deeper understanding of what was going on and why I was continually losing the battle with food.

> *Identifying an issue in our lives can be helpful. Understanding the issue can be transformational.*

With a deeper understanding, I was able to significantly reduce self-criticism. Every time I overate, I used to beat myself up about it. I would keep uttering the words, 'Why do I keep doing this to myself?'

Although I thought I had identified an issue at this stage, I had discovered a root cause.

Having found the root, what I now needed was action. I needed a new process. One that could break those two deeply embedded habits. Even though it seemed like less of a requirement to alter my mindset around exercise, the two habits were so intertwined that both needed to be addressed.

## Breaking the Habit(s)

As I set out to change the habits that existed so profoundly within me, I recognized one of the first significant obstacles – an incredibly strong association exists between 'food' and 'enjoyment'.

This isn't just limited to taste. Although we want to eat food that we like the taste of, there is something deeper that exists with food. It frequently forms part of any social occasion and can act as an accompaniment to many things we like doing.

Enjoying food was completely natural to me, as it is for all of us. Whether food is in abundance or scarcity, we all want to enjoy eating. And if we're lucky enough to choose, we all want to eat the food we like.

Despite what I'd learned about inner change being the priority, I discovered this time that external change was required. I had to make changes in my external environment in order to develop a new process and break free from my lifelong habits.

To get started, I kept track of everything and made notes each day. This highlighted to me that there were two key scenarios I most often found myself in when I ate: eating alone or eating at home with my son.

When I ate alone, it would not be uncommon for me to sit and read the newspaper in the morning or watch a football game in the evening. I no longer had a social life, so these were a couple of simple pleasures that I'd held on to.

The problem with these pleasures was that I created an association between 'eating' and 'distractions', so was not mindfully eating.

By giving my attention to other things beyond eating, I was encouraging myself to eat more until whatever I was doing was finished. For example, the distraction of a football game would mean that I'd be tempted to eat more during the full 90 minutes that it lasted.

A lot of food can be consumed in 90 minutes.

What I needed to do as part of my new process was to disrupt this. I had to separate 'eating' and 'distractions'. I had to separate eating from doing everything else. I had to just sit and eat. So, I tried.

It wasn't easy at first, because it felt like I was losing one of the few pleasures that I had left in life. This led to many more necessary diversions. It was particularly difficult when I was tired and had endured another long and lonely day in pain. The lifelong habit of eating with freedom, and the adopted habit of eating for comfort due to my struggle, made any type of change incredibly tricky.

*Making changes in life and sticking to them is far easier when things are going our way. It's when times are tough that we're truly tested.*

The resistance to change was so profound that I found myself having an argument inside my mind: 'Why can't I sit in front of the TV on a Friday night and eat a big plate of food that I enjoy the taste of?'

There was real depth in this argument, considering I'd made it through another week in constant pain. Was it too much to ask?

This battle exemplifies the greatest conflict any of us will ever fight: a battle of the mind. Whether we are fighting pain, coping with others mistreating us, dealing with insults, being bullied or trying to let go of someone or something, it is the state of our mind that matters most.

*One of the greatest pieces of armour that any of us can ever have, is a well-developed mind muscle.*

Despite such a raging battle in my mind, everything I'd been through had prepared me for this moment. All the pain, all the necessary diversions, all the days of struggle, they all contributed to providing me with the training to develop my mind muscle. Therefore, I turned to what I knew would allow me to achieve progress - repetitions.

I kept practising and practising. Failing and failing. Learning and learning. And because I treated all failures as necessary diversions, I was able to avoid self-criticism and self-judgement. Progress was slow, but I did expect this, because I was trying to change the habits of a lifetime.

Eventually, with countless repetitions, I did improve.

What I discovered was that the more that I ate without doing anything else, the more at peace I felt. Eating mindfully was aligned with working with my pain, rather than provoking it, which was something that I gratefully found to be very peaceful.

I no longer uttered the words, 'Why do I keep doing this to myself?'

I still experienced pain from food, but it was less.

Like so much of how I've been able to achieve progress with my pain, there is a simplicity at the core of what I'm doing. I was basically just sitting, eating and doing nothing else. But, just like the other ways in which I've achieved progress, there is a distinct discrepancy between simple and easy.

My new process was simple. My new process wasn't easy.

This is a very apt way to sum up how I've been able to achieve progress with my whole life. It also exemplifies how I live my life each day. I live it very simply. Whether it is the mind, nutrition, exercise or even entrepreneurialism, I have found incredible value in simplifying whatever it is I'm dealing with.

I believe that this value can only be extracted, however, if it's recognized that a simple life doesn't necessarily mean an easy life. What I mean by this is that by simplifying our lives, we can remove complication and grow as human beings.

This, to me, is progress.

Despite the simplicity of my new process, following it every day created another challenge. It is a challenge that I still face today. But each morning when I wake up, I look no further ahead than the day that is in front of me. I don't tell myself that I'm going to have to overcome this battle with food every day for the rest of my life.

I tell myself that all I need to do is win the day.

*By changing our relationship with food, we can replace a form of self-harm with a form of self-calm.*

What I want to highlight with great compassion is that the self-damaging behaviour around food that we experience isn't our faults. There is no fault, and there is no failure. There is just the condition of the mind muscle. Because none of us is typically trained in or even made aware of developing the mind muscle, when we try to make changes to deeply embedded habits around such powerful elements as food in our lives, we are destined for failure.

We are destined for a lifetime of necessary diversions and learning.

We shouldn't blame ourselves for a form of self-harm if we don't understand what we are doing. Or how to authentically change this.

*Self-harm should not directly equate to self-blame.*

We need to first become aware that the mind is a muscle, then go about doing as many repetitions as we can until this muscle becomes more developed. If I convert the 11 years it took me to authentically change my relationship with food into days, it took me 4,015 repetitions.

Malcolm Gladwell in *The Outliers* said that it takes 10,000 hours to master a skill. To change my relationship with food took me more than 96,000 hours.

But I did it. I changed my relationship with food.

# 19

# My Individual Diet for My Individual Design

Certain words and principles are repeated over and again in this book due to how much they mean to me – **individuality** is another one of them. After so many years of following others, my way of eating is now completely based on listening to my own body.

It's a constant work in progress, because I'm always learning, and every day I wake up I learn more. What I eat today may not be what I eat tomorrow – I am a student of nutrition and life and an expert in neither.

It must, therefore, be recognized that what I eat now is specifically reflective of my own journey with food. As well as the individual design of my unique body. It would be a very flawed approach to mirror what I eat because that would deprioritize individuality.

The information that follows should be treated as a reference, not a template, and we each must find our own way.

*Leading is more powerful than following.*

What I openly admit is that I don't have it all figured – not even nearly. It's something of a miracle that I've been able to make progress with an extreme health condition, when no practitioner could help. But still,

I claim no expertise in human health or digestion.

With that said, I don't believe that there's a need to claim expertise. If we only ever shared what we could definitively prove as scientific fact, then so much opportunity for learning from each other would be lost. It's not about proving what we've learned but rather about just sharing our experience.

I haven't found 'the' way. I've found 'a' way.

**Scientific research may be reputable, but it's not individually applicable.**

More than ever in modern society, we've become so afraid of saying three simple words which can be empowering: 'I don't know.' That's unfortunate because it can help us achieve more self-confidence through becoming comfortable with admitting that we don't have all the answers. And the truth, which is now in denial more than ever, is that none of us will ever have it all figured out. In nutrition or in life.

I believe with great passion that we'd all be better served, and be able to serve others better, if we simply admitted that we're all students of life. We'll never stop making mistakes and we'll always be learning, so exchanging information without judgement should be what we strive for.

**Humans are the most intelligent beings on this planet, but we are far less intelligent than we think. Or rather, far less aware.**

This book is not one of advice – it's an individual story that I share with faith that it will help others in some way. I neither deserve nor need plaudits. What I've written isn't right or wrong, good or bad, better or worse – it's about perspective, and you need to decide how you use the information contained within.

This applies to what I eat – I'm not right or wrong and I can't entirely explain it – I'm just sharing my real-life experience with you. I didn't choose this path, but I've tried to do something with it – I didn't want all this pain to be for nothing and realized that if pain was the ultimate teacher, then why not shared what I've learned. Whether or not it's what people want to hear.

We should never forget that true open-mindedness is having the ability to accept opinions that are directly opposed to what we believe.

**It is from those who disagree with us that we can learn most.**

## Simple Eating, Simple Solution

I've never known what triggered my pain in the first place, and I may never know, but there is absolutely no question about this – my body hates complexity.

My body is my own and my pain is unique to me, but I believe there to be universal value in the simplification of a diet. This is because complication causes confusion, in both mind and body, and if we have no idea what each food is doing to our body, then we will have little chance of figuring out what's going wrong.

For example, one of the major problems with many processed foods is that they contain so many extra ingredients, which are often hard to pronounce, unnatural and counterproductive to good digestion.

Interestingly, even those with opposing dietary viewpoints agree about the benefits of simple eating.

Meat eaters who eat with awareness seem to focus on just eating meat with no sugary accompaniments or condiments. Plant-based eaters who eat with awareness, seem to focus on eating vegetable dishes with no complicated sauces. There may well be disagreement on whether we are designed as herbivores, carnivores or omnivores, but there is agreement on the benefits of simple eating.

What I now realize with my own body is that, for years, my head office had been screaming to my gut office: 'Keep it simple, stupid.'

Because my mind muscle was less developed, though, I had less awareness. My mind was less in tune with my body. That is no longer the case, and although I haven't found a cure for my condition, my state of health in both mind and body has improved.

As described earlier, I now think about food as a puzzle – the more pieces there are in the puzzle, the more complicated it will be and the longer it will take to figure out. If there are fewer pieces in the puzzle, the process will be quicker, and the solution more easily sought.

Translating this to the body, it means the digestive system will operate more smoothly, and fewer blockages will occur, if we give it a less complicated food puzzle.

I can only go by my own experience, but I do encourage others who have had digestive issues – and even those who haven't – to explore the simplification of a diet. I honestly believe there is more value to be derived from simplifying the way we eat than following any commercial diet designed by someone else.

We also need to remember that health and longevity are based on more than just what we eat – genetics play a part, as does environment as well as our ability to keep stress in balance. There is no definitive and there are no rules.

Nobody else has the right to tell us to follow a specific diet, because nobody else is our designer. We are not even our own designer.

I know that many people believe they're doing some good in the world by trying to express their passion for a way of eating, but I really do believe that it's better to be a role model than a preacher. I think what is often overlooked is just how much damage can be done by overbearing opinions and judgemental behaviour.

It's a very lonely place to be fighting digestive illness, which is invisible to the eye, and compassion is often lacking.

*A person who offends us is also another human being. Someone who has experienced pain and struggle. We shouldn't judge before we know and because we will never know, we should never judge.*

The best influences I've had in my life are those who focus on how they live their own lives each day. They set an example but avoid aggressive persuasion. They respect individual decision-making and understand we are all unique.

Consider how much better the world could be if we removed judgement.

How much better could the lives of people be if we learned from each other?

How much further forward could we be with publicly available and reputable nutritional information if we encouraged sharing without accusation?

What should also be remembered is that a lot of the scaremongering about the risks associated with certain ways of eating excludes the consideration of quality of life. There is no point in living to the age of 100 if every day is a day of digestive misery and pain.

Existing is not living.

**If we are poor in our gut, we will be poor in our life.**

Low carb, low fat, meat, plant-based, raw – none of this is more important than letting our body be our guide.

Simple eating, simple solution. Individual courage, path to progress.

## Filling Up the Bucket

As I continually learned to prioritize what my body was telling me, I started to visualize in my mind what was happening as part of the digestive process after I'd eaten. This was when I created the analogy of filling up the bucket. It's derived from the idea that time is needed for the body to create more vital stomach acid.

What I imagined was the stomach being a kind of bucket. One that needed to be refilled continuously. So, just like it takes time to refill a real bucket, it also takes time to reproduce stomach acid.

The following illustration provides a playful example of this:

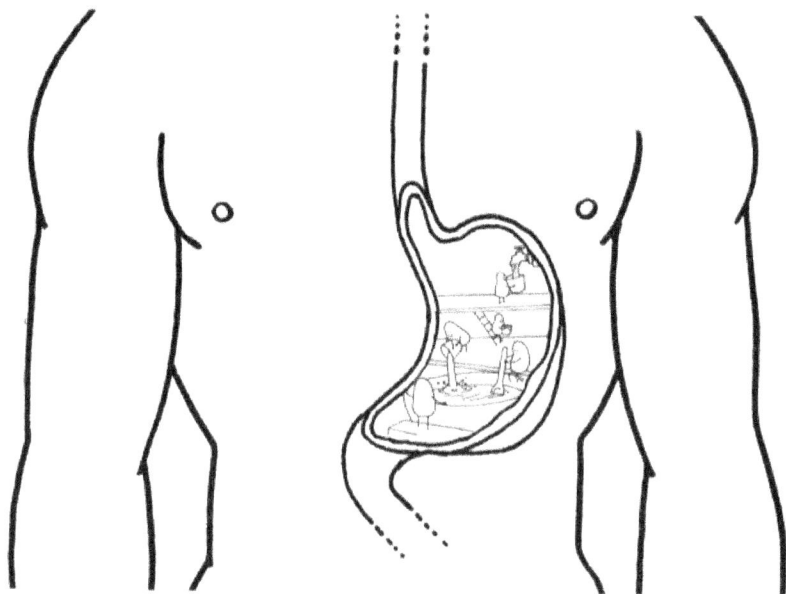

One of the reasons that I found this analogy so helpful is because my body has taught me just how much it hates 'food on top of food'.

I'd long since been left confused and frustrated by my health condition, but there were certain aspects which were clear to me. One being that my body reacted badly when I didn't give it enough time to digest food before starting to eat again.

The playful characters in the above illustration highlight this. As little workers in my body, if they're not given enough time to keep filling up the bucket, they're put under too much pressure and the bucket runs dry.

If the bucket runs dry, then this can lead to a breakdown.

A breakdown can cause clutter to build up.

A build-up of clutter can result in constipation, and constipation always leads to more pain.

Put another way, my gut office becomes furious with my head office.

The filling up the bucket analogy is aligned with other important lessons in this book, such as eating mindfully and not overeating. If we overeat, especially unnatural foods, then there's more chance of problems occurring in the gut office. If we also eat while in a stressed state, then our gut office will not be able to perform efficiently.

The little workers in the diagram will represent an unhappy workforce.

What's important to note is that this analogy is of course not factual. Stomach acidity and the workings of the digestive system are complicated considerations. All I'm doing is planting another seed of thought, which may be helpful, through a light-hearted diagram illustrating how important stomach acid is for digestion. If, however, you eat a clean, natural and simple diet, then you may well be able to eat more frequently with less time in between.

It still comes back to eating simply and naturally and finding the courage to be individual.

The filling up the bucket analogy also relates to changing our relationship with food. Whereas once I found pleasure in stuffing myself to the gills with tasty food, I almost find it pointless now. My mind now perceives it as a form of madness to overeat and try to get so much joy from eating. This is an incredibly powerful mindset to adopt for personal health.

The idea of limiting our pleasure from food may indeed be a foreign concept because practically every culture seems to emphasize the social event of eating. But it can be authentically transformative to our state of health.

*By taking charge of what we eat, we take responsibility for our health.*

I must reiterate again, though, I am not encouraging a negative relationship with food. I am encouraging a positive relationship with food. One which stops food having such a control over us. One where our mind is developed enough that it can make the decision to give our body what it needs, rather than what we desire.

The act of eating to me now is just something that I do. I am somewhat ambivalent towards it. It's like taking a shower or shaving. Neither of these are sources of great pleasure in my life, but I certainly don't dislike them. It feels nice to have a warm shower and be cleanly shaven.

Combining various lessons in this book has been as helpful to me as I wish it to be for you. It exemplifies how small changes, when applied together, can make a significant difference. The filling up the bucket analogy encouraged more small changes in my life, and as a seed of thought, it's one that I continue to nurture.

## Supplements or Substitutes?

One of the contributor factors that always complicated my journey was with medicines and supplements, which might explain why I'm more negative than positive about both. And while it may seem like I'm vehemently against medicine, I'm not. There is no doubt the lives that have been saved and the advances in health that have been made due to pharmaceutical products and medical care. I've also met some wonderful doctors and have nothing but respect for those who study so hard to follow a career dedicated to helping people.

What's interesting now, though, is that there seems to be a trend where more and more doctors are breaking free from the system because they didn't sign up to be 'drug dealers', in their words, and this is what they feel they've become. It's also interesting to hear so many admit that the nutritional education provided to them, as part of their training, is limited and questionable.

My wish is that doctors and all healthcare practitioners are given more support and freedom in the future to fulfil their original intent – helping improve the quality of life of others.

In terms of supplements, they do also have their place and can be helpful. However, I just wonder if we should place more emphasis on preventing illness, rather than just treating it. As Benjamin Franklin wrote:

**'*An ounce of prevention is worth a pound of cure.*'**

I'm also a firm believer in the natural over the artificial. I support lifestyle change over medicine and food over supplements.

My experience with both medicines and supplements has been very similar. I spent a lot of time taking them and a lot of money on them. All with little to no benefit. From a certain perspective, they even made matters worse as they acted as a distraction from making changes in my life.

Although neither medicine nor supplements helped me, I did discover a distinct difference between the two: medicine has a more potent and identifiable effect than supplements. The effect of supplements can be so mild that it's often difficult to know if they're doing anything at all.

Most supplements I took showed no effect. I was bombarded with exaggerated stories based on words like 'cleanse', 'detox' and 'healing', but I never felt any cleaner, any more detoxified or any healthier after taking them.

For all I knew, I could have been taking placebo after placebo.

Maybe I was.

Unfortunately, there wasn't a placebo effect on my bank account. That was very real.

A useful way to elaborate on this point is to consider the difference between medicine and supplements in ailments that are very common.

If we have a headache and take a painkiller, which results in the headache going away, then we can say with conviction that this medicine was effective. The risk of taking a placebo is less because medicines are stronger and show more distinct signs of effect.

Now consider tonsillitis. There is little doubt that antibiotics offer a highly effective form of treating this infection. For example, every time I contracted it, I was given antibiotics. And every time, it worked.

Where supplements come into the picture with tonsillitis treatment, is with the theory that they help replace good bacteria. So, it's now becoming more recommended that they're taken after a course of antibiotics because antibiotics kill the good as well as the bad. They attack infection but also damage good bacteria. This is no surprise considering the name:

'Anti' meaning 'against', and 'biotic' relating to 'living organisms'. Therefore, antibiotics meaning 'against life', in a simplified definition. As you'd imagine, the probiotic supplement industry loves this.

The difference between the medicine and the supplement in this example of tonsillitis is that the former shows a profound effect, but the latter doesn't. Antibiotics clearly cure tonsillitis, but taking a probiotic afterwards has a little identifiable impact. Of all the times that I've had tonsillitis in my life, I only took probiotics on the last couple of occasions, and there was no difference in my recovery when I did and didn't take them.

So, although I do understand the theory behind probiotics and introducing good bacteria, I've personally never experienced any health benefits from taking them.

What's important to add, however, is that I haven't had tonsillitis or any other common ailment such as a cold or flu for years. This will be particularly surprising considering the extremely simple and limited way I now eat. I also used to get terrible hay fever in the summer and that's also completely gone – I've almost forgotten what it's like to sneeze!

**What we don't eat can be as important as what we do eat.**

Change in my life has replaced the need for medicine and supplements.

I crack a wry smile when I think about this irony; my pain condition is a chronic condition, yet due to illness, I never get sick anymore. As Hippocrates said, 'Nature is the best physician'.

My own experience and what my body has taught me is that natural is unquestionably the preferable route. This is why I personally no longer take any medicines or supplements.

I choose to live a natural life.

I choose to change.

My individual choices, however, are not aligned with market trends as the global supplement industry is approximately $60 billion, and demand continues to grow. However, do we really know what these supplements are doing? Or are we just buying into the marketing hype?

The answers to these questions are up for debate, but what's an indisputable concern is when natural food is replaced with artificial supplements. To supplement means to 'add', not 'replace', and what's surprising is just how many athletes take them, despite professional advice. They seem to put their zombie face on, hold their hands out and swallow whatever is promoted to them.

> *Education over supplementation is a far more effective route to better health and fitness.*

What might make many people change their mind about supplements is if they knew the truth behind how new supplements are brought to market. The following four stages show the testing processes for new supplements being introduced to the UK market:

- **Level 1:** Anecdotal evidence promoted by celebrities and athletes
- **Level 2:** Case series or observational studies
- **Level 3:** Randomized controlled trials
- **Level 4:** Systematic reviews and meta-analysis

Level 1 is the weakest form of testing and becomes more stringent as each stage progresses towards level 4. What would, therefore, make sense is if all supplements went through all four phases of testing before being released for public sale. But this isn't the case – the majority only go through Level 1.[5] In other words, practically anybody can create a supplement and bring it to market.

Raising our awareness and understanding about supplements is, therefore, important for both our health as well as our bank balances. Even if a supplement isn't damaging to our health, if it isn't providing any benefit, it is needlessly putting us under financial pressure.

Although it may seem like I'm all doom and gloom about supplements and medicines, I'm certainly not on some hell-bent mission to show that either is the root of all evil. Far from it. I am just honest about my journey, what I've learned and where I've ended up.

The fact that I don't take any painkillers for my pain is a personal choice. The fact that I've chosen a natural path is a personal choice. Each of us must find our own way. With or without medicines or supplements.

---

[5] https://nutritionsociety.org/publications/sport-and-exercise-nutrition; accessed 9 July 2019 (information is contained in the book rather that at the link to this website).

# 20

# What I Eat – The Truth

To end this section on nutrition, I'm now going to provide specific detail on what it is that I eat. By revealing what I eat, I know I will invite conflict, controversy and unanswered questions. But this isn't something that should be construed negatively. Like every other part of this book, I'm simply telling my story as it happened.

The way that I've ended up eating is the reflection of a long and painful journey. One which has been led by desperation rather than choice. And even though my efforts are clearly dedicated to taking care of my body, I've been pushed to extremes which have taken me into the unknown. Because of that, I've ended up taking certain risks. I believe these have been unavoidable because any time we leave the beaten track, we incur more risk as we don't know what lies ahead.

***An extreme health condition makes it impossible to avoid the extreme.***

The start of my explanation on how I've ended up eating the way I do relates to my usual frustration, loneliness and, as ever, the worst thing to deal with - pain. After my attempt at healing on a plant-based diet and other efforts to live with less pain, I reached the point where there seemed like there were no more roads to go down.

I used to say that I'd eat dog shit if it made me feel better. I would!

After persevering for seven months on a plant-based diet, I accepted that it was another failure. Or rather, another necessary diversion. I tried everything that I could and gave it my best shot: tofu, lentils, peas, beans, nutritional yeast, quinoa, soy, fruits, vegetables and all types of powders, butter and foods that I could blend.

Nothing worked. Yet again, it was an expensive experience.

It seemed that my body just couldn't cope with such a high-sugar, high-carbohydrate way of eating, even though I was only consuming natural sugars. Along with chronic pain, I had all sorts of other negative physical reactions that made me look and feel awful.

Once I started to reintroduce animal products, I decided to go in the opposite direction and significantly reduce my carbohydrate intake. But even though it made so much sense, due to the lower sugar content, my body still would not respond. I made progress, as I modestly reduced the chronic pain, but I became so constipated that a new pain developed in my ascending colon. The same type I'd experienced during my fast in the Cambodia yoga retreat.

I honestly felt like I was damned if I do and damned if I don't.

If I ate in a way that reduced my chronic pain, then I increased another type of pain and could never go to the toilet. If I ate in a way that reduced the other pain and helped to release my bowels, then I was living in agony with chronic pain.

There seemed to be no way out of pain.

To help relieve constipation on a low-carbohydrate diet, I regularly visited my colon cleanse therapist. She was a lovely, knowledgeable lady, so I never minded going there. I just knew it wasn't a good sign that my bowels weren't able to function on their own. In the meantime, I kept trying to eat more and more fibre, but the more fibre I ate, the more constipated I became.

During one colon cleanse, my therapist told me that I'd probably lost a kilo in greens. A comment that I discovered had considerable depth, when I went to the gym for three hours the next morning on an empty stomach.

I felt euphoric as my body was so relieved to get rid of all the waste that had got stuck. As relieved as I was, the same problems immediately returned as soon as I started eating again. I was faced with having to choose between living with horrific chronic pain or spending my life constipated with searing colon pain.

It was another edge in my life and, once again, it would be where the authentic change took place.

## A Pivotal Moment

The catalyst for this change arrived when I woke up one morning with chronic pain and colon pain and feeling terrible overall. This was when intuition kicked in and, to this day, I don't know why, but I decided to have some red meat for breakfast.

What happened next was extraordinary.

Within 45 minutes of eating meat, my bowels released, and my pain reduced. It screamed in the face of everything I'd learned about fibre easing constipation and red meat making it worse. It was this pivotal moment which led me to the final part of my journey towards what it is that I eat today.

Literally, as soon as I was off the toilet, I started to study the Inuit diet and any other traditional ways of eating. I wanted to learn about any diet which minimized or excluded carbohydrates. I read book after book and waded through huge amounts of information.

This was when I decided to try a zero-carbohydrate diet. A last chance saloon attempt to live with less pain.

**Desperation is a powerful motivator.**

My journey on a carnivore diet can be split into two parts - the first three months and the next six months. This nine-month period was crazy, frightening, shocking and confusing but also educational. If I didn't have such an extreme health condition, there is no way that I would have stuck at it. The adjustment process was too radical.

As I was out of options, there was little choice but to persevere. I was also aware that if nothing else, the lessons learned could be shared in this book. I ended up learning so much that there would probably be enough for a standalone book, but the most important lessons are covered in the next section.

Before moving on, though, I need to disclose what it is I eat. It certainly won't take long because it's that simple:

I eat beef and drink water.

Even in consideration of my strong belief in the benefits of learning about electrolytes, I learned that beef does have a well-balanced electrolyte profile. I don't even add salt – my whole diet is literally just beef and water.


## The Lessons

The reason I noted a nine-month time frame is because that's how long it took my body to adapt. And upon finishing this book, further adaptation continues, and many challenges remain. It's therefore important to emphasize that I haven't found a cure for my pain, but I have been able to reduce it. Considering I lived at an 8 or 9 out of 10 for so many years, it is a blessing to be living at a 3 or 4. So to summarize my journey so far:

- **Months 1–3:** I ate red meat (of varying kinds), salmon, organ meats and very occasional low-carbohydrate foods such as avocado and mushrooms. I drank only water.
- **Months 4–9:** I ate only grass-fed beef and drank only water.

The reason that I wasn't strictly zero-carbohydrate for the first three months was because I wasn't convinced that eating this way made any sense. To go from avoiding saturated fat like the plague to eating it by the spoonful takes an incredible mind shift.

*If we want to change our body, first we need to change our mind.*

Only when I got through enough research to learn how flawed all nutritional studies are was I persuaded that we may have been led down a long, health-damaging path of low-fat dieting that started in the 1960s. This isn't about accusations and conspiracy theories, but rather just learning about the realities of trying to create an accurate nutritional study.

To conduct a truly flawless nutritional study on a large enough volume of people over a long enough period is almost impossible. Especially when budgetary constraints and so many variables are involved.

*Nutritional studies are scientific 'theory', not scientific 'fact'.*

To put it more simply – it doesn't encourage much confidence to say that red meat is bad for your health if the people being studied are also smokers and drinkers and take limited exercise.

Beyond all this debate, though, the reality for me was that I was at the end of my tether. I had literally tried everything for more than a decade, and there was a very clear message that my body was screaming to my mind: give me more fat and less fibre.

Once I accepted this and shut out the noise and scaremongering, then I was able to fully commit to excluding all carbohydrates.

Once again, I have discovered further alignment with other lessons in this book and particularly around changing our relationship with food. Eating just beef every day is no source of enjoyment for me, so I just get it done. From a certain perspective, and keep an open mind here, it's one of the most natural ways to eat because it's like animal behaviour.

There are no questions about what to eat next and no issues with temptation – I eat until I know it's enough and store the rest for later.

At the end of my first three-month period, I did have a meal of sweeter carbohydrate foods because I knew that I was going to commit to beef and water only. This reminded me about how much more difficult it is to change our relationship with food when sugar is involved – of any kind. For those eating a higher carbohydrate diet, unfortunately, I don't have the answers to this.

As much as I've found that this way of eating has helped me, what I can't deny is the severity of the adjustment process. Every time I tried something new, I seemed to react much worse than anybody else. For example, I experienced heart palpitations for six and a half months before they calmed down.

That is an astonishing period to go through every day with your heart beating irregularly and why I must state with conviction that I'm not a doctor and cannot provide medical advice. Professional care must be sought before committing to any radical change in diet, and even I ended up back at the doctors, which is something I hadn't done in years.

I underwent an electrocardiogram test and that came back fine, but while I was there, I took the opportunity to get blood tests done to see what else was happening. When the result came back, my LDL (low-density lipoprotein) cholesterol, known as the bad cholesterol, was higher. But my HDL (high-density lipoprotein), known as the good cholesterol, was also higher.

As much as it may sound insane to others, I just couldn't pay attention to my cholesterol – I'd finally found a way that allowed me to live with less pain and look and feel physically healthier. I did spend some time studying cholesterol, but there is that much disagreement around it that it just seemed to be another minefield of information.

In any case, what would I do if a doctor told me that after looking at a set of test results that I was in grave danger, while I felt better than I had in 12 years? Would it be insane to heed a lab result over my own body? We should remember that just because people get it wrong, doesn't mean they get it wrong on purpose. Human beings are naturally flawed.

I am aware that it makes no sense and I am aware that it seems like I should be nutritionally deficient – especially in vitamin C. But as much as I do OK with liver, which contains more vitamin C as well as being nutrient dense, it just doesn't sit as well with me.

The only meat I eat is untrimmed ribeye steak because it has a higher fat percentage and seems to have the least impact on my pain. Typically, it contains 70 to 80 per cent fat, which is important because if I dip below about 70 per cent, then I get constipated. The beef I buy is grass fed and always from the same farm in the north of England, situated in an area of natural beauty. This also means that I only eat locally produced food, so it doesn't have to travel far to reach me.

*Share of Disposable Personal Income Spent on Food, 1960 to 2016 (US)*

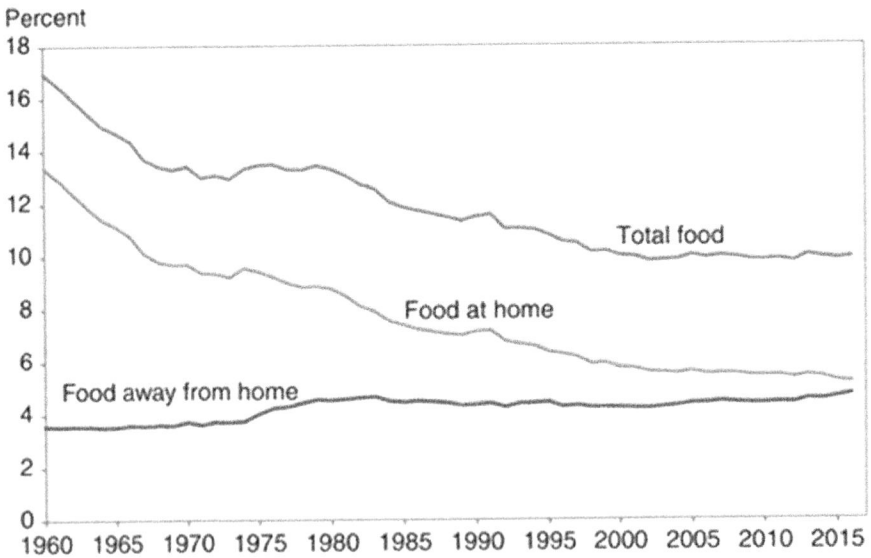

*Source: United States Department of Agriculture, Economic Research Service, Food Expenditure Series, July 2019*[6]

Eating this way certainly isn't cheap, but it does raise another in-

---

[6]  https://www.ers.usda.gov/data-products/chart-gallery/gallery/chart-detail/?chartId=76967

teresting point. Our parents and grandparents spent a much higher percentage of their disposable income on food, which to me, simply means that they were making a greater investment in their health. We seem to have developed a habit of trying to save money on food in order to pursue damaging lifestyles.

Beyond all this, though, I live with less pain by eating this way – is there really anything else I need to say? Even the most cynical person would struggle to argue this point, considering the content of this book.

So, this is where I am today. I haven't found a cure, but I have made progress. I wake up every day and basically just live for that day. Every day is different, and that will always be the case. For everyone.

Any day that I get to live with less pain is one that I'm eternally thankful for. And any day that I get to spend with my son when I'm less distracted by pain is a blessing of infinite proportions. Therein lies another important lesson related to a topic I covered earlier in Chapter 9: I now worry less about tomorrow.

I also continue to learn and read new research and follow the experience of other zero-carbohydrate proponents. More than anything else, though, I continue to listen to my own body.

*Continued exploration is as important as finding a result.*

## My Beliefs

My whole journey with pain has taken me through a quite unbelievable amount of trials and tribulations with food. However, one of my greatest beliefs remains in eating simple, natural food. Yes, my path has led me to question sugar in all forms, but this hasn't changed my attitude that the state of global health would be far improved if we just went back to eating more naturally. Whether fat or carbohydrates.

My beliefs around what we have been taught from a nutritional perspective have, however, changed dramatically. Whereas once I trusted the information that was being provided to me, I now have little trust at all. The effect of industry, money and greed is a reality that we need to start becoming more aware of.

The cold, hard truth is that there is far more profit in a group of sick people than there is in a group of people who are fit and healthy.

I accept that this sounds like a conspiracy theory, but I'm simply going by my own experience. Whether we have been duped into believing that fat is bad for us or not, there is no doubting that an overhaul of publicly available nutritional information is desperately needed. Most are decades out of date.

In consideration that this is unlikely to happen any time soon, what I encourage others to do is take the time to learn.

Your life does depend on it.

**Greater knowledge leads to greater health.**

Whichever way any of us eat, there will always be propaganda. There will also always be critics, no matter what choices we make or what choices we are forced to make. For example, two common criticisms of eating an all-meat diet are that it increases the risk of colon cancer and heart disease.

Consider these questions, though:

- Wouldn't colon cancer have wiped out human beings a long time ago due to such a high consumption of meat?
- How is it possible that we made it beyond being cavemen when, for periods, meat is all that was eaten?
- How could we have survived so long if eating saturated fat leads to heart disease?

Yes, there will be a long list of arguments to counter this and I may be accused of oversimplifying, but I retain my belief that so much value can be extracted from simplicity. I am posing simple, common-sense questions to plant the seed of thought that perhaps fat, and even saturated fat, isn't that bad after all. My body seems to like it.

I can't know exactly why this is nor explain everything. What I do know is that by eating this way, I've reached a deeper level of self-acceptance. I accept that this is the way the world made me, and I accept that everything written in this book, is exactly what needed to be written.

I also revert to those four words which have served me so well in dealing with stress:

I didn't create me.

**As an entrepreneur, I am a creator, but as a human being, I am a creation.**

We should not judge others and we should not be judged. Life is not a movie script where we get to decide exactly what happens and how it all ends. If my life was a script, then it would have read, 'Go to a yoga retreat, follow a plant-based diet, discover spirituality and heal my pain.'

What a great story.

If it had worked out this way, then not only would it have been an easier story to tell, it would also have been a less painful and costly one. In the two years since I returned from Cambodia, I've endured some of the worst periods of physical pain along with the emotional pain of letting my only son move to a different country.

No one has all the answers, and no one will ever live a perfect life. How we eat should not define us. Even though I've made progress with my health without medicines or painkillers, there isn't a movie-style ending.

I didn't win back the girl, and I don't bring the family back together.

**A movie is a fantasy. Life is real.**

In terms of what the future holds, I don't know what lies ahead. No one does. I will most likely take some more blood tests and have a heart scan, which is thought to be a good predictor of cardiac disease, but what difference does it really make?

Could I really go back to eating in a way that means living with unbearable pain? Honestly speaking, I don't think I could. Even if a medical professional told me I am at a high risk of mortality by eating this way, I just don't think I could take going through my 40s in the same way as my 30s – overcome by pain.

If I were given a choice to have 10 more years and thrive or live a longer life in pain, I would choose the former without a moment's hesitation. And I would say thank you very much when I checked out at 50 years old.

What should be remembered, though, is that there is a completely different perspective that needs to be considered. What if, by eating this way, I'm enhancing my health and eating in a way that I was supposed to all along? What if I'm reducing my risk of heart disease and cancer?

There are certainly physical signs of this on my appearance, as the rate at which I was prematurely ageing has almost certainly slowed down. My hair is also thicker, and I have more mental clarity.

Further to this, I've eradicated flatulence and bloating and seen an improvement in my gum and dental health, along with a whole host of other physical symptoms. I also have a much healthier colour in my cheeks, which is rather wonderful after walking around looking like a ghost for so long.

Last, I must point out that I'm no pioneer of this way of eating, which is not only in reference to other cultures such as the Inuit. If social media is anything to go by, the sheer volume of people who follow a zero-carbohydrate diet is incredible. I've been in contact with people who have been doing it for decades and even raising their kids this way.

Stories of miracle healing and recovery from such illnesses as Lyme disease, arthritis, obesity and a whole host of other medical problems are abound. Of course, I can't verify any of this, but the volume of people makes it unlikely that they're all lying.

The lesson, however, remains the same. Don't take my word for it and don't take anybody else's – learn for yourself. Avoid propaganda and follow your own journey – no matter what I write here about my experience, have the courage to be individual.

*If the mind commits to a lifetime of learning about the body, then the body will experience a better lifetime.*

## A Nutritional Seed of Thought

Before leaving this chapter, I'd like to plant one more seed of thought. It's important, so please take note, because it illustrates how I was finally able to connect the dots of what I've always described as an anomaly.

Throughout this section, I've continually described how a plant-based diet didn't work for me, but in the interest of retained authenticity, honesty and no agenda, I want to elaborate on the distinct difference between my experience on a plant-based diet when I was in Cambodia versus following the same diet when I returned to London. You may think it contradicts earlier points I've made, but all that matters is the truth. And everything I write is my truth.

In short, when I followed a plant-based diet in Cambodia, I coped with it reasonably well. I even had some really good days. This is why I committed to the new regime with such determination when I got back to London and stuck with it for months on end. I remembered the good days in Cambodia, so I educated myself on formulating a nutritionally rich plant-based diet with the required supplementation.

However, instead of continued progress, my body completely broke down. Along with extreme chronic pain, I had all sorts of other reactions, which seemed to reflect an autoimmune disease: bloating, pale complexion, flatulence, itchy skin, watery puffy eyes and dark circles, and many more symptoms. It was like my body had shut down.

So, why when I was eating the same food in Cambodia didn't I experience any of these reactions? I had some bad days in Cambodia along with the good ones, but they related solely to an increase in chronic pain. I didn't experience any autoimmune type reactions.

I now believe that the answer to the above question is one of the biggest and most painful necessary diversions I've ever had to go through: focusing too much on nutrition and not nearly enough on my environment meant I suffered greatly. I also now understand that eating a mango that's fallen from a tree in Cambodia is utterly different to eating one that's flown halfway around the world and bought in a shop in London.

### How food is treated may impact how it treats our body.

My deterioration on a plant-based diet was instantaneous on my return to London, but I didn't recognize it at the time because all my focus was on nutrition. The seed of thought I therefore want to share is this: if you're gluten intolerant or experiencing any other type of negative reaction to food, you may well find that you can eat the exact same food in a better environment with your stress more in balance.

I now truly believe that so many illnesses could be improved or even alleviated if we returned to a more natural environment. Even if this is an unrealistic ambition in modern society, this is still a consideration for parents with children that struggle with persistent digestive conditions and sickness.

Gluten has long since been an obvious problem for me, yet, when I was in Cambodia, I ate glutinous-containing oats without the usual extreme reaction. This personal experience may be worth considering whatever your health struggle. For example, an asthmatic is likely to fare better living by the sea and surrounded by nature, as opposed to residing in a city with high levels of pollution.

It seems obvious, but how many of us choose the medicinal route over the natural path to a better quality of life? Can't we see the woods for the trees?

As I write these words, I admit that I do so hypocritically because I still live in London. Why? Because every decision I've made has reflected my knowledge at that time. I'm also a father and couldn't just keep prioritizing what was best for me over D. The only way that our son could live in Slovakia with his mum was if I stayed in London.

*Today, we know more than we did yesterday and tomorrow, we'll know more than we do today. Life is a never-ending education, so avoiding self-judgement is imperative.*

What I also accept is that had a plant-based diet worked for me in London, then I'd never have gone down the low-carb and eventually carnivore route. As hard as this has all been, every failure has been an intensely educational necessary diversion, and I can now honestly say that I've done it all. I've tried all known diets and eaten in every way that I could find – many more than I've been able to document in this book in consideration of trying to manage the length.

My dietary journey is therefore complete, and a full picture has formed in dedication to this book.

## What's Next for Me?

Now that I'm able to connect the dots, I have a clearer understanding of why a beef-and-water-only diet has worked better for me; it's the simplest way of eating that doesn't expose me to junk such as flavourings, colourings and pesticides. As I pointed out in Chapter 19, what we don't eat can be as crucial to our health as what we do eat.

However, even a beef-and-water-only diet hasn't come without consequences, and there is another truth that I want to share – one which is a reminder that we must always recognize our individual design.

As I described earlier in my book, my whole journey with chronic pain started in 2007 when a Slovak doctor told me I was at high risk of oesophageal cancer. Since then, the statistical data I have looked at, along with feedback from UK doctors, is that although I have Barrett's esophagus – which is a precancerous condition – the amount of people with this condition that go on to develop oesophageal cancer is only about 0.5 per cent.[7]

Of course, this doesn't change the fact that I do have this precancerous condition and I can openly admit that a repercussion of adjusting to the carnivore diet has been stomach acid painfully flowing up into my oesophagus.[8] I am therefore knowingly aggravating this condition, so why would I do such a thing?

It would be a harsh irony if it ended where it all began.

There's no need to spend any more time answering the above question because I believe the desperation of my journey with chronic pain is clear enough. Instead, I want to provide some advocacy for a plant-based diet because it did completely eradicate my acid reflux. Even when I was in agony in London, I was able to lie down flat without acid coming back up my oesophagus.

Therefore, it could be said that I was reducing my risk of oesophageal cancer by following a plant-based way of eating because it was less provocative to an already confirmed precancerous condition.

Then again, switching back to the beef-and-water-only diet, I have experienced an incredible improvement in other areas of health. Some I've already noted, but others include solving all my autoimmune type reactions and healing other areas in my body. The pain that I experienced for years in my ascending colon has been completely

---

[7]  https://www.asge.org/home/for-patients/patient-information/understanding-gerd-barrett-39-s

[8]  It's becoming more common for practitioners to talk about having low stomach acid rather than too much and I have been tested for this. My stomach acid has been confirmed as not being too low. I've also tried using a betaine hydrochloride supplement which worsened the situation by causing even more acid to rise up and cause more heart burn. Interestingly, though, in relation to my point in Chapter 19 about the potential placebo effect of supplements, I found that a betaine hydrochloride supplement did have a profound effect.

eradicated, and I no longer get constipated. Ever!

This is why I've persevered because maybe, given enough time, my stomach might adjust in the same way as my colon and bowels. But I also accept my medical diagnosis of having a weak lower oesophageal sphincter (see Chapter 12 describing the door-type mechanism at the top of the stomach) and that perhaps I can't sustain this meat-based way of eating. A tough reality considering a significant reduction of chronic pain but a reality all the same.

Where I've found peace in all of this, once again, is through finding my purpose. I've no doubt some people will fare better on a plant-based diet, but I've also seen some extraordinary stories from others who have improved their health dramatically on a carnivore diet. For example, I've heard stories of women who were told they'd never have children miraculously giving birth. The perplexing affliction of fibromyalgia being overcome by people who'd suffered for decades.

My wish is simply that by sharing my story honestly, it will allow others to make better choices based on the truth rather than propaganda.

I also believe I'm a more rounded person for having fairly sat on both sides. I've learned a huge amount from the vegan community and been inspired by people committed to spreading messages of love and compassion across the world. I've also learned a huge amount from the carnivore community and been fascinated by the potential of regenerative agriculture.

In many ways, I see my body as the ultimate testing facility. It's been battered and bruised by all these diets, but all this pain has also provided many extraordinary lessons – all of which are included in this book.

When my work is done with this book and all that is required to make people aware of it – perhaps one day I'll be lucky enough to get a little piece of land and live off it. Somewhere close to my son.

Maybe I'll even be able to create a place of harmony where people of different beliefs can come together and share their views with an open mind about nutrition, health and life. No judgement and nothing to prove.

Perhaps that's where I'll find the needle in the haystack I described in Chapter 3.

*By helping others, we can help ourselves.*

# V

# The Physical Body

*Fulfilment can't be found in the mirror.*

# 21

# The Power of Exercise

To make progress with pain, I've not only had to work hard at developing my mind and learning about nutrition, but I've also had to exercise my physical muscles too. So, in Part V, we'll be delving into the unique aspect of exercise and how it can be a powerfully effective natural form of pain relief. This is certainly what I've experienced. Right from when my pain began back in 2007.

Although, like everybody else, I have my preferences regarding the type of exercise, I've found that any kind of activity is beneficial in pain management. You don't have to run a marathon to reduce pain. A walk in the forest will do just as well and also relax the mind.

**How we treat the body will affect the mind.**

Whereas my journey with food has been about trying to avoid increasing my pain, while accepting that all food does to some degree, my journey with exercise has been about actively reducing pain. Therefore, working out provides me with a great deal of positivity and without it, I'm not sure I would have survived my pain.

This probably explains my passion for encouraging others to explore exercise in pain management, too, as it can really pay dividends for your well-being.

Nutrition and exercise now hold an equal level of importance. If I were to ignore one or the other, then I would suffer. This happens with many people who place too much emphasis on one and not the other. For example, an early morning run won't count for much if you spend the rest of the day eating foods with poor nutritional value.

Without nutritional education, the impact of exercise will be limited. I know this to be true because in the past, I exercised three to four times a day some weeks because I was eating for enjoyment and comfort, which meant that I was experiencing more pain. The more I ate, the more I needed to exercise to reduce the pain. As crazy as this sounds, a lot of people force themselves to exercise more so that they can eat more. However, until we change our relationship with food, we'll keep going around in circles.

When we have a positive relationship with both food and exercise, then the impact on our lives can be incredible. There can be a movement away from prescription and/or recreational drugs, as well as food that corrupts our health. Of all the medicines, supplements and whacky treatments I've tried, nothing has come even close to being able to reduce my pain as much as exercise. Not surprisingly, physical exercise is very special to me.

## Exercising the Mind

What differs in my approach to exercise now is that I use all my muscles, including my mind muscle. Most people focus solely on the body and are unaware the mind plays such a huge part. Everything is connected.

**The body won't change without the support of the mind.**

The change that I'm referring to here is, again, an authentic and lasting change that can't be easily reversed or undone. Even when faced with struggle or temptation.

It's now more important than ever to develop the mind muscle so that we can make better decisions for our body. This doesn't just relate to nutrition but also with how we exercise. We are bombarded with pro-motions and advertisements of short-term physical transformations, which are misleading at best and dishonest at worst.

There's also something of significance missing in these promotions because no attention is given to internal change. There's nothing wrong with physical goals, but they must not take priority over our internal health and state of mind. And if we develop our mind, then we can learn to exercise as a blessing more than a burden.

Even though I've always loved sports, I truly believe that anyone can learn to enjoy exercise. Getting started can be tough, but the rewards are limitless: better health, uplifted mood, a more positive outlook on life, a sharper mind, an alternative to eating and drinking and a great way to spend time with family and friends.

Even pain hasn't been able to stop the positive power of exercise.

By making a change in our minds, we can remove any resistance to physical progress. All those occasions when we just don't feel like exercising or make up any excuse possible to avoid doing so can be minimized or wholly relinquished. We never need to make excuses if we genuinely enjoy what we're doing.

To some this may sound like I'm speaking a foreign language, but learning to see exercise as a blessing is a skill of the mind. In other words, it's something that can be learned, rather than talent bestowed upon the few. Developing the physical body is about practice and repetitions. Learning to enjoy exercise is no different.

More practice will lead to more enjoyment.

## My Individual Physique

Clearly this book isn't about vanity, but I wanted to enclose an image of my physique because I understand that we live in a visual world. Plus, I'd like to share some of my experiences on a zero-carbohydrate diet. The following image was taken when I was trying to monitor the physical effect of reducing carbohydrates and increasing fat.

I've never tracked my progress by photos (which is reflected in the slightly odd look on my face and skewed camera angle), but this was one of my few photos. It's at least authentic and not professionally manipulated (the same as the fasting photos I shared in Chapter 17).

One of the interesting elements is that I still managed to retain a lean physique, despite eating so much fat – my rough split on a low-carbohydrate diet was about 5 per cent carbs, about 30 per cent protein and about 65 per cent fat. What this image and the body images included in Chapter 17 show is that it's possible to maintain muscle mass on either a plant-based diet or a meat-based diet. The quality of protein is another subject, but I retain the view that we would all be better served if we removed judgement and openly learned from each other.

The most fascinating experience I've had with my body, however, has been moving to a zero-carbohydrate diet. I was shocked during the first few months of eating only beef when I gained so much body fat. My belly was literally hanging over my trousers, and in my whole life I'd never experienced this.

I've learned not to judge, though, and rather saw this as an opportunity to gain more insight on how the physical body works.

One theory I'd read was that the body hangs on to fat because it's been starved of it for so long. I was sceptical about this because I'd heard so many of these reasons, which are often just used as sales tools for new diets. What I discovered, however, was that there was some depth to this theory. I tested this by significantly increasing my daily exercise schedule to three to four hours per day, while also including plenty of change and cardio.

The result? My body shape stayed pretty much the same. I couldn't shift the fat.

Then I went the other way and reduced my exercise to only 30 to 45 minutes per day. The result was the same, and my body shape didn't change much. Even when I ate a lot more fat, my body fat didn't seem to increase by much. There was always this general margin between about 15 per cent to 20 per cent where it never went above or below.

No matter what I did, I couldn't beat the body.

It was as if my body had found a natural condition and was doing everything possible to stay that way, which did make sense because having visible abs and a body fat percentage of less than 10 per cent is not a natural state. This is the same with building excess muscle – we need to force this and it's not something the body wants.

As I finish this book, it is starting to settle down, but it seems like there are many months to go before my body believes that I'm not going to starve it of fat again. I guess it's understandable considering I've been lean my whole life.

# 22

# The Six Authentic Principles of Physical Fitness

Despite the typical nature of today's advertising campaigns in the fitness industry, which usually focus on short-term, unrealistic gains, I believe the authentic principles of physical fitness remain unchanged throughout time. There may now be more advanced approaches, but this is no substitute for the grit we need to find 'within' ourselves when it really counts.

The 'within' that I am referring to is that inside the mind.

***There is no scientific advantage that can overpower the strength of the mind.***

The six principles I follow are:

1. Discipline
2. Consistency
3. Perseverance
4. Intensity
5. Change
6. Awareness

These principles have allowed me to make genuine progress physically, but they also hold synergy with how I've learned to deal with my pain.

In this chapter, I'll be focusing on the connection between my life, my pain and my physical condition. This isn't just because of the core relevance of my journey with physical pain in this book, but also because it has taught me a considerable amount about these six principles.

I've learned to become more disciplined and consistent, with better direction in my ability to persevere. I've also learned to be more intense without a need to be more aggressive, while gaining a deeper appreciation for change and becoming more aware.

**By avoiding the flawed shortcuts to physical fitness, we avoid the wasteful shortcuts in life.**

These six principles are, of course, not my creation. Apart from awareness, the other five are commonly associated with physical fitness. They're not easy, but they don't have to be complicated. As with nutrition, significant value can be found in simplicity.

The reason that I define these principles as authentic is due to the lasting change they provide. For example, I had discipline before my pain started, but I also had plenty of setbacks as my wilder side took over. This also meant that I only sometimes achieved consistency. My pain has provided authenticity to my discipline as I no longer set myself back and now perform with more (authentic) consistency.

So, let's look at each of the principles in turn:

## 1. Discipline

When I tried to find a way to define discipline, as it related to my journey with pain and exercise, I found it difficult to put into words. Then when I checked *The Oxford English Dictionary*, I realized that the official definition is very fitting: 'The practice of training people to obey rules or a code of behaviour to correct disobedience.'

This description closely matches how I've learned to see my pain as a kind of teacher in my life. Simply put, when I upset this teacher, I get disciplined.

If I don't exercise often enough for my teacher, I experience more pain. If I don't eat what is specifically suited to my individual design, and as my teacher requires, I experience more pain. This even applies to the subject of time; when I spend my time in areas that are not dedicated to my path of purpose in life, then my teacher deems me disobedient and I experience more pain.

My teacher is easily upset!

Although this strict teacher in the form of my pain is unique to me, there is once again a more universal perspective worth considering. If we neglect exercise or ignore any level of discipline, then we may end up experiencing more pain in our lives. Physical, emotional or mental suffering.

Without discipline, we can live a life of frustration. We can continually fall short of goals that deep inside of ourselves, we know we can achieve. We may continuously give in to distraction, which can hinder us from reaching our potential.

There is always something that can hijack our attention if we're not disciplined. And this really is the story of my life. I knew within myself that I could achieve more than I was. What I didn't understand was my potential or what it meant. I wanted to 'be somebody' or 'do something', but although I had the drive, I lacked the direction.

I had dreams I wanted to reach, but what kept them in the distance was continually giving in to distractions. I had discipline, but it was sporadic, so periods of focus would be followed by blowouts and extreme partying.

My discipline is now authentic because I keep my focus every day with 0 Days Off. My pain makes sure of this.

Authentic discipline is a strange example of why trying to get rid of our pain can be a flawed process. I know how crazy this statement sounds, considering the content of this book and the devastating effect pain has had on my life, but pain can guide us. It can not only act as an alarm in the body, alerting us that something is wrong, but it can also push us towards our potential.

**Pain can be what breaks us, but it can also be what makes us.**

One of the keys to successfully reaching any goal in life is committing enough time to its pursuit. If we are ambitious, then we may find that there is a requirement to work towards those goals every day. This might mean that we need to sacrifice things in our lives that we enjoy, or that are fun. And in fact, I've often been asked, 'What do you actually do for fun?'

The truth is that I don't really do anything for fun. At least not in the original sense that I was brought up to believe. I didn't know that fun could be about fulfilment and that by having the discipline, I could achieve a different kind of fun.

This took me many years to accept, but what I now do is utilize the power of perspective.

Before my pain, I apparently had an exciting social life. My weekends were wildly entertaining, and my adventures took me around the world. I made lots of great friends and had lots of fun. Yet, I always felt an emptiness inside of me. These experiences weren't feeding me. I was unsatisfied and dissatisfied, and I knew when being honest with myself that the fun I was having was coming at the cost of not reaching my potential.

This changed as I grew older and experienced more pain.

From a profound perspective, this is where I've learned that pain can play an extraordinary role – it was forcing change in my life.

My understanding of wanting to 'be somebody' or 'do something' has evolved considerably. I now understand that need to be the centre of attention and always last to leave the party were perfect examples of how misguided I was in trying to fill a void in my life.

Such attempts to be different lacked depth, so they could never fill the void. They could never fulfil me.

It's important to understand that I'm not saying give away your life to work – especially when you're young. The point I'm making is that higher goals can't be achieved without discipline. I miss having a social life and I miss the old banter in the pub with friends, but by adjusting my perspective I can avoid feeling sorry for myself. I don't spend any more time in the pub, and so I can commit more time to reaching my goals.

This directly applies to exercise – instead of having a hangover, I'm out exercising. I have authentic discipline because I exercise every day, and with an adjusted perspective, that is a different type of fun. A far healthier one.

Exercising every day won't suit everyone, but I would argue that it's easier than stopping and starting. Once we're in our groove, we enjoy it more and can avoid the demoralizing feeling of having to repeatedly start again.

The simple fact is that if we do something every day, then we will improve. In mind, in body and in life.

**The difference between achieving our dreams or not can be whether we are (authentically) disciplined.**

## 2. Consistency

*The Oxford English Dictionary* defines consistency as, 'consistent behaviour or treatment; the quality of achieving a level of performance which does not vary greatly in quality over time.' This is what I now have with 0 Days Off – a level of commitment which doesn't vary. I wake up and spend time on 0 Days Off every single day.

Consistency is linked with discipline too. By avoiding distraction and resisting temptation each day, we practise discipline. By repeatedly committing to a goal that we strive toward, we show consistency. In this way, discipline and consistency complement each other.

However, I face a specific challenge with consistency because one of the hardest aspects of dealing with chronic pain is its relentless consistency. All day, every day, without fail. Although this can help keep me focused and on track, it's also a heavy burden to bear.

Can any person keep going without a break?

This conflict helps explain the nature of my 10-year search. I tried everything to find a cure, because I sensed that if I didn't, then either the degenerative nature of illness would get me, or I would submit to suicide.

I was trying to find an end to my pain before it pushed me to end my life.

The concept of finding an ending is crucial when working toward a goal. If we don't have an end to aim for, then we don't have a goal. We just keep going. This is something I struggled with over the years. If my pain was never going to end, then how could I take value from the principle of consistency? It just seemed negative.

This also supports my objective way of thinking about suicide because, as I mentioned earlier in the book, what is the point in committing to a lifetime if all the time in that life is going to be in pain?

The way I unlocked this considerable challenge of the mind was again to adjust my perspective.

Changing my relationship with pain was the key, but in this case, it didn't quite fit the lock. A slight adjustment was needed to think about pain as a coach, which helped provide a theme of familiarity about my love of sports.

By perceiving my pain as a coach, I began to think about the attributes which make up the greatest coaches in the world; qualities such as tenacity, talent, intelligence, courage and determination are all excellent examples. But the one that stood out the most to me was – consistency.

The best coaches keep going. Whether in victory or in defeat, they manage to maintain the same high standards. They may reach many individual goals along the way, but as soon as they reach the summit, they already have their eyes on the next peak.

Their dedication to improvement is relentless, and here I find synergy with my pain.

One of the ways these great coaches can live this way, and consistently achieve, is that they shorten their horizons. Top sports coaches don't talk about the next year's game – they focus on today's game.

They aim to win today's game, and that's it.

They aim to win the day.

This is now my perspective; I try to win the day. I try to win the day consistently.

No matter what our pain, this perspective can offer great value. If the goal is simply to make it to the end of that one day, then that is entirely different from trying to imagine how to make it through next year, which only provokes more stress.

With a well-developed mind muscle, when tomorrow comes, the same way of thinking is adopted, and the aim remains to win the day.

What I propose here can also be directly applied to physical fitness. If we adopt the idea that all we need to do is win the day – or win the workout in that day – then we can derive far more benefit than if we keep looking ahead and getting demoralized by long-term prospects. With this perspective, we can also retain our level of fitness, as we're not aiming to solely reach one peak and stop exercising. We can avoid constant ups and downs, which incur setback after setback, as we realize that it takes far longer to regain physical fitness than it does to lose it.

**It's easier to exercise at the plateau than to keep climbing the mountain.**

Learning to exercise with authentic consistency will also naturally encourage us to adopt the mindset that exercise is a blessing. It won't be such an upheaval because we won't have to keep starting again.

In my individual case, I have used the consistency of exercise to counter the persistence of pain.

## 3. Perseverance

Acting with authentic discipline and consistency is a feat within itself. But sometimes – even when applying the power of perspective with both of those principles – it isn't enough. This is because there are times when we just need to put everything else aside and find a way to keep going. We need to rely on perseverance, which *The Oxford English Dictionary* defines as, 'doing something despite difficulty or delay in achieving success.'

For me, of all six authentic principles, this is the raw one. This isn't necessarily about resisting temptation or setting up a plan to repeat something in order to improve. It's just about continuing to put one foot in front of the other.

In terms of physicality, this is the 11th repetition (rep).

Not everyone will experience the 11th rep in the gym. For some people, the gym just isn't for them. But the mindset behind the 11th rep isn't exclusively reserved for gym users as it can apply across our lives. When we hit the 10th rep and our arms – or lives – are shaking, we must find a way to make it past the 10th and get that 11th rep up.

No matter how lucky we are, we will all be faced with the 11th rep at some point in our lives. We will all face moments where things are so tough that our only two options are to either give up or persevere.

Losing our health is one of the most notable examples of those moments.

> *In the battle with illness, perseverance may be the most potent weapon in our armoury.*

The enormity of perseverance has been monumental for me as I've needed it every day for more than 12 years. I still need it today. I honestly can't remember a single day when I didn't need to persevere and, although every day is different, every day requires a necessity to persevere.

Like consistency, however, my thoughts around perseverance are mixed. The word 'delay' in *The Oxford English Dictionary* definition represents another frustration for me because my pain isn't in delay; it's never-ending.

I have accepted the likelihood that the only ending to my chronic pain will be death, so if life becomes solely about persevering until death, then this is no life at all.

Once again, this is where the power of perspective is so crucial. Despite the real possibility that I will endure chronic pain for the rest of my life, the perspective I adopt is that it's because of pain that I will reach my potential in life. It's also because of pain that I'll end up living a life that is about so much more than my own.

I will get to positively influence the lives of other people, and that isn't something to be underestimated.

The other reality is that without perseverance, I would never have made it this far. I would never have been able to finish this book, and I would never have been able to achieve my dream of becoming an entrepreneur. So, by hanging on, I've reached new heights.

All of what I am proposing here relates to physical fitness too. If we can hang on and endure, then we will be rewarded.

Consider the mindset, mood and emotional state of someone standing at the bottom of a hill. There may be trepidation, lethargy and negativity as they prepare to run up it. Then halfway up, when their legs are shaking, and thoughts of giving up are dominating their mind, the whole experience may still not be enjoyable.

However, when they reach the top – having hung on and endured – everything changes. All feelings of negativity are replaced by positivity and a sense of achievement. Any doubts about whether the effort was worth it immediately vanish, and there isn't a single person on the planet who would regret having made the run once reaching the top.

This is the magic of perseverance; it can not only help us reach our goals in physical fitness, but also in life. And as we become more accustomed to pushing through exercise, we will become more accustomed to pushing through in life. By doing so, we learn to authentically persevere.

As a last thought on authentic perseverance, there is a response that I always give to people who say that they can't be bothered exercising: 'Remember how you'll feel when it's done.'

**Perseverance can be what gets it done.**

## 4. Intensity

The next principle describes the behaviour of my pain towards me with accuracy. The word 'pain' is even included in *The Oxford English Dictionary* definition of intensity, 'the quality of being intense; "the pain grew in intensity." The measurable amount of a property, such as force, brightness, or a magnetic field.'

It's a principle that once again invites conflict, but one which through more in-depth understanding can provide significant value.

One of the obscure characteristics of my pain is that it responds to opposing approaches. When my mind is under intense stress, my pain worsens. When my body is under intense stress – through exercise – the opposite occurs.

The harder I train, the more relief from the pain I experience.

There is an important physiological consideration that I am aware of here. That is regarding endorphins. Even though my journey has become about more than just the physical, such as perceiving my pain as a teacher or coach, the effect of endorphins in the body offers an essential source of learning.

Endorphins are technically defined as brain chemicals, which are known as neurotransmitters. These neurotransmitters pass signals from one neuron to the next. A more user-friendly way to think about them is that they are a natural drug within the body.

A drug which can cause us to experience the same feelings and sensations as if we were taking actual drugs, such as euphoria and pain relief. From the day that I made the decision to stop taking any kind of manufactured painkiller, endorphins have been invaluable to me.

Endorphins, however, are limited to the physiological. They connect with the mind but don't relate to a mindset. Therefore, to extract the most value from the principle of intensity, I've had to seek a deeper meaning. The aim is to capitalize on the physiological effect of endorphins as well as a more developed mind muscle.

The way that I achieve this, as I've described previously, is to see my pain as a teacher or coach. This is because the more intensely I train, the more pleased my coach is, and the less I'm disciplined.

Therefore, I value the 11th rep greatly. This is the rep which can add intensity. More intensity can mean more muscle pain, but it can lead to less chronic pain in my body. I am using positive pain to counteract negative pain.

Exercising with intensity has always been my go-to place when my pain has been very bad. I am so persuaded of its positive power on the mind and body that I believe it applies to any type of pain. For example, if the pain is emotional, and we're struggling with low mood, then exercise can provide a natural lift. If pain is mental, and we're struggling with trauma, then exercise can provide a positive distraction for the mind, while helping to give us a more optimistic outlook on life. Even if the pain is of a spiritual nature and we're hurting in our soul, then physical practices such as yoga can make a positive difference.

Although I could be challenged for referencing other types of pain here, it should be remembered that one type of pain often creates another. My physical pain has caused significant emotional pain due to what – and who – I have lost from my life. My physical pain has also caused significant mental pain due to the thousands of days that I've endured without respite.

All of us will be subjected to varying types of pain, but exercise offers a natural and effective way to deal with it. And I've learned that exercising with intensity can be even more beneficial.

**The more we get out of a workout, the more we take in from a workout.**

Training with intensity shouldn't be confused with aggression. We don't need to be angry when we aim for the 11th rep. The idea that bodybuilders are fuelled by aggression is often confused by the impact of steroids. It's the drug that causes mood alteration, not the actual exercise.

I train with a peaceful intensity. I exercise with a passion, not anger. I'm in a positive state of mind, not a negative state of mind. Getting to the 11th rep takes effort, but it doesn't mean aggression. And when I put the weight down, I feel an overwhelming sense of peace.

My pain is reduced, my coach is pleased with me (I'm in less pain) and I enter a good space.

I experience this with all types of exercise; after I hit the sixth hill repetition on my bike, having only aimed for five, I feel at peace. After I complete the 100th lap in the swimming pool when I only aimed for 80, I feel at peace. After I finish back-to-back 90-minute yoga classes – meaning three hours all in – I feel at peace.

This experience with high-intensity exercise has also taught me an incredible lesson in life:

**Our successes in life don't need to be at the expense of others.**

High intensity doesn't need to mean high aggression. We can live our lives with an authentically intense passion, without damaging the lives of others. Despite my negative experiences in business, I don't believe that business or life needs to be about getting ahead at the consequence of others.

To conclude on the principle of intensity, I'd like to share a story from a charity cycle ride for International Childcare Trust in Kenya.

During one particularly tough day and about halfway through the ride, all the cyclists were struggling. This was, after all, supposed to be a charity cycle ride. Not a professional event.

'We're not bloody professional cyclists!' was a cry from the camp.

During one of the pit stops, I sat and spoke with the chairman of the charity. He was a charming gentleman who was known affectionately and jokingly as 'the Hef' (short for Hugh Hefner), due to his quick wit and sustained good looks in his senior years. As we chatted, he asked me earnestly whether he should gather everybody round to speak with them or try and organize a diverted route. I asked him to wait until the end of the day and then see what everyone said.

As each cyclist crossed the finish line that day, there were floods of emotion. Tears of elation. This was a direct reflection of the intensity of the physical exercise that they had just completed. Had we pursued an easier route, then the reward would have been far less. We had authentically persevered and been greatly rewarded through the exhilarated feeling of not giving up.

Beyond all the emotion, there was something so powerful to be learned. If this could be achieved through intensity on a bike, then imagine what could be achieved through intensity in life.

Not aggression. Intensity. Authentic intensity.

After the initial emotion of finishing had subsided, the mood that night during our social gathering was so high it would have been easy to think that we were on drugs. In a way, we were. Physiologically, we were all flying on endorphins, and spiritually we were all flying on having been part of something dedicated to improving the lives of others. The experience of the cycle was physically rewarding, and the purpose of the cycle to raise money for underprivileged children was spiritually rewarding.

**The greater the climb in humanity, the greater the reward for humanity.**

## 5. Change

Although very simple, *The Oxford English Dictionary* definition of change is very apt: 'Make or become different.'

When we want to change our lives, we seek a different outcome. We can't control the outcome, but we can become tired of the outcomes that recur in our lives, which leave us feeling empty with no purposeful direction.

I didn't want to change my life, but the change occurred. And although I can't claim it was of my own volition, that doesn't really matter. What matters is how I live my life today, not how I lived my life in the past.

I can't change the past, but I can continue to make positive changes in the present.

Change is an incredibly important word to me. That's clear from how I've placed great emphasis on its power throughout this book. Although the mind is where the authenticity of change takes place, change is also important in my approach to exercise in terms of variety.

To improve fitness levels, develop more physically or even improve flexibility through a practice such as yoga, variation is vitally important. This doesn't devalue repetition, but rather highlights the importance of both. Whether we are working out our mind muscle or physical muscles, both repetitions and variety will add value.

If we want to achieve a better balance with stress, we may need to practise letting go. This is because it can help to remove clutter from the mind and create space to achieve more balance with stress. Therefore, we need to repeatedly let go and do the required repetitions with the mind muscle.

Practising letting go is, however, not the be all and end all of managing stress. There are many more issues in our lives that can be stress provoking than just trying to let go of things that bother us. We need to practise detachment, taking responsibility, being present, acceptance and various other exercises for the mind. The variety within our practice is valuable in keeping the mind muscle sharp.

This way of thinking also applies to physical fitness. By repeatedly training with variety, we follow an effective process of getting physically fit. We combat the challenge presented by the body's ability to remember and learn – known as 'muscle memory' – and face this head on. An example of body learning is when we participate in any new exercise. In the following 24 to 48 hours after exercise, muscle soreness occurs. Hence why people who've never been on a bike before, struggle to sit down following their first-ever cycle!

Each time a new bike ride is completed, though, the soreness decreases (excluding any notable increase in intensity). From one perspective, this is good, because it helps us avoid limping around after every time we get on a bike. From another perspective, it creates a challenge.

The challenge is that, because the body learns, it slows down our progress in physical fitness. Therefore, the fitter we get, the more difficult it is to make gains.

How we deal with this challenge is by continually surprising the body. In this way, exercising differently for 15 minutes every day can be more powerful than exercising the same way for one hour every day.

In my own exercise program, I cycle, swim, go to the gym and practise yoga. I also enjoy walks in the forest with my son, which is made tougher when he runs down a hill and needs me to carry him back up on my shoulders. Therefore, I have plenty of variety included in my physical regime.

However, even with the variation in my exercise type, there is still a need to apply variation within each. Take swimming for example.

One of the distinct benefits that I've found with swimming is that it provides a cooling effect on my body. This sensation, along with the actual exercise of swimming, helps to reduce my pain during particularly bad days. Because of this, I swim more regularly than I used to. As such, I have improved.

Repetition in the form of swimming lengths means that I can now swim farther for longer without stopping. However, eventually I hit a plateau and stopped improving.

To tackle this challenge, I introduced a second swim stroke, butterfly. By alternating lengths in the pool between front crawl and butterfly, I drastically increased the intensity of my swimming session over a shorter period.

Variety allowed me to keep improving.

**Change leads to more progress.**

What's important with this example is once again the authenticity behind it. My commitment to change in exercise is authentic because it's lasting. It's an ongoing process and an ongoing challenge. It isn't just a case of telling myself that now I've introduced some variety in my workout, then I don't need to consider any more variation. Far from it.

Continual change is needed. The same with life.

The mind and body are always evolving and therefore need to be constantly challenged.

If we can commit to continual change through exercise, then we rise to the challenge posed by muscle memory in the body. Not only does this help keep us sharp physically, but it also helps keep us mentally sharp.

If our willingness to change ceases, then we can become stagnant. This might stop us growing and/or prevent us from improving.

Authentic change is now at the core of how I live my life and work with my pain. It's also at the heart of how I approach exercise.

**If you can change your mind, you can change your world.**

## 6. Awareness

Of the six authentic principles of physical fitness, the last one is the one that seems like the odd one out. *The Oxford English Dictionary* gives the definition of 'knowledge or perception of a situation or fact.'

There is a less obvious connection between exercise and awareness because awareness is usually more associated with the mind, but I've found a significant connection between the mind and exercise in what it has come to mean to me. What was once a fun combination of pastimes, sports and training, has now become about something much deeper.

Exercise improves my quality of life because it is the most effective way for me to reduce pain.

Considering what I endured during my 10-year search, and the frighteningly continuous deterioration of my health, it's therefore of little surprise that exercise holds such a special meaning to me. It also explains why I've been able to look beyond the tangible and see my pain as a type of teacher in life or coach when I train.

This is an act of awareness, and using exercise to satisfy the demands of my coach is what holds spiritual depth.

Depth with exercise, however, isn't limited to those types most typically associated with awareness. Yoga being an example. Yoga has taken me on a journey of awareness, but I've found depth in all types of exercise. Even one that so rarely brings up spiritual reference, such as weightlifting.

When I lift weights, I don't do so with an aggressive mind but with one that has learned about and been positively influenced by the teachings of Buddhism. I've learned to live more presently. My efforts to be more present in life are also now reflected in my gym time.

**What allows us to have a present-moment practice . . . is practise.**

Exercising with a more present mind has also resulted in being able to train with more intensity. Something that pleases my coach (my pain) because I can push beyond my limits and hit the 11th rep. And it's in this moment of the 11th rep when a truly present mind is required – a more present mind is a more powerful mind.

There is no room for distraction because if the mind wanders, the body gives in. So not only does the 11th rep encourage a present mind, but it can also lead to a state of meditation.

For those who don't like the gym, this concept of weightlifting connected to meditation may be difficult to understand. But it can be applied to any type of exercise. The last lap after a long swim. The final 100 metres at the end of a marathon. The final exercise in a tough Pilates class.

Distraction – and even extreme pain – can be removed entirely from our minds as we become totally focused on getting over the finish line.

We can become intensely aware.

Combining these two principles of intensity and awareness opens up possibilities in so many other areas of life too. No matter what we're doing, if we can get our minds into the same state as when we are in the moment of the 11th rep, then the results can be quite incredible.

We can become more present in our work or more present with our family. More present in anything. Once again, this isn't about being aggressive. The 11th rep and intense awareness are about being present and finding peace. Both of which can lead to more balance.

Let's take writing this book as an example - I wouldn't have been able to get through it without this 11th rep mindset. In fact, this book has been more like my 15th rep. It's taken that much out of me and has required all six principles in abundance. I've had to be disciplined, consistent and persever. I've had to work with intensity, commit to continual change and write with awareness.

What the 11th rep has also brought to my life is a greater sense of gratitude. I am genuinely thankful to be able to exercise, and hugely appreciate the positive effect that both my mind and body experience during and after the 11th rep.

I am perhaps at my most grateful in those immediate moments following the 11th rep, when I'm entirely at peace and want for nothing else. No more money, no more material things, no more anything.

I feel my mood lift, my energy increase, my pain decrease, my frustrations diminish and get as close to 5 or 6 on the stress scale (see

Chapter 7) as I possibly can.

Awareness may not seem like an obvious principle of physical fitness, but when considered from a certain perspective, it's as important as the other five. *The Oxford English Dictionary* definition of awareness is very simple, but it's also very fitting.

# 23

# Fulfilment

Why are we here? What is our purpose? What do we seek?

We ask many of these types of questions when we start to discover greater depth in our lives. But despite the different paths we can follow, I do believe that we are searching for a shared destination – fulfilment.

It's something I reference throughout this book. Along with achieving more balance, I believe fulfilment is one of the ultimate goals in life. More so than financial gain, qualifications and even happiness because I don't believe they hold the same level of nourishment as fulfilment.

It may seem strange to find fulfilment in this section about the body. However, it isn't out of place here. It's all about how we try to achieve fulfilment and how we get there.

Fulfilment is often not recognized as one of the ultimate goals in life. It doesn't take much for us to divert from the path to fulfilment and get distracted by other goals, such as money or committing to jobs that we believe will provide financial security. We can also fall into the mindset that physical appearance is what matters and that the better we make ourselves look physically, the better our lives will be.

None of this can represent authentic fulfilment, though, because none of this has depth. Fulfilment isn't an external consideration – it happens within. It happens in our minds and, as I've experienced, it happens within our souls. This explains why making money or getting six-pack abs doesn't satisfy this feeling or need for more.

No matter how much money we make or how aesthetically we sculpt our physique, it will never be enough.

**The search for fulfilment is an internal journey.**

I realize this statement might be open to misinterpretation, so let me explain by saying money and self-image are both important. We need to pay the bills and we live in a visual world – none of us can change the way the world works. But the reason I can state my views with conviction is due to the insights of my journey because I've lived a life that was barren of fulfilment.

Only through my pain did I discover what fulfilment really meant.

Before my pain began in 2007, I was on a path that would never ever have provided authentic fulfilment. I was living a selfish life based on goals that lacked depth. No matter how many pay rises I received, I always wanted to make more. Whenever I got an end-of-year bonus, I felt like I was trying to force myself to appreciate it more than I did.

What's interesting about my journey is that teaching and coaching in my younger years held more depth and were meaningful, but then I let money become my master and pursued it as a primary goal.

Throw in my antics to get laid as often as possible, and my life goals had about as much depth as a desert puddle! Yet, these were real goals for years and, had my battle with pain not started, they would have remained.

**The irony of pain is that it can be a curse and a blessing at the same time.**

Pain is what caused me to authentically change my entire life, and that allowed me to discover fulfilment.

That doesn't make me heroic or an extraordinary person who con-sciously decided to better himself. I was afflicted with a health disorder and had to change or die. Whether by my own hand or by continuing along a very damaging life path.

Looking back on my life before pain, my two main flaws about fulfilment – or the lack of – were these two elements of money and physical appearance. Only through pain was I able to completely readdress their meaning.

## What We Need Comes from Within

The problem with money is that it doesn't improve our lives internally. For example, despite the benefits of private medical care, money doesn't guarantee good health. In fact, as exemplified by my 10-year search, money can mean abdicating responsibility for our health.

Money can be the reason we don't change our lives as well as the reason we lose sight of gratitude and appreciation.

> **It's better to be miserable underneath the arches, than to be miserable in Park Lane.**

These are not my own words, but I like them very much. It's an excellent reminder of how much appreciation can be lost with money. If we're sitting underneath the arches without a penny to our name, then someone giving us a simple cup of tea would mean so much. If we have pots of money in a mansion in Park Lane, then even the most expensive gift would mean very little. This is why one of the last acts I did for my mum before she slipped into her final hours was to give her a cup of tea. She received the tea and said, 'Ooh, that's lovely.'

Our relationship with money and health can also be cyclically damaging, like buying health tokens. We want to buy these tokens, through medicinal drugs and medical care, then we go and blow them all on a bad diet and damaging lifestyle. Once we run out of tokens, we then want to buy more so that we can do it all over again.

All of it means that we avoid authentic change in our lives, and this creates a barrier to discovering fulfilment. We need to remember that what truly makes us great is who we are inside: confidence, self-esteem, positivity, humility, emotion, determination, kindness, love and everything else that makes each of us a unique human being, all occur inside of us. We can't gain more confidence and better self-esteem by making more money, because developing better self-esteem is achieved by developing the mind muscle.

It is an inner practice.

I only became aware of the futility of money in achieving fulfilment, through committing to working out my mind muscle and doing the required repetitions. It took a long time and required a lot of pain.

Now to physical appearance, and why I chose to place this subject of fulfilment here. To sum it up in a few words: fulfilment can't be found in the mirror and can only be found in the mind.

## Creating Fulfilment

One of the most poignant lessons that I learned on my journey through training my physical body is that no matter how physically developed I got, I could not achieve authentic fulfilment. Even with purposeful training in dedication to this book, the shape of my body never provided me with fulfilment. In fact, the more in shape I became, the more self-critical I became. Again, this is because fulfilment is an internal state, not an external act.

I'd also like to share the following story that may help to emphasize my point here.

As I approached Christmas 2017, I started to feel apprehensive because my love for the Christmas period had been replaced with a Scrooge-like misery and a wish to get it over and done with. The typical themes of the festive season such as parties, having fun, letting loose, eating and drinking were all a recipe for disaster to me.

However, I was also much further down the road with *o Days Off*, and my mind muscle was more developed. So as Christmas approached, I thought more deeply about the concept of time and started to think:

'If my time is going to be spent abstaining, fighting temptation and generally waiting for it all just to be over, why not use my time with more purpose? Why not give my time to others?'

So, I decided to volunteer for a couple of days at a homeless shelter.

When I arrived on Christmas Eve, I was blown away by just how many volunteers there were. It was heart-warming to see so many people willing to give up their time. Especially at that time of year.

I played my part, but the most poignant experience for me was when I sat down with one of the guests and engaged in conversation with him. As much as all the jobs that needed to be done were important, what each volunteer really wanted was to interact with the guests and feel like they were making a difference.

As we talked, I started to think that I should guide the conversation towards something more meaningful. Perhaps I could use some of my own experience with life struggle to plant a few seeds of thought in his mind. But clearly, he didn't want this.

All he wanted was someone to sit and talk to. Right there and then I realized I was making a difference. Not by giving profound advice, but just by listening. And it really was no burden to me – we literally sat and talked about football for hours. He was a lovely chap and a real encyclopaedia on football history.

When I finished my shift that day, I went home and gathered my thoughts on this experience. It was then that I realized that I'd achieved an extraordinary sense of fulfilment. I hadn't achieved anything extraordinary, yet I was extraordinarily fulfilled.

This is because the fulfilment I was feeling was happening within.

I learned so much from this experience:

First, it made me consider a universal element of fulfilment that we all share as human beings. Even though the path to fulfilment is individual, there is a common path to fulfilment that we all share through the act of helping others.

It feels great. It feels whole.

Second, I found a very close connection between this experience and chronic pain. This guest was thankful for the time we spent together because I engaged with him. I was genuinely interested in what he had to say, and I turned my phone off to pay him the respect he deserved. And give him the attention he needed. This is what those with chronic pain want more than anything else from others – honest engagement and genuine attention.

Of all the times I sat with people in the earlier years of my illness and tried to make them understand what I was going through, perhaps the line that I heard most often was, 'What is it you actually want?'

What I wanted was the same as the guest I met in the homeless shelter, and that was someone to listen.

Fulfilment for me is, therefore, simply about helping others. No matter the outcome of how many copies of this book get sold, writing this book has been one of the most fulfilling experiences of my life. Because the purpose behind it is to help other people.

To summarize, exercise can be a profound and meaningful act if we focus on the experience it provides. Not the outcome of physical appearance.

# VI

# The Authentic Entrepreneur

*Integrity will always pay dividends.*

# 24

# Entering the Ring

If I were to line up everybody I've ever known and ask them to describe my character, one word would come up over and again – graft. I am a grafter, and hard work has always been at my core. I believe a strong work ethic was instilled in me from a young age.

My first job was delivering newspapers in Annan before school each day. Waking up early and cycling through the streets, no matter the weather, was a great lesson in earning my own money. And being Scotland – it was pretty much cold, raining and dark most mornings.

My paper round earned me between £5 and £10 a week, depending on whether I also did the Sunday newspapers. Not only was the work experience invaluable, but I also got an early lesson in managing my finances. Certainly not on spreadsheets, though, and I didn't even have a bank account at that time.

It was literally an 'under the mattress' scenario.

Beyond earning money, my paper round also taught me about exercise. I was already interested in sports, but the physical exertion of delivering newspapers on a bicycle also showed me how working out can create a positive start to the day. Something which remains embedded in me.

Even though the weather was unwelcomely harsh on my fingertips when I started each morning, I always finished my round in the same way: sweating and with a sense of real achievement. The last few houses on my route were at the top of a hill aptly named, the 'Back of the Hill', which was so steep that we struggled to run up it during our pre-season football training sessions. Cycling up it had my legs working overtime.

Looking back, it was distinctly representative of life and the journey of an entrepreneur. What is daunting at the bottom – with questions of doubt as to whether it's possible to make it – can be overcome by elation and a sense of fulfilment when the summit is reached.

What I didn't know then is that cycling up that hill every morning and completing the paper round were the makings of the entrepreneur in me. Many necessary diversions lay ahead, and my understanding of fulfilment would evolve, but these were the initial steps.

**The first footsteps through the snow mark the path.**

Although my paper round was a paying job, the first business I set up was selling erasers at school. An illegal one I must admit, as the erasers were acquired through stealing them from local newsagents. This was before the world of CCTV and the eye-in-the-sky cameras, so shoplifting was a lot easier.

I am not, of course, advocating shoplifting, and in any case, I'm guessing that sales of erasers would be rather dismal with the kids of today's generation. My journey into the criminal underworld was also thankfully short lived and by the time I was 16, I'd picked up a (very legal) job at the local supermarket stacking shelves.

Although I was earning my own money, it didn't mean that I got to keep it all. With Dad leaving when I was 16, and my brother heading off to university later that year, life at home was tough – both financially and in terms of my mum's state of health.

I remember the day my dad left very clearly. My brother and I bounded downstairs one morning to hear Mum screaming. She'd received a letter from the bank informing her that she no longer had access to the joint bank account – my dad's way of breaking the news that he was leaving.

Although I chose to maintain a relationship with my dad, I still believe that not facing his responsibility was damaging and cowardly.

Beyond all the heartbreak and emotional carnage that ensued, the reality was that bills had to be paid. My mum had been a housewife throughout their marriage, so the money that she earned from the cleaning job she took on when he left wasn't enough. Even so, I was still very proud of Mum for rolling up her sleeves and working for minimum wage during a tragic time in her life.

She too was a grafter.

As the household income changed overnight, I had to contribute 'dig' money. This being money paid by children to their parents while still living at home. Typically, my friends paid £10 per week, which included those who worked full-time. But I needed to pay more because the money was simply required. I didn't complain, though, because I could see how much my mum was struggling. On many levels.

For example, when I was home for the holidays from university, I always gave her half my weekly pay. My usual job was working at a local housebuilder as a labourer, which earned me £120 per week. I gave £60 to Mum, which, although left my net earnings a bit short, didn't stop me enjoying the job.

I never discounted my education but just preferred being outdoors than in the library. I always felt far more energetic when I was up early and physically exercising, whether it was cycling through the streets or building houses.

All these early work experiences were influential in shaping my character. I learned about independence, discipline and the value of completing a task on my own. I also learned about the sense of achievement that work can provide when money is earned with honesty, integrity and graft.

Without this grounding, I would never have been able to become an entrepreneur.

I also would never have been able to persevere for long enough; to change my relationship with pain.

## The First Round

As I grew up and entered adulthood, I held many more jobs, but my first real step into the business world came when I got back from travelling in 2004. I moved to London at the start of that year and can still recall walking into Liverpool Street Station – wearing a backpack with a flimsy CV in hand and £500 in my bank account.

Naive is an understatement, and beyond the fiercely competitive nature of London as a city, I didn't realize that all the money I had to my name would barely be enough for a month's rent.

**Without naivety, we'd never go anywhere or try anything new.**

The scarcity of any notable work experience meant that I had to take the option that many people do when they start a career: work in sales.

My first job in London was selling advertising space for a magazine in Notting Hill. The location might sound glamorous, but the reality was far from it. I was literally walking into every shop and retailer that was on my patch and trying to persuade them to buy advertising space in one of the company magazines. This type of advertising didn't really work so it was a hard pitch, but I learned how to deal with rejection and move on quickly.

**The tougher the challenge, the greater the lesson.**

The experience was valuable and helped me land my second job a year later. This is where my career in property started, and I'll always remember what the managing director said after he negotiated my salary:

'Eddy would have taken magic beans if I'd offered them to him.'

A humorous quip, and made in good taste, but it truly reflected how desperate I was to get away from advertising sales.

The property company I worked for was a small brokerage introducing new build development projects in Central and Eastern Europe to UK investors. It was high risk, as the properties hadn't yet started construction or were still being built, but I liked the job and sold a lot of properties. It still involved cold calling but was better than pounding the streets of Notting Hill.

### *Repetition is an important stepping-stone to success.*

The business grew from estate agency into fund management, and my hard work rewarded me with a stint in Bratislava. Instead of just brokering deals, the company had taken on investment capital to buy land and become a developer, allowing me to work on all sorts of interesting projects, including a ski resort in the High Tatra mountains, and I enjoyed learning a lot.

The problem was that I kept taking on more and more work but had no idea how to deal with stress. Every time a new task came up – hotel leases, commercial space, bank finance, planning – I was eager to be involved and take on more. There was nothing wrong with this, but my lifestyle of work hard, play hard was causing internal damage.

This is where the story of this book all started and sitting in front of a doctor in Bratislava being told that I had a 50-50 chance of getting oesophageal cancer.

The other problem was that, despite being passionate about my work, I was completely unaware of the true goings-on in the company. I had no idea how investor monies were being managed nor whether exorbitant management fees were being taken.

This was to be the catalyst for how my time ended with the company after four years of hard graft. What raised initial concerns were rumours that had been swirling around about how investors' equity was being put at risk. Also, how motivations had become more geared towards those at the top profiteering from management fees rather than building projects of value. I didn't really know what was going on, but I did see that I didn't want to be part of it.

Despite the disappointment of how this all ended, I learned a huge amount – perhaps more about what not to do in business as well as what to do, but both types of lessons are equally valuable. When I went to see the ski resort for the last time, it was sad to see it end up as a few unfinished buildings.

To me, entrepreneurialism was about creativity and building something, and in the end, we didn't build anything.

In truth, I took it too personally and got far too caught up in it all. I should have worked less and spent more time learning the Slovak language and embracing the culture. I took far more responsibility for my work than I did for my own health, but my mind muscle was undeveloped, so there is no self-judgement here.

Regardless of how desperately I wanted to build something, I was just an employee and never had any influence.

**An authentic entrepreneur is someone who builds, creates and adds value for self as well as others.**

My time in Slovakia wasn't only about work as it's also where I met D, and without us meeting, I wouldn't have a son. There was also plenty more adventure as I travelled across Slovakia and took business trips to countries I hadn't been to before, including Russia. I thought the Scots could drink but found the Russians took it to a whole new level with vodka!

Love, travel, hangovers, health issues, disappointment, life lessons - my time in Slovakia seemed to have it all. It was a roller-coaster ride, and when I got back to London, I was genuinely ready for some stability.

I'd gambled on joining a small company, which I believed was entrepreneurial, and had lost out badly. I felt sure that I wanted a safe and secure job in London to at least get me back on my feet and help regain my motivation.

## The Second Round

Slovakia was a great adventure, but it also left me beaten up. The career disappointment had been accompanied by health challenges, and my battle with pain had become progressively more difficult. I wanted to reduce stress and take less risk.

However, when it came to the crunch back in London, I ended up in another small brokerage company – this time focusing on UK property – and gambled again on working for what I believed was an entrepreneurial business. This decision perfectly exemplifies the 'glass ceiling of fear' that I discussed in Chapter 4 – I wanted to be an entrepreneur, so I put myself in challenging situations, but had too much fear to set out on my own.

Once again, I helped grow the business from a brokerage into fund management and once again, my hard work was rewarded. This time with a shareholding as I became a partner. The problem with this promotion was, up until that point, I'd focused on building investment funds and securing investor capital, but by becoming a partner I got to see the whole business. And what I saw I didn't like.

**Damage to the soul can manifest as sickness in mind and body.**

The business model had questionable ethics and there was a focus on making money in property from people in vulnerable situations. I tried to justify it as a service as much as I could, but I couldn't avoid the truth eating away inside of me - how could I make money from people in pain when I myself had experienced so much pain?

The answer to this question is paradoxical because I had created a connection between money and trying to recover my health during my 10-year search. The longer I stayed with this business, the more my soul was corrupted and the further internal damage I experienced, but I was afraid to leave because I'd lose my income.

In terms of why I sold my soul, I don't think I can answer that without it sounding like an excuse. Perhaps I had to get greedy before I could understand greed. Perhaps I had to let money become my goal before I could discover life goals of real depth. I knew what I was doing, though, and nobody forced me into it.

Eventually the decision to leave was made for me, and after eight years of building the business, I was called into a meeting and told by one of the other partners that I was being pushed out. Not only that, but I had to hand back my shares at zero value. Shares which were worth hundreds of thousands of pounds.

As much as I now accept that everything happened for a reason, and this event is what forced me to commit my whole life to 0 Days Off, the way it was handled was despicable. The partner who delivered the news knew everything about 0 Days Off as well as my mission to help others and used this situation against me.

Ending a business partnership isn't easy, which is why many legal battles ensue, and because there was no justifiable reason to take my shares, they had to rely on circumstance. So, they waited until I separated from D and took on the financial obligation of a new apartment then swiftly made their move. Bearing in mind this was preceded by comments such as, 'If you need to take a break, then do so' and 'We've got your back,' the news hit me like a wrecking ball.

They didn't have my back – they stuck a knife in it.

My reaction of turning pale and begging to be told the news wasn't true was similar to when I was sitting in front of the doctor in Bratislava.

**We often fear losing money as much as we fear losing our health.**

What followed was one of the worst periods of my life, where I lost everything in a short space of time. My stress levels were at an all-time high, and my personal situation meant that there was no way that I could fight a legal battle. I was drowning in fear and their plan had worked, so I gave in and signed the papers they forced upon me. I'd committed 12 years to what I believed were entrepreneurial businesses.

How different might my life have been with a more developed mind muscle and the courage to start my own business?

## On the Canvas

To paraphrase Winston Churchill, our darkest hour can become our finest hour. My first round in business had left me beaten up, but my second round almost knocked me out. I was laid out on the canvas, and it was as if I could hear the referee counting me out: 1,2,3 . . .

There were days during those two weeks of being pushed out of the business where I'd literally lie on the floor looking up at the ceiling. I'd overcome obstacles in my life before and faced challenges head-on, but what now? I had a health condition that, despite a decade of trying, I couldn't get past.

I'd worked tirelessly to build a business that allowed me to work flexibly so I could continue my pursuit of reducing chronic pain, and now I had to start all over again – could I muster the strength?

As the referee counted up to 10, I felt like I couldn't move. The little boy who wanted his mummy when she died was the same one now laid out on the canvas – lost and alone. After more than a decade of battling pain and 12 years of commitment to entrepreneurial ventures, which ended with devastation, I felt like I was looking over to my corner and signalling for the towel to be thrown.

At a count of 9, though, I remembered the one single choice that I'd been faced with through all my years of battling a relentless health condition: keep going or give in.

This was really a pivotal moment in my life as I was forced to start relying on faith. I could either believe that there was no reasoning behind all of this, or that everything was happening for a reason. As I wrote in Chapter 5, if we can find purpose, we can extract great value.

*Sometimes what seems like the worst possible thing that can happen, is exactly what needs to happen.*

Looking back, and now that I'm able to connect the dots, I now perceive this experience very differently. My mind muscle is now more developed, and if such an event happened again, I would endure far less fear, keep stress more in balance and make my way through to acceptance more promptly.

Today I live with less pain and, although I can't know what a fair shareholding payout would have meant, I can know that it would have made today a different day. If time travel was possible, would I risk the reduction of my pain today for more money in the past? We have to be very careful about wishing we could change something because we would also alter everything else.

Money is essential in society, but having it in excess will always detract us from seeking more depth in life and taking responsibility for our health. My perseverance, while having six months of heart palpitations due to adjusting to my zero-carbohydrate diet, wasn't just about having a desperate health condition. I had no more money to try any new diets, so having less money took away my choice of retreating. I live in less pain today because of everything that took place – it's all connected.

Further to this, having less money forced me to learn on my own because I couldn't afford any more medical help. This journey of learning taught me much more than just about chronic pain – this book is a testament to that. The content isn't reserved for those who suffer from chronic pain, and there is more I've learned about life.

Last, we must remember the futility of revenge – due to the nature of the business, there were an endless number of ways I could have destabilized the company, but what would that have achieved? By taking revenge we cause as much damage to ourselves as we do to those we're acting against. Think about how much time is wasted between two sides going back and forth with each avenging the previous act.

An English Buddhist monk, who was giving a playful talk about revenge, said it best, 'What's the point in taking revenge . . . Karma will take care of the bastards in any case.'

## The Final Round

My discovery of faith was reflected in the decisions I made after everything was tied off. This is what led me to the yoga retreat in Cambodia, and it literally was a case of typing 'long-term yoga retreat' into Google and choosing the first option that came up. It was all meant to be.

I found it very hard to be apart from my son for two months, but sometimes a calling is stronger than emotional pain. D was also supportive, despite our recent separation, and showed what an incredible person she is. She had every right to tell me that working full-time and taking care of our son would be too much, but not once did she take this attitude. She saw how much pain I was in and knew that I needed to go.

It would be later that year that I would see how much pain she was in, which led to moving our son to Slovakia.

Her behaviour during this period was literally the opposite of those I defined as partners in business – she was helping me in pain while others were capitalizing on my pain. She remained a blessing in my life after we separated and is the epitome of kindness and selflessness.

Although Cambodia was a spiritual experience, the realities of life remained, and when I got back to London, I had to earn a living. Therefore, I decided to contact some investors and set up my own property company. It wasn't difficult because I'd always treated them with integrity.

As this was to be my first full venture with me at the steering wheel, I wanted to build a business on higher principles than I'd previously experienced.

I named the company 'Niap Developments' – with 'niap' being 'pain' spelled backwards. Nobody ever figured that out but I guess it is a unique play on words.

I created the following five basic principles for Niap Developments:

1. Treat the investor's money the same way that I treat my own
2. Invest my money alongside investor's money, allowing shared risk and equal incentives
3. Take no fees and work solely on a performance basis
4. Provide legal security to investors
5. Work with total transparency

I did my best and ended buying a few properties in London for refurbishment, which were profitable, but the impact of Brexit had a negative impact on the housing market. No matter how many people talk about making 'good' investments, it's impossible to beat the market.

My reaction to this change in the market was, however, a good example of how much more developed my mind muscle had become. Instead of trying to force the business to continue, and risking investors' money, I accepted that everything was happening for a reason and stayed more balanced in stress. This didn't mean perfectly balanced in stress because I'd sold everything to set up this company and invest alongside my investors, but I didn't subside to fear like in the past. This change of market conditions is also what led me to put it all in to 0 Days Off.

My property company was relatively short-lived but, as always, I learned a lot. At one stage, I completely ran out of money, and if you want to test your problem-solving skills, then this is one way to do it. I even went back to what I'd learned about fasting and calculated how long I could go without food. But I learned that running out of money isn't the end - giving up is.

> **One of the greatest lessons around managing money is having no money.**

I will always remember showing D my cash-flow position and strategy, and let's just say that the horrified look upon her face reminded me that some parts of being an entrepreneur are best left with the entrepreneur!

What's important to understand here is the difference between risk and gambling. I didn't own the properties I was renovating and rather allowed investors to take ownership as security. My personal finances could, therefore, never affect the investment even though I had my own money on the line.

My risk was my own and I put my investors first.

In the end, I worked it all out and did right by everybody. I made far less money personally due to taking no fees and sharing the investment risk, but I learned something about myself that took me back to the days where my working life started out: I'd rather work hard and make less money than cheat people and make more.

**If we act with integrity, we can rest in peace.**

# 25

# A Year to Live

Although Niap Developments was my own business, and I'd finally achieved my lifelong ambition of becoming an entrepreneur, I still felt something missing.

This book was what provided me with fulfilment, and in a certain respect, there was an entrepreneurial element to it, but my only aim was to pass on authentic information. I didn't think of this book as an entrepreneurial exercise, and I still don't care about sales. If it reaches the people who need it most, then it's a success to me.

However, because the book wasn't what I deemed an entrepreneurial creation, I had an urge to do something else. It was as if all the frustration from those years of playing the part of a 'pretend entrepreneur', which meant helping others build their businesses, was now exploding.

On top of this, I had also become acutely aware of time. Having battled pain and illness for so long, I realized that there is no time like the present. The problem I discovered was that fear remained an obstacle in my mind. My reaction with my property business when the market changed showed how I'd made enormous progress in being able to find meaning when external events went against me, but too much fear remained.

Therefore, I sought the dramatic.

I gave myself a year to live.

I sat in front of the mirror and broke the news to myself.

Despite how drastic this sounds, and how I couldn't fully persuade my mind that it was true, I was planting another seed of thought. One which if nurtured would help reduce worry about the future and keep my focus on my desire, intent and process instead of the outcome.

This allowed me to adopt a very powerful mindset.

**_When time is more limited, we use it more optimally._**

## Living the Dream

What may seem like an obvious question is why would anyone commit to entrepreneurial ventures if they had a limited amount of time left? Especially when the first year of a new business is always the toughest. The answer is simply to live their dream.

When I was growing up and fantasizing about all the ventures I could create, it was never actually about the money. Despite my old pals perhaps thinking that I wanted to be a millionaire, it really wasn't about wealth.

It was about creation. It was about trying to do something different and be someone different.

I had all sorts of entrepreneurial ideas when I was younger. And had my venture into the criminal underworld of selling erasers at school been more guided, I may have pursued them far earlier in my life. There were many things I was unsure of when I was younger, but I always knew I wanted to create something of my own, and I always knew that I wanted to follow a different path.

I always wanted to be an entrepreneur. It was my lifelong dream.

Therefore, by focusing on my intent, desire and process, it didn't make a difference if my time was short. Because I was acting with a present mind and spending what time I had on being creative.

This limited time also provided positive pressure. The thought of having less time pushed me to want to make every second count. I was reminded of all those stories I'd read and motivational speeches I'd listened to of people who had thrived in life after being diagnosed with a terminal illness.

The bad news is what woke them from their slumber and forced them to live life with much more energy and purpose. Even to the point, on some occasions, they overcame their illness.

**Falling down leads to rising up.**

## Why Wait?

In my own journey, there was a version of bad news that I'd been receiving every single day for more than a decade. Every morning when I woke up, I was given the bad news that I still had to live with chronic pain. Therefore, why wait for a doctor to tell me how limited my time was?

Why should any of us wait for this?

The reality is, we all need to accept that our time is finite.

We are all mortal, and we will all die. But this isn't a bad thing. It's just a real thing. The thought of death can either be negative and suffocating if it means we live in fear, or it can be positively encouraging as we try and get the most out of each day.

It's about perspective and our attitude toward time.

This is why I found the spoken words of giving myself a year to live so powerful. The physical act of saying the words was like a hammer that smashed through fear, and a bolt cutter that snapped away from the shackles of doubt. I still had no idea what lay ahead but committed to living each day with faith.

Everything would work out as it should.

**The power of faith is greater than the constraints of fear.**

## Entrepreneurial Freedom

One of the most powerful elements of living with more freedom is that it allows our creative selves to flourish. Our fear around failure reduces, and we learn to be less affected by what others may think. These are invaluable attributes to an entrepreneur because being able to shut out the noise from naysayers around us, as well as the naysayer of doubt within, can open the floodgates of creativity.

This is what I experienced.

The urge that I felt from a young age to create something genuinely entrepreneurial was an urge that was never going to go away. Once I accepted this, I found the courage to turn this urge into reality.

As I thought more deeply about what it was that I wanted to create, two subjects came to mind - nutrition and clothing.

Nutrition was the obvious one due to my long battle with food, but there was also a strange calling to the world of clothing. I visualized designing a clothing brand which could help carry the key messages of 0 Days Off around the world, such as the mind is a muscle.

Without delay or any more procrastination, I established 0do Clothing and 0do Foods (0do starting with a zero being the abbreviation of 0 Days Off).

The main challenges I faced with 0do Clothing were that I didn't have a clue about starting a clothing company and I was on a tight budget. With less fear and more awareness of time, I wasn't deterred and sought to find a designer who could help me create an initial concept. I couldn't afford an established designer, so I had to find another way.

## Authentic Products

I made out a list of all the top fashion universities around Europe and started looking for a student designer. One responded very positively by letting me place an advert on their job board, and within a couple of months, I'd found a student designer who created some initial concepts.

I think V-Neck is not modern so I stuck with a simple crew neck w a thick ribbed neckline.

the word the side is quite i think we will add more make sense of placement.

Odo

I love the quotes.

I think we can use them in various places around the body I don't think we necessarily need to finalise the exact placement now as it is minor but I would like to use one at the front and one at the bottom of the back

Side note: Take a look at the off-white, they place int's of wording on their streetwear garments, might be nice to add " the mind is the muscle" o n the bottom of the back.

i'm definitely thinking a mix between two fabrics the top being thicker (maybe a neoprene) and the bottom a light water proof fabric

I really like this silhouette, the zip up anorak is VERY in right now and simple and to wear

"PURPOSE IN PAIN":

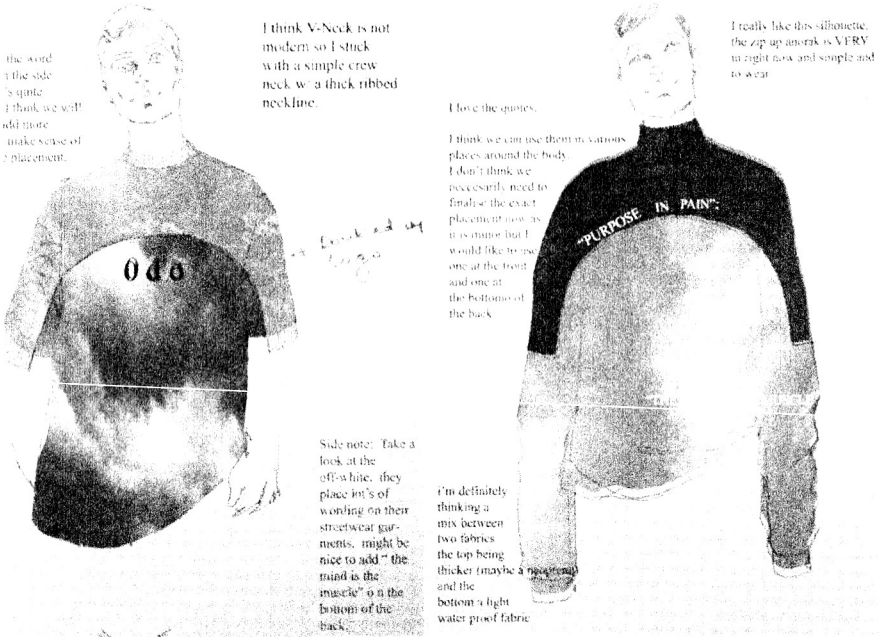

At a total cost of £200 for the advert and initial design work, I felt like I'd adhered to the frugal requirements of a fledgling entrepreneurial venture.

Once I reached this stage though, I realized that my financial constraints meant I couldn't take 0do Clothing much further if I also wanted to commit to 0do Foods. I also felt it was through nutrition that I could add the most value to people's lives.

Therefore, I fully committed to 0do Foods and worked with the same creative people who designed my book website (www.zero-daysoff.co.uk). They'd become very special to me and had developed a real passion for helping me take 0 Days Off forward and help others.

What they ended up creating (www.odofoods.com) was exactly in line with my own thinking. They were always able to capture the heart of 0 Days Off and reminded me why it's so important to work with people who are driven by more than money.

Where I faced a much bigger challenge was with creating a product. I had no experience, and most of my initial ideas went nowhere. I incurred lots of failures, but I was used to this by now and had already redefined failures as necessary diversions. I knew it was all part of the learning process.

The biggest lesson I learned was that I needed an A–Z of food development. On top of a product, I also required the knowledge on how to take it to market. This was when I came across a wonderfully creative company which offered a full suite of services. From the first call with the founder, I knew we were in sync.

It just seemed meant to be.

However, as glad as I was to find this company, and as much as I was continuing to act with faith, I couldn't avoid the realities that any entrepreneur faces. Over the next 18 months, we came up against obstacle after obstacle as we struggled to create something that stayed aligned with the principles of 0 Days Off.

*Sticking to your principles can be one of the most significant challenges in life.*

After much perseverance, though, we finally ended up with a low-carbohydrate product. It excluded nuts and seeds, included only natural ingredients, was suitable for most diets, and ticked all the 'free-from' boxes, including gluten-free.

Of course the product couldn't be completely aligned with my own nutritional direction, as I had reached a point of excluding all carbohydrates, but I wasn't trying to create something exclusively for me. I was simply trying to create a natural food product and encourage people to eat less sugar.

My intentions, however, didn't alleviate entrepreneurial pressure. From a certain perspective, it was madness to set up this business in my situation – I had no income, my property business had stalled, I was writing this book and I had to fly back and forward to see my son. All required time and money, and the reality of my pain remained.

The situation should have buried me in stress, but this is where another irony existed with my pain. I'd learned so much through developing my mind muscle that I was now far better equipped to manage stress. I had a desire to create something of value, I set an intention to put the wheels in motion and I followed a process to make it happen. That is where my focus remained, rather than with the outcome of whether the enterprise would be a commercial success.

I simply had faith that everything would work out as it should.

odo Foods is still in its infancy, but I've taken steps toward making the first product available through interested retailers. What the future holds I can't know, and that is out of my control. I took it as far as I could before switching my focus back to finishing this book. Regardless of whether entrepreneurial efforts are based on adding value to the lives of others or not, sharing what we've learned will always be the ultimate gift.

**Have the courage to share your story.**

## Changing Our Relationship with Risk

My entrepreneurial journey incurred a lot of risks, which I would never have been able to take without changing my relationship with pain. This was always the starting point for all other changes in my life.

Risk-taking produces enormous fear, and previously, I was no differ-ent. This is an unfortunate reality, however, because it can prevent us from reaching goals that we are perfectly capable of achieving. For example, there is significant risk associated with climbing Mount Everest, but this doesn't mean that it can't be done. And it's because of the associated risk that makes it so rewarding.

It's the same in entrepreneurialism.

What's fascinating is that the risk of losing money – or taking financial risks – is often more frightening than anything else. More than scaling Everest.

More than death!

The fact that people commit suicide due to financial loss is a tragic representation of just how poisoned our relationship with money has become in modern society. It seems that as soon as we let money become our masters, we let ourselves become slaves.

I'm not saying that money isn't essential. As an entrepreneur with no trust fund to dip into or anything to fall back on, I know the importance of counting pennies. I use the same razor blade to shave until it's so blunt that I'm practically scratching my face off! However, by changing our relationship with risk, we can develop a much better relationship with money. We can see money as something that helps us achieve our goals, instead of making money the actual goal itself.

Like any other authentic change of relationship in this book, changing our relationship with risk isn't easy. There is, however, a useful lesson from the teachings of Buddhism that can help: 'treat every day of life as if it's a game.'

What this encouraged me to do on my own high-risk journey was to start looking at the financial figures on my spreadsheet through a different set of eyes. I left behind a fearful set of eyes, which always worried about 'what if', and developed a more courageous set of eyes, which relied on faith.

**We gamble with hope but can learn to risk with faith.**

This new perception resulted in less stress caused by thoughts of bankruptcy and helped me look at my numbers as part of a game I could play. If I played well, then I would stay in the game, and if not, then it would be 'game over!'

The more I practised this way of thinking, the better I became at playing. I learned to play with less fear and more freedom.

I worried less about losing (money).

Why?

Because it was just a game.

I fretted less about the future.

Why?

Because it was just a game.

I blamed others less for things that didn't go my way.

Why?

Because it was just a game.

I also genuinely asked myself, 'What's the worst that can happen?' If I got knocked out of the game, it didn't mean that my life was over.

Just that I'd run out of money.

> **We can always start again and play a different game, but we only get one life per game.**

Although running out of money is undesirable and can create hardship, when we think about it more deeply, is it a tragedy? How we answer this question depends heavily on what type of relationship we have with risk and money.

If we've dared to take a risk and follow our dreams, then how can running out of money be a tragedy? How can it even be a failure? Especially if the ventures that we set out to create are aimed at adding value to the lives of others.

Perhaps the greater risk is not following our dreams.

What I accept in my own case is that there are other factors to consider if I run out of money. I have responsibilities as a father, my son lives in a different country and I have a health condition that can affect my ability to gain and maintain employment. But even with such heavy considerations, I still no longer let stress burden me. I simply have faith.

I have faith that everything will work out as it should, and that because I can't control the outcome, it's not worth getting stressed about it. This doesn't mean that I never get stressed, but rather that I now stay closer to a 5 or 6 on the stress scale rather than kill myself with worry up at a 9 out of 10.

I just try and accept that all I can do is play the game every day to the best of my ability. That's all any of us can do.

What's also worth remembering is that 'game over' will indeed eventually mean 'life over'. We will all run out of time, and we will all die. So, why not try and play the game with childlike freedom and courage?

## A Turning Point

In my own story, this is again where pain has played such a paradoxical role in my life. Without my pain, I never would have written a book or become an entrepreneur. I never would have been able to play my game with freedom and courage. I never would have reached my potential.

What is true for all of us is that sometimes the very thing that we think is taking away our life is precisely what is needed to help us truly live.

> *Rock bottom will always be a turning point because there is nowhere else to go except stay there or start heading back up.*

I sometimes think of my pain as that which took away the rope when I was climbing the mountain towards my goals. I had so much fear in my life before my pain started that I always retreated down the mountain when the weather changed. I wasn't necessarily afraid of taking risks, because I repeatedly put my hands on the rope, but there was always something missing.

I needed a better relationship with risk. I needed something to reduce my fear and stop me from looking down.

This is what my pain provided – it took away the rope and gave me no choice but to commit to the ascendency. And because there was no rope to get up or down, I had to go all in.

Maybe that's the only way that any of us can reach our peak in life. For our rope, fallback or safety net to be taken away.

What this may unveil, as it did for me, is that deep hate for our pain can be accompanied by a strange type of love. For example, I have a deep hate for my pain because it has stripped my life of so many things. Like a sculptor with a chisel and hammer in hand, it has chipped away and chipped away until the stone carving remaining reflects a shadow of a life that once was.

I also feel a great sadness in me, for never once have I been able to hold my son in my arms without the distracting curse of chronic pain.

The strange love that I feel for my pain is based on reaching my potential in life. This book is my potential. I could not have done any more, and I could not have done any better. Writing the book has been challenging enough, but going through everything that provided the content has taken all of me.

And more.

Where I, once again, find more profound meaning in all of this is in the perspective that my pain is a type of teacher. One who showed more belief in me than anyone else, by staying by my side every day and pushing me to climb without a rope. The pain took away my fear.

Perhaps this is true for all of us – perhaps pain is the ultimate teacher in life that can help us overcome fear.

I never wanted to live with pain, but having accepted it as my teacher that may never leave my side, I have found life-altering benefit in deciding to learn rather than run. Listen rather than hide. For me, every relationship change I have made – including with risk – has all started with changing my relationship with pain.

What I've also become aware of is that the legacy I leave behind in death will be shaped by the pain that I have experienced in life.

Isn't that the case for everyone?

# VII

# Conclusion

*An end is also a beginning.*

# 26

# To Be Continued

Despite being the concluding section of this book, I don't see it as the end. Whether from the perspective of my own life or any reader who comes across this book, there is a continuation.

Life goes on.

In reaching this point, however, I have become aware of the power that a book can carry. A book can hold an air of immortality. It can outlive our own existence and continue to touch the lives of people after we die. I find this thought incredibly inspiring.

To think that even after I'm gone, this book can still add value to the world provides me with great fulfilment. I, therefore, say to anyone who is procrastinating over whether to write a book - just get on and do it. You will never be able to control the outcome in terms of popularity and book sales, but what you can do is create a desire, set an intention and follow a process.

Everything else will work out as it should.

> **A book is never a success or failure. It's just liked by some and not by others.**

In terms of the content of this book, has it all been worth it? Has all my pain been worthwhile, if this book will continue helping people after I die? The way in which these questions are answered is the same way that so many other questions get answered in life – there is no definitive yes or no answer. There is, rather, perspective.

From a selfish perspective, it certainly hasn't been worth it. The raw and ruthlessly damaging nature of living with pain has made every day a grinding battle. It has made smiling an effort and laughing a rarity.

From a selfless perspective, it has been worth it. I've spent my time on something that I know in my heart will help people in some way. Finding purpose is one of the most powerful ways to deal with pain.

This book represents my purpose. I started out writing it as a way to help others in pain, but it ended up helping me along the way too. Writing has been cathartic, as it provided me with meaning in the darkest of times when I felt like I couldn't go on.

**If you can find purpose in the pain that you're experiencing, then you will experience less pain.**

My reference to pain in this message is universal. Pain comes in varying forms, and each of us will experience our own, but I propose that the type of pain matters less than finding purpose.

If you lose someone close to you but find meaning in their death, this can offer a healthier way to grieve. If you have a traumatic experience but share what you've learned with others, then they can benefit as well as you. If you live with addiction but open up about your struggle and speak with other addicts, then you will use your time in a more valuable way.

What's so important to remember is that finding purpose is never instantaneous. It isn't something that immediately happens as soon as the hard times arrive. It took me years to find my purpose, which is why I continually go back to the words by Steve Jobs: 'You can't connect the dots looking forward, you can only connect them looking backwards'.

When we look back upon a tragic event or experience, we do so with a different set of eyes than when it happened. That's where I am today. I look back at everything that has happened since 2007 with an entirely different perspective. I didn't choose this journey, but I now accept the purpose behind it. People have often said to me over the years, 'How can you write such a book if you haven't found a cure?'

I struggled to answer this in the past, but my response today is: 'It is exactly because I never found a cure that I wrote this book.'

I can now look back and connect the dots.

## Our Health Is Our Only True Wealth

By connecting the dots, I've gained a deeper understanding of what really matters in life. This is why my entrepreneurial journey hasn't buried me in stress, despite the risk and pressure of ending up with no money. I'm now far less affected by financial pressures, and as I reach the end of this book, I would like to elaborate on a few reasons why:

### My Health Has Improved

I could literally write this as the sole reason and just finish the book with these words. There really is no need to go any further, because when considered with deepened thought, absolutely nothing else matters more than health. For our loved ones and for us. Because without our health, we can't enjoy, embrace or appreciate anything. A sunset loses its stunning appeal. The flowers in spring lose their beautiful scent. Our children's laughter loses its innocent magic. Love becomes distant, and affection becomes non-existent.

With our health, we can live with freedom. We can laugh, joke, enjoy and show love with great expression.

Many people take their health for granted. That is, until they lose it. This is exactly what happened to me. So many things that I complained about in the past now seem of little importance because I've learned to appreciate the simplest of things in life.

A hug. A smile. A kind word.

When we really think about it, the only true freedom we have is with our health and in our minds. I would even argue that living in a prison cell with good health provides a better quality of life than living with debilitating pain.

This is because pain can be a type of sentence. It can keep us locked in a different kind of cell but takes away our freedom in a very similar way. The improvement in my health felt like this cell door gradually opening. And with it came a renewed sense of freedom that made financial burden seem less significant.

## Pain Has Given Me a Shield of Armour

Living in pain is very difficult, but one of the positive repercussions of any form of struggle is that it does make us stronger. I haven't cured my pain, but I have learned to reduce it. And because I've made it this far, I've gained strength from experience.

For example, it's possible that after this book is released, previous business associates may come after me in some way. I would hope that they would see my honest account of events as an opportunity for change in their lives, but this is a hope and not something I have faith in because it's a long way back for a mind poisoned by money. Perhaps in time.

What they or any other critic need to understand, however, is that I've already reached the promised land. I no longer need plaudits and have gone all in with 0 Days Off – in the truest sense possible – so have nothing else to lose.

I believe that everyone who reads this book will be impacted in some way – be it positive or negative, inspired or misunderstood, I will have made an impact. I will have made a difference.

This is all I ever wanted. This was my ultimate life goal. This was the void that I could not fill until my pain began.

No matter who comes after me or what criticisms come my way, I genuinely feel bulletproof.

## Money Can Create a Stranglehold over Our Lives

Money is important, but the truth is that the more money we make, the more we want to make. And the more money we have, the less we appreciate it. Further to this, the more money we collate, the more we fear losing it.

Upon finishing this book, I discovered a certain beauty about being relieved of money and material assets. I know this may sound crazy to some people because we need money to live, but it almost felt like I'd let go of trying to protect the crown jewels, and instead just started to take in the natural view around the castle grounds.

**_Losing money can be stressful, but once we let go of it, a wave of peace and relaxation can wash over us._**

What is worth remembering is that beyond a certain point, the impact of money on our lives starts to wane considerably. This being the case at sums much less than we'd expect.

Someone who has no money and wins £5,000 would feel such a sense of appreciation that the elation would be overwhelming. Life would be genuinely transformed because they could buy food and dramatically improve their quality of living.

Someone who has £1 million and wins another £1 million may well be pleased with the result, but their life wouldn't really change, and their sense of appreciation would be limited. The truth is if we make money our goal in life, we will live a life dominated by stress.

## I Have Achieved Fulfilment

Although my life savings are all but gone, I feel at peace because I have dared to invest those savings in a cause which I believe will add value to the lives of other people.

In writing this book, I have become fulfilled. This will remain the case, regardless of how it is received or how many copies it sells. I had a desire to help other people and find some purpose in my pain, I set an intention to take action and I followed a process of learning and writing. The outcome is out of my hands.

If the ultimate goal in life is to achieve fulfilment, then despite having less money, I feel like the world's richest man.

## I Have Become the Person I Always Wanted to Be

When D and I were together, I often used to say, 'I just want to be a good man.' She would always tell me that I was a good man, but deep within myself, I never agreed with her. I felt too much guilt and shame.

She also once told me that our mistakes are not our fault because we are all created with flaws. As a man, therefore, I shouldn't blame myself for mistakes that men make. It was an extraordinary show of kindness and insight, but as my story has told, I was never able to appreciate the love she showed me.

Now, however, I am deeply at peace with the man that I've become. I've settled my emotional debts with D and have left behind the heavy baggage of guilt and shame. I now realize that one of the hardest things I ever had to do was forgive myself for what I didn't know. I didn't have the knowledge, and my mind muscle was underdeveloped.

If other people could understand this, I believe they could achieve far more self-acceptance too.

These reasons help explain why I feel less stress, despite my financial pressures. I have achieved more in my life because of my pain than I ever would have without it. That may well be the case for all of us, which is why changing our relationship with pain can become so powerful.

Pain has taught me many things, not least of which that our health is our only true health. Without it, we are poor. With it, we are wealthy beyond our imagination. This being true, we need to learn to appreciate it. And sometimes the only way to truly appreciate our health is to first lose it. Just like love.

## After 4,300 Days in Pain . . . the Tide Turned

Despite how long it has taken me to make genuine progress with my own health, I wish by sharing my final desperate attempt to reduce pain serves as encouragement for how much can be achieved in a shorter space of time. It's only really in the six months leading up to the completion of this book that my health has improved.

Coincidence?

At the end of 2018, despite having come so far, I was totally exhausted. The second half of the year had taken a heavy toll on me, and I greatly underestimated just how much I would miss my son. Being completely honest, I didn't handle it well, and the experience reminded me that stress can come from many directions.

Even a broken heart.

After two tiring trips to Slovakia in quick succession in December, I was utterly worn out. I looked in the mirror when I got home to London and saw a pale, gaunt, prematurely aged face looking back at me. What I realized at that moment was incredibly difficult to accept – I'd built 0 Days Off but didn't have the health to take it to the world.

I'd certainly made progress, but any author or entrepreneur will understand just how much energy is required to take a book or enterprise forward. Especially in the formative stages. And without good health, trying to promote a book or build a business is practically impossible.

As I stared in the mirror, though, I didn't feel sorry for myself. Such feelings of self-pity were long gone. I just felt a heavy sadness but more than anything else, deep frustration. Surely there was 'someone' out there who could help me even slightly improve my condition? Or surely there was 'something' that I hadn't tried?

The problem was that I was out of time. I simply couldn't afford to pay for any more therapists or try any more ways of eating. Plus, I honestly felt like I'd turned over every stone. More therapies and new diets would just be going over old ground.

I had reached another edge. And once again, it was at this edge where authentic change took place. This time in the form of what seemed like a final epiphany.

When I thought about finding that 'someone' out there, I realized that the person of great wisdom I was seeking was staring right back at me in the mirror. Who else had studied for more than 4,000 days without respite? Who else knew my body better than me? Who else had persevered through so many necessary diversions?

I was a student who remained a student, but one who had also become a teacher.

I needed to learn from my own teachings because we all have a studious teacher inside of us.

This provided an answer to the second thought, relating to what I hadn't tried. The 'something' that I hadn't tried was 'everything'. I hadn't yet applied all the lessons in my own book at the same time.

I'd been to a yoga retreat and benefitted from a peaceful and natural environment. But I had eaten foods that were misaligned with my individual design.

I'd learned to eat foods more aligned with my individual design in London. But I lived in a stressful city with reduced time in nature.

So, I decided to embark on one final journey.

## A Last Roll of the Dice

Within a few weeks of staring at myself in the mirror, I found myself swimming in the Red Sea in Egypt. It made no sense financially to take this trip, but I was prioritizing my health over my bank balance.

It was the final leg. The last roll of the dice. The endgame.

As I set off to the airport to catch a cheap flight to Hurghada, I felt a surprising sense of calmness within me. Even though I was struggling in pain, I knew that this was the final stage in a very long journey. Upon my return, I would finish the book and give it to the world. Either by my own hand or just through faith that it would find its way.

From the moment I arrived in Egypt, I committed to applying everything that I'd learned. Not through a pressurized approach, but in an approach that can best be described as a 'disciplined sense of peace'.

The following paragraph is the longest in the book, but it is also one of the most important. This is what I did for 14 days and nights in Egypt:

Meditated. Swam in the Red Sea. Exercised. Ate only those foods aligned with my individual design. Drank only still bottled water. Calmed my mind before eating. Watched the sunrise and the sunset. Reminded myself of the purity of my deed when I was missing my son. Let go of the past. Stopped worrying about the future. Stayed present-minded. Focused on chewing every mouthful before eating. Rested when I needed to rest. Slept more when I needed the sleep. Wrote. Read. Minimized time on all electronic devices. Went for quiet walks to reflect how far I'd come. Had faith that everything was happening with purpose. Focused on my desire, intent and process. Stopped trying to control the outcome. Appreciated the natural beauty around me. Forgave myself for past mistakes. Gained more self-acceptance. Ate slowly in peace without distraction. Spent time in the sun. Accepted that every day is different and that every day would always be different. Felt self-compassion and self-love. Told myself every day that I deserved to live in less pain.

The result? A cure?

Unfortunately, not. But from a certain perspective, something just as powerful . . . wisdom.

I believe that I reached a point of knowledge, and acceptance, in Egypt that represented a new beginning. A first step toward reducing my pain in the summer of 2019 as I finally finished this book.

### *Gut health is about more than the gut.*

What I also became aware of during my time in Egypt was just how much influence the world and the natural environment can have on our health. The world can create us. The world can make us sick. The world can heal us.

The world that can make us sick is most often the world that we create as human beings. The pollution, the pesticides, the reliance on medicines, the manufactured, the greed, the material assets, the stress, the processed, the drugs and many, many other examples of our modern way of living.

The world that can heal us is the natural world. The food, the fresh air, the sea, the sun, the love, the friendships, the calmness, the quiet, the hydration, the simple things and many, many other examples of what the natural world can provide.

I became very sick in this world, but through a completely natural approach and bucketloads of perseverance, I found 'a' way.

## Pain Is Everyone's Teacher

Finally, I would like to share two meaningful trips that I took during my time in Egypt.

The first was when I took a trip to Cairo. As much as the Pyramids were awe-inspiring and the museum was interesting, it was Old Cairo that caught my heart. I was one of the few tourists there that day, and this allowed me to truly embrace the local culture. What I felt there was an overwhelming sense of community, and I was reminded with an extraordinary influence just how important community is for our health.

I had lost mine, and as I stood there very far from home, I longed to be back in Annan playing football and going home to see my mum. Like many men who had lost their way, I pined to be a boy again.

When I left Annan, it was to seek adventure and try to 'be someone'. What I became aware of in Old Cairo was that 'being someone' is not about grand achievements or fame and fortune. It's about the small gestures that are practised in daily life that truly make a difference.

I finally understood I didn't need to leave Annan to 'be someone'. That 'someone' was already inside of me.

The second experience was when I took a trip to the desert with a local guide. During the excursion, we visited a local family who lived in the most basic of environments. They lived off the land, and the land didn't give them much. The following photos show this but cannot completely encapsulate the conditions.

Despite these people having so little, I felt a bizarre sense of envy build up inside of me during my visit. They had far less than me, but at the same time, they had so much more. Every day, they had to struggle just to get by, and every day, they faced real challenges. But every day, they faced these challenges together.

They were a family. They woke up together, they cooked together, they travelled together and they struggled together.

They weren't wealthy, but, despite the conditions, their health was good. They ate less food, but what they did eat was sourced from the natural environment in which they lived. I had come from a place of far more material riches, yet standing in the desert, I was without my family, and I was in search of my health.

As I said my goodbyes and thanked them for their warmth, I gave them a donation. I was left to wonder, however, whether it was I who was truly the poor one.

Later that day, I sat with the guide by a campfire. Just the two of us exchanging pleasantries as the sun set in the background. It seemed as if we had the whole desert to ourselves, and I almost felt at home. It was a barren, natural environment, but it was as healing as any forest or sea.

*The healing power of nature can occur in any natural form.*

As I sat there completely at peace, a question came to my mind, which I had asked many times since lying on that doctor's bed in Slovakia when my journey started in 2007 – 'Why is there so much pain in the world?'

It was then that an answer came to my mind – 'Because without it we would never learn.'

After more than 12 years of pain, my life had ended up as barren as the desert in which we sat. Yet, I'd learned more in those 12 years than I would have learned in 12 lifetimes without my pain. It was then that I also remembered when it was that I'd given myself a year to live (in March 2018 as described in Chapter 25).

The date was 6 February 2019.

I'd given myself a year to live, and the world listened. In the 12th and final month, my journey with this book ended exactly how it was supposed to. In the 12th and final month, the tide turned.

Against insurmountable odds and being pushed to the brink of suicide on more than one occasion, I have managed to reduce my pain. I am now dedicated to helping others do the same. From Slovakia to Egypt and plenty in-between. That's my story.

*'Your pain is the breaking of the shell that encloses your under-standing.'*

Kahlil Gibran, *The Prophet*

# About the Author

Edward Stevenson has an undiagnosed chronic pain condition which started in 2007. After trying and testing every possible diet, therapy and physical training method he could find, Edward now shares his wisdom of everything he learned in *0 Days Off* to help others find purpose in adversity.

**You can connect with me on:**

🌐 https://www.zerodaysoff.co.uk
🐦 https://twitter.com/edward0daysoff
📘 https://www.facebook.com/0daysoff
🔗 https://www.instagram.com/0daysoff1

28623968R00180

Printed in Great Britain
by Amazon